This Book is Due...	This Book is Due...
MAY 2 7 '05	
SEP 2 0 '05	

Mt San Jacinto College Library
1499 N. State Street San Jacinto
Ca 92583 (909) 487-6752

Las obreras

Chicana Politics of Work and Family

Las obreras
Chicana Politics of Work and Family

Aztlán Anthology Series
Volume 1

Vicki L. Ruiz, Volume Editor
Chon Noriega, Series Editor

UCLA Chicano Studies Research Center Publications
Los Angeles

Library of Congress Cataloging-in-Publication Data

Las obreras: Chicana politics of work and family/ Vicki L. Ruiz, editor
        p. cm. — (Aztlán anthology series ; v. 1)
    Based on Aztlán: a journal of Chicano studies, 20, nos. 1
and 2 (1993) with an updated introduction and four new essays.
    Includes bibliographical references.
    ISBN 0-89551-094-4
    1. Mexican American women — Political activity. 2. Mexican
American women — Employment. 3. Mexican American
women — Social conditions. 4. Mexican American families.
I. Ruiz, Vicki. II. Series.

E184.M5 027 2000
305.48'86872073—dc21   00-022132

This book is a reprint of Aztlán: A Journal of Chicano Studies 20, nos. 1
and 2 (1993). © 1993 The Regents of the University of California. An
updated introduction and three new essays have been added. Oxford
University Press has generously given permission to reprint "Claiming
Public Space," an excerpt from Vicki L. Ruiz's From Out of the Shadows:
Mexican Women in Twentieth Century America (1998).

Cover art by Yolanda M. López
Our Lady of Guadalupe: Margaret F. Stewart
1978, oil pastel on paper
Collection of Shifra M. Goldman.
Courtesy UCLA at the Armand Hammer Museum of Art and
Cultural Center.

U Chicano
C Studies
L Research
A Center
Publications
2307 Murphy Hall
Los Angeles, California 90095–1544 USA

aztlan@csrc.ucla.edu

Center Director: Guillermo E. Hernández
Publications Coordinator: Wendy Belcher
Business Manager: Lisa Liang
Assistant Editor: Renee Moreno
Production: William Morosi

CONTENTS

Acknowledgments

First, I would like to thank all of the authors who contributed essays to this volume, especially the younger scholars who entrusted me with their first publication. Thanks also to Yolanda López for graciously allowing us to reprint the inspiring image of her mother. Chon Noriega deserves special mention for providing the impetus for this amplified, revised anthology. Wendy Belcher has been a terrific production editor; her efficiency and gentle prodding are greatly appreciated. On the Arizona State side, the administrative staff in the Department of Chicana and Chicano Studies, Susan Alameda and Araceli Albarrán, protected blocks of my office time so I could identify new essays and draft the introduction. In addition, Laura Munoz, a Ph.D. student in history, has been a superlative assistant. Laura, *gracias por todo.* I also acknowledge *mi esposo* Victor Becerra—his abiding love, patience, and humor sustain my spirits. More than words can convey, I appreciate his insight, commitment, *y corazón.*

Preface

With this volume, we inaugurate the Aztlán Anthology Series. The series is designed to build upon work published in previous issues of *Aztlán: A Journal of Chicano Studies* in order to address specific debates and concerns within the field. Our goal is to make available previously published essays and new scholarship in a format that serves the emerging needs of research and the classroom. We welcome your suggestions for future anthologies.

The UCLA Chicano Studies Research Center Publications is especially pleased to be able to collaborate with Vicki L. Ruiz, who guest edited the special issue on "Las Obreras: The Politics of Work and Family" for *Aztlán: A Journal of Chicano Studies*, volume 20 (1991). The volume quickly sold out its print run and has continued to be in strong demand for classroom use ever since. The Aztlán Anthology Series allows us not only to bring that volume back into print but also to update and expand its contents to reflect subsequent changes in the field. For our inaugural book, then, Ruiz has added a revised introduction and four new essays, including several from up-and-coming scholars whose work will help redefine Chicana and Chicano studies as we enter the twenty-first century. *Las Obreras: Chicana Politics of Work and Family* is at once a proven resource and a new guide toward an interdisciplinary understanding of the "memory, voice, and lived experiences" of Chicanas within Aztlán, within the family, within the workplace, and within the nation-state. It is imperative, as Ruiz notes in her introduction, that we hear these voices if we are to understand, and thereby engage, the complex dynamics of power, public space, and social change.

Chon Noriega
Series Editor

Introduction

> When I had my younger children and I was still
> negotiating, I would take nursing breaks . . .
> everybody had to wait while the baby ate. . . . I think
> it made employers sensitive to the fact that when
> we were talking about benefits . . . and a contract,
> we're talking about families and we're talking about
> children.
>
> —Dolores Huerta,
> as quoted in *A Century of Women*[1]

The intersections of everyday politics and social change run
through the chapters assembled in this volume. Represent-
ing two generations of Chicana studies scholars, the authors
simultaneously honor and problematize the lived experiences
of Latinas in the United States. Cradling the memories of their
mothers and grandmothers, they illuminate the multivalent
subjectivities and obligations of *mujeres* as they strive to integrate wage work, family life, and community engagement.
The dynamics of power permeate the realm of decision making whether one is situated at work or at home. We must move
beyond a celebration of *la familia* to address questions of power
and patriarchy, the gender politics of work and family.

As the editor of *Aztlán*'s first volume on gender and now,
six years later, this amplified anthology, I selected essays that
address these questions in ways that bring out the discordant
voices of the past and present. The volume represents the collective work of Chicanas/Latinas trained in a variety of fields—
history, literature, American studies, psychology, economics,
and sociology. Blending cultural studies and social science
perspectives, it provides a sampling of the exciting Chicana/
o studies scholarship on women and work. From turn-of-the-
century domestic workers in the Yucatán to a Mexicana making her home in present-day North Carolina, this collection
profiles women across classes, occupations, generations,

borders, and time. It balances the task of piecing together a partial collage of Mexicana/Chicana experiences with that of confronting issues inextricably connected to the power of the state and the power of patriarchy in creating institutional and psychological boundaries "for" women, and women's conscious decision making, given specific historical, political, economic, community, and familial contexts. These issues cannot be boiled down into a dialectic of accommodation and resistance but must be placed within the centrifuge of negotiation, subversion, and consciousness.

Those of us committed to Chicana/o studies owe a particular debt to anthropologist Patricia Zavella and cultural studies theorist Chela Sandoval. In *Women's Work and Chicano Families*, Zavella provided the first extensive critical examination of power dynamics encountered by Chicanas on the factory floor and in their living rooms. She revealed the intricate negotiations, networks, and decisions made by Mexican cannery workers in the Santa Clara Valley.[2] Complementing Zavella's feminist ethnography, Chela Sandoval provides an interpretative frame for interrogating power relations in motion. In her words, "The differential mode of oppositional consciousness depends upon the ability to read the current situation of power and of self-consciously choosing and adopting the ideological form best suited to push against its configurations."[3] Building on the works of Patricia Zavella, Chela Sandoval, Margarita Melville, the late Magdalena Mora and Irene Ledesma, as well as other *compañeras*,[4] the chapters in this collection can be divided into four sequential categories— confronting the state, negotiating the family, situating stories, and taking charge.

> The women had come from various parts of Sonoratown. . . . There were more than thirty Amazons. . . [They] approached the workers {scabs}] and began seizing the shovels, picks, and tamping irons.
>
> —*The Los Angeles Times* 1903[5]

The state, as represented by any form of institutional power established within the polity, has exerted considerable influence over the life choices and possibilities available to Mexican women. In my chapter in this volume, "Claiming Public Space at Work, Church, and Neighborhood," I illuminate the ways in which women's bonds at work, in church, and through the neighborhood serve as conduits for social justice and collective identity. Building community takes many forms, from the Unidad Para Siempre (a rank-and-file caucus emerging from the 1972 Farah Strike) to Sister Rosa Marta Zarate's current organizing efforts through *capulli* (a network of self-sufficient economic cooperatives that blend Latin American liberation theology, MesoAmerican traditions, and community development projects).

This tapestry of resistance has historical roots on both sides of the political border separating Mexico and the United States. As Emma Pérez documents in her chapter " 'She Has Served Others in More Intimate Ways': The Domestic Service Reform in Yucatán 1915-1918," Mexicans were not insensitive to or unaware of public policy for redressing long-standing grievances as well as improving their standard of living. Through carefully crafted case histories, Pérez shows the impact of legislation on individual lives. However, governing bodies in both Mexico and the United States have usually taken an adversarial role concerning the rights of Mexican women.

As part of global student movements of the late 1960s, Mexican American youth joined together to address continuing problems of discrimination and stratification and, in the process, they transformed a pejorative barrio term, "Chicano," into a symbol of pride. Focusing on the women involved in el Movimiento Chicano, historians Virginia Espino and Marisela R. Chávez provide two distinct studies of claiming public space while confronting the state. Espino's chapter " 'Woman Sterilized as Gives Birth': Forced Sterilization and Chicana Resistance in the 1970s" portrays in very human terms the forced sterilizations of Mexicana immigrants in the delivery rooms of the USC/Los County Medical Center. She explores how these procedures were brought to light and the ways in which Comisión Femenil Mexicana took action. A tactical coalition developed between working class Mexicanas and the Chicana professionals affiliated with the Comisión. Indeed, newly minted attorney and Comisión member Antonia Hernández represented twelve immigrant women who sought redress for their suffering through the courts.

In " 'We Lived and Breathed and Worked the Movement,' " Marisela R. Chávez provides insight into the dynamics of el Centro de Acción Autonomo (CASA), the signifier of Marxist thought inside the movement. Although women were committed to organizing workers into unions, conducting research on immigration, and conducting social services for undocumented individuals, they also chafed at their *compañeros'* traditional gender expectations. As a daughter of CASA, Chávez has had unparalleled access to former *militantes* and her chapter complicates the categories of gender politics, feminist identities, and collective memory within an organization once steeped in revolution and now ignored in nationalist narratives of the Chicano Movement.

The dialectic of structural barriers and collective action also resonates in Mary Pardo's "Creating Community: Mexican American Women in Eastside Los Angeles" and María Angelina Soldatenko's "Organizing Latina Garment Workers in Los Angeles." Pardo examines the ways women have taken power into their hands at the neighborhood level. Mobilizing for lights and recreational leaders at local parks, for example, may seem like a small victory, but such action reflects the community consciousness and organizing abilities of Mexican women. While not considered "work" within a traditional definition, women's grassroots groups provide valuable civic labor. Soldatenko offers an insider's view of life in Los Angeles garment plants and the coercive power of the state and the ILGWU in undermining the material conditions and organizing potential of Latina operatives. Soldatenko does not mince words: "The segregation at work along gender/ethnic lines occurs simultaneously with the gender/racial exclusionary practices of organized labor and the sanctions of the state . . ., which exacerbate the exploitation of Latina garment workers." Challenging persistent stereotypes of docility and apathy, the chapters in this section underscore Mexicana/Chicana leadership, both manifest and latent, in community groups and labor unions.

> A woman has enough to do in the house . . . You can't serve two masters, and one of them has to be your husband.
>
> Women like to work here. At home the man is boss, but not while you are at work.
>
> —Mexicanas interviewed by Paul Taylor,
> *Mexican Labor in the United States*[6]

Although expressed over seventy years ago, these sentiments still ring throughout contemporary Latino communities.

The intersections of work and family belie any one pattern or set of patterns. Women bring attitudes from home to the workplace and from work to home. Empowerment and conflict exist side by side as women struggle to rationalize and integrate wage earning with domestic responsibilities. Fraught with contradictions and subtexts, the voices emerging from the chapters by Beatriz M. Pesquera, Denise A. Segura, and Yvette G. Flores-Ortiz reveal the plurality of discourses among Mexicanas/Chicanas as they negotiate the politics of work and family. In " 'Work Gave Me a Lot of *Confianza*:' Chicanas' Work Commitment and Work Identity," Beatriz Pesquera paints a nuanced generational and occupational profile of women workers and their perceptions of job and domestic obligations. Richly textured and theoretically articulate, her chapter defines the connections between occupation and identity among factory, clerical, and professional workers.

Denise A. Segura and Yvette G. Flores-Ortiz appear to contradict each other when Segura contends in her chapter "Ambivalence or Continuity? Motherhood and Employment among Chicanas and Mexican Immigrant Workers" that Mexicanas feel less guilt about working outside the home than Chicanas who have been socialized into the 1950s television sitcom model of nuclear family roles. Conversely, in "Levels of Acculturation, Marital Satisfaction, and Depression among Chicana Workers: A Psychological Perspective," Yvette G. Flores-Ortiz finds that Mexicanas tend to suppress anxiety, even developing psychosomatic illnesses, while Chicanas tend to be more open in terms of expressing conflict over role expectations and thus, experience fewer symptoms of depression. I leave it up to the readers to interpret the evidence for themselves. Certainly, though, these chapters point to the conceptual vacuum inherent in the feminist edifice of separate spheres. In other words, "the inextricable nature of family life and wage work in the histories of immigrant wives and women of color explodes the false oppositions at the heart of the public/private dichotomy."[7] Integration, rather than separation, offers a more prescient construct in exploring the dynamics of Mexicana/Chicana work and family roles.

> And there were so many snakes. At night while we
> walked, we could hear the snakes hissing. . . .
> During the day while the sun was very hot, we would
> seek refuge under the small bushes and just when

we were about to sit down, there in front of us were two or three snakes coiled . . . [María Salas describing her six days in the desert with her six children as they ventured to *el otro lado.*]

—Quoted in Margarita Decierdo,
"Mexican Migrants in North Carolina:
María Salas Shares Her Story"

This volume seeks to address the question of voice, both figurative and literal. Scholars cannot "give" voice to people, but they can provide the space for them to express their thoughts and feelings in their own words and on their own terms. In our interpretations, we cannot put words in peoples' mouths or, like some early ethnographers and contemporary journalists,[8] run roughshod over their lived experiences. Evident in works such as Norma Cantú's *Canícula,* Arturo Islas's *Migrant Souls*, and Pat Mora's *House of Houses*, fiction can create an interpretative window into the past.[9] Tejana folklorist Jovita González offers an intriguing example in "Shades of the Tenth Muse" (1935), a short story she penned on the eve of her marriage to educator and civil rights advocate Edmundo Mireles. In recovering this story hidden in the archives, literary critic María Eugenia Cotera crafts a fascinating analysis of González's life and work. Bridging a feminist past and present in "Engendering a 'Dialectics of Our America': Jovita González's Pluralist Dialogue as Feminist Testimonio," Cotera draws the reader into Jovita González's world as she crossed the threshold "from independent female and institutional intellectual to that of wife and political helpmate."

Drawing on her own California girlhood, writer Mary Helen Ponce reinscribes Chicana memories through the texts of her imagination. "Campesinas," "Onions," and "Granma's Apron" express the ways memories crystallized in literature proffer nourishment for our spirits. As journalist José Cardenás declared in his profile of Ponce, "It's *good* to be back at Grandma's house with its kitchen smells and the chaos of untold numbers of family members running in and out."[10] Indeed, the narratives of Mary Helen Ponce exemplify the interplay of fiction and collective memory in constructing identity.

Though filtered through the lens of time and mediated by the interviewer, oral histories reveal day-to-day rhythms, negotiations, and challenges. In "Mexican Migrants in North Carolina: María Salas Shares Her Story," Margarita Decierdo provides a warm and intuitive portrait of a Mexicana adjusting to life in a southern agricultural community. Similar to the Tejanas interviewed by Norma Williams,[11] Salas's life history accentuates women's role in the preservation, production, and transmission of culture. Indeed, her narrative coincides with Antonio Gramsci's commentary that "tradition, in short, is a mosaic."[12] Situating stories embodies cultural production and for all of the authors in this anthology, situating stories is a political act.

> He'd say "You know, my socks; they never matched."
> I'd say, "Who cares? There's a war going on . . . there's
> things to be done . . . Get real . . . Your socks don't
> match, get pantyhose." [Martha Cotera referring to a
> "turning point" conversation with her husband Juan.]

Narratives of resistance provide strategies for the future. In the final section, "Taking Charge," *testimonios* by Chicana activists elucidate "the synapses of struggle" to quote historian Mary Ann Villarreal. Tejana feminist Martha Cotera, in her interview with Villarreal, reflects on her life as an organizer, sprinkling in well-placed *consejos* and pulling no punches. Cotera's political instincts come to the fore as her words speak to power—the power of confronting sexism within La Raza Unida while simultaneously confronting racism within Texas feminist groups. Cotera makes an eloquent plea for history: "Enlarge the ranks, and sensitize at least that generation of men to women making history." She continued, "Maybe there's a way without destroying the souls of activist women to put ourselves in that history without destroying the real issue, which is to act." Mary Ann Villarreal's deftly edited oral narrative honors Cotera not by painting her as some sainted icon but by drawing out her humanity, candor, and courage.

Approaching oral interviews from the format of a raw transcript, Guadalupe M. Friaz in " 'I Want to Be Treated as an Equal': An Interview with a Latina Union Activist" gives a firsthand account of labor organizing from the ground floor. It is an unvarnished account of the daily grind that can certainly demoralize, if not destroy, "the souls of activist women." Friaz frames the questions to underscore the impact of race, class, and gender on individual perceptions and choices.

The concluding chapter by Gloria J. Romero, " 'No se raje, chicanita': Some Thoughts on Race, Class, and Gender in the

Classroom" offers a compelling narrative of our collective struggle to make a difference. Romero eloquently delineates the nexus between pedagogy and theory in the classroom. She courageously articulates the contradictions our students and we face, with each other and within ourselves. The chapter is empowering testimony, one that grapples with the process of transmitting ideas and creating a climate conducive to intellectual openness and community engagement. Romero illuminates the processes through which we learn to recognize the political subtexts in the classroom and to deal with them in a constructive, purposeful manner. Gloria Romero will now take her considerable skills as an educator, scholar, and grassroots organizer to the California Assembly as a newly elected Democratic state legislator.

Memory, voice, and lived experiences are central to Chicana Studies scholarship. More than shared stories, testimonios enunciate gender as profoundly political acts. In the words of theorists Shoshana Felman and Dori Laub: "To testify is thus not merely to narrate, but to commit oneself, and to commit the narrative to others; to take responsibility—in speech—for history."[13] Both on the theoretical and individual level, the following chapters document and interpret the lives of Mexicanas/Chicanas as they have struggled to claim their space on the factory floor, in the neighborhood park, at the lecture podium, and at the kitchen table. Listen to the conversations; hear the voices of *las mujeres de Aztlán.*

Notes

1. From an interview with Dolores Huerta, United Farm Workers' Vice President. In Alan Covey, ed., *A Century of Women* (Atlanta: TBS Books, 1994), 47.

2. Patricia Zavella, *Women's Work and Chicano Families: Cannery Workers of the Santa Clara Valley* (Ithaca, NY: Cornell University Press, 1987).

3. Chela Sandoval, "U.S. Third World Feminism: The Theory and Method of Oppositional Consciousness in the Postmodern World." *Genders* 4 (1991): 15.

4. Margarita Melville, ed., *Mexicanas at Work in the United States* (Houston: Mexican American Studies Center, University of Houston,

1988); Vicki L. Ruiz and Susan Tiano, eds., *Women on the U.S.-Mexico Border: Responses to Change* (Boston: Allen and Unwin, 1987); Norma Williams, *The Mexican American Family: Tradition and Change* (New York: G. K. Hall, 1990); Adela de la Torre and Beatriz Pesquera, eds., *Building With Our Hands: New Directions in Chicana Studies* (Berkeley: University of California Press, 1993); Pierette Hondagneau-Sotelo, *Gendered Transitions: Mexican Experience of Immigration* (Berkeley: University of California Press, 1994); Mary Romero, Pierette Hondagneau-Sotelo, and Vilma Ortiz, eds., *Challenging Fronteras: Structuring Latina and Latino Lives in the U.S.* (New York: Routledge, 1997); Mary Pardo, *Mexican American Activists* (Philadelphia: Temple University Press, 1998); and Irene Ledesma, "Texas Newspapers and Chicana Workers' Activism, 1919-1974," *Western Historical Quarterly* 26, no. 3 (Autumn 1995): 309-31. Of course, the beginning point on Mexican women and work is the 1980 anthology edited by Adelaida del Castillo and Magdalena Mora, *Mexican Women in the United States: Struggles Past and Present* (Los Angeles: UCLA Chicano Research Center Publications, 1980).

5. *The Los Angeles Times* (25 April 1903).

6. Paul S. Taylor, *Mexican Labor in the United States*, Vol. 2 (Berkeley: University of California Press, 1932; rpt. Arno Press, 1970), 198.

7. Ellen Carol DuBois and Vicki L. Ruiz, eds., *Unequal Sisters: A Multicultural Reader in U.S. Women's History* (New York: Routledge: 1990), xiii.

8. Examples include Ruth Allen, "Peon Women in Texas," *Sociology and Social Research* 16 (1931-1932): 131-42 and Debbie Nathan, *Women and Other Aliens: Essays from the U.S.-Mexico Border* (El Paso: Cinco Puntos Press, 1991).

9. Norma Cantú, *Canícula: Snapshots of a Girlhood en la Frontera* (Albuquerque: University of New Mexico Press, 1995); Arturo Islas, *Migrant Souls* (New York: Avon Books, 1990); and Pat Mora, *House of Houses* (Boston: Beacon Press, 1997).

10. *The Los Angeles Times* (7 November 1998).

11. Williams, *The Mexican American Family*.

12. Alberto Maria Cirese, "Gramsci's Observations on Folklore," in *Approaches to Gramsci*, ed. Anne S. Sassoon (London: Writers and Readers Publishing Cooperative Society, 1992), 219.

13. Shosana Felman and Dori Laub, *Testimony: Crises of Witnessing in Literature, Psychoanalysis, and History* as quoted in Ivette Romero-Cesareo, "Whose Legacy?: Voicing Women's Rights from the 1870s to the 1930s." *Callaloo* 17, no. 3 (1994): 784.

Part One:
Confronting the State

Claiming Public Space at Work, Church, and Neighborhood

Vicki L. Ruiz

During the second week of May 1972, Elsa Chávez, a twenty-six-year-old El Paso garment worker, left her post at the Paisano plant of Farah Manufacturing. Joining 4,000 Farah employees in El Paso, San Antonio, and Victoria, Texas; and Las Cruces, New Mexico; Chávez became part of a twenty-two-month strike for seniority rights, higher wages, pensions, and union recognition. Management's manipulation of production quotas sparked the most indignation among Mexican women who formed the backbone of Farah's line personnel.

Chávez's anger is easy to understand. Imagine that you have been hired to sew belts on to slacks. To get a raise, you must meet a quota of 3,000 belts per day, which translates into sewing six belts per minute. Forget your lunch hour, for if you fall too far behind in fulfilling your quota, you will be fired. As a "checker" of freshly sewn garments, Chávez felt fortunate that she did not have to meet a quota; yet she understood the situation of the seamstresses with whom she worked. "Some of my fellow workers . . . were very nervous because they were always told, 'Hurry up' . . . 'You're going to be fired.' There was so much pressure that they started fighting for the bundles." Although Chávez perceived herself as earning good money and facing little personal harassment, she too walked out.[1]

Successful union organization depends, in large measure, on a sense of solidarity and community among workers. Effective political and community action requires the intertwining of individual subjectivities within collective goals. Claiming public space can involve fragile alliances and enduring symbols, rooted in material realities and ethereal visions. On a situational, grassroots level, informal and formal voluntary organizations do serve as conduits for women's collective identity and empowerment. For the Mexican women whose voices are in the foreground of this study, the individual bonds formed at work, at church, or in the neighborhood reflect a mosaic of subjectivities, strategies, and goals but remain rooted in collective struggles for recognition and respect.

Gender and social justice—doesn't that equal feminist consciousness? As contemporary Mexican women know all too well, it depends on whose feminism and whose context. As one Farah striker bluntly stated, "I don't believe in burning your bra, but I do believe in having our rights."[2] Mediated by gender, race, culture, and class, activism transforms individual conceptions of self, changes that alter people's lives with subtlety or drama. Labor disputes raise the stakes in the precarious politics of work and family. Drawing on the insightful scholarship of Laurie Coyle, Gail Hershatter, and Emily Honig on union pamphlets and newsletters, on local media coverage, and on oral history, an examination of the Farah strike provides a powerful case of community building through union organization.

When she joined her striking coworkers, Elsa Chávez had little inkling of the struggles that lay ahead. Farah Manufacturing was the largest private employer in El Paso; its chief executive officer Willie Farah had a reputation as a patriotic, civic-minded business leader; and labor activism found few friends in a conservative border city notorious as a "minimum wage town."[3] Indeed, the May 1972 walkout was not the culmination of an overnight organizing drive by representatives of the Amalgamated Clothing Workers (ACW) but the result of a protracted campaign begun in 1969. Events on the picket lines outside the El Paso plants quickly convinced the ACW that the strike could not be won within the city limits. Willie Farah responded with armed security guards walking with unmuzzled police dogs, and he obtained a court order upholding an 1880 law stipulating that pickets must stand at least fifty feet apart. From 800 to 1,000 people, many of them women, were arrested, some during midnight raids at their residences. Instead of the usual $25 bail set for misdemeanor offenses, those arrested during the Farah strike were required to post a $400 bond.[4]

Within a few months, the 1880 picketing law was declared unconstitutional, and Farah was ordered to "call off" the dogs and desist from interfering with peaceful picketing. Farah decided to take his case to the U.S. Supreme Court, but in August, Justice Lewis Powell ruled against him by affirming the decisions of the lower court. At the same time, the National Labor Relations Board charged Farah with such unfair practices as intimidation and harassment.[5]

But if Willie Farah found little solace outside his native El Paso, he found plenty of local support. Both El Paso dailies offered him a friendly hearing. And when El Paso's Catholic bishop Sidney Metzger openly supported the strikers, an area Protestant minister Paul Poling wrote a highly charged anti-union pamphlet endorsed by thirteen other clergy. Yet, despite being insulted at street corners where they picketed department stores, in their neighborhoods, and in letters to the editor, the Farah strikers continued their vigil.[6]

As one El Paso activist reflected, "We thought when we went out on strike that our only enemy was Farah . . . but we found out it was also the press, the police, the businessmen. . . . This strike was not just for union recognition."[7] The Farah strike distilled the racial and class cleavages within El Paso, cleavages evident in both the daily lives of the strikers and the opinion sections of local newspapers. Letters to the editor typically chastised the Farah strikers for their ingratitude, ignorance, and gullibility to outside agitators. Or, as one retired El Paso retail saleswoman (F.T.T.) wrote,

> Mr. Farah did not invite one of the people who are working for him to come and work for him. They all asked for a job and should thank God that they got one. If they think they are such hot stuff and qualified for a better job then why don't they quietly fold their tents and leave? . . . The Farah family has worked hard for what they have and no one has the moral right to harm them. I would like to give my boot—and you know where—to those picking [sic] in front of The Popular.[8]

Although their letters appeared less frequently than those of their opponents did, strikers and their supporters responded in kind, and the editorial pages impart a sense of the polarity of opinions surrounding the "morality" of the Farah dispute. In a spirited letter critical of media coverage, Irma Camacho wrote, "The Farah struggle, since its conception, was a moral fight for human dignity, since then through the use of your newspaper, the controlling 'powers that be' have stolen what objectivity there could exist and have subjectively used the facts to place economic value over human rights."[9]

Realizing that "the strike won't be won in El Paso," the Amalgamated Clothing Workers called for a national boycott of Farah suits and slacks.[10] Supported by AFL-CIO unions, campus activists, celebrities, and liberal politicians, Citizens' Committees for Justice for Farah Workers sprung up in cities from the Pacific coast to the Atlantic seaboard. In addition to holding fundraisers, these groups organized picket lines in front of department stores that carried Farah products. During "Don't Buy Farah Day" on December 11, 1972, an estimated 175,000 people, predominately AFL-CIO members, held rallies and parades across the country. United Farm Workers President Cesar Chávez visited the workers, as did Sergeant Shriver, the Democratic vice-presidential nominee of 1972. The Farah strikers also listened as U.S. Representative Edward Roybal from California spoke of his youth as a garment presser and ACW member. Support even crossed party lines with Nelson Rockefeller's public endorsement.[11]

The national boycott slowly began to have its desired effect. Sales declined from $150 million in 1972 to $126 million in 1974. As an article in *Texas Monthly* revealed, some retailers gladly took Farah slacks off their racks not in response to pickets but in retaliation for Willie Farah's "high-handed methods of doing business."[12] While the boycott undoubtedly contributed to bringing Farah to the bargaining table in March 1974, the dedication of the Mexicanas holding the line cannot be underestimated.

As weeks turned into months, the Farah picketers turned to one another for support, friendship, advice, and action. Critical of ACW support in El Paso, one group of women formed a rank-and-file committee within the union. According to Coyle, Hershatter, and Honig, the "members . . . shared a strong sense of themselves as workers and a desire to build a strong and democratic trade union." The women "put out their own leaflets, participated in marches and rallies, helped to found the Farah Distress Fund, and talked to other strikers about the need for a strong union." This caucus continued its work after the strike's successful settlement under the name *Unidad Para Siempre*.[13]

The strike, however, divided friends and families, because a little less than one-half of the original workforce had walked out. In my interview with her, Elsa Chávez recalled how this schism affected her personally:

> I had a fiancé there—we were going to get married, but he was from the inside, I was from the outside. So, we broke up because he didn't want anything to do with the strikers. After the strike, he came back and (then) I told him "good-bye."[14]

Chávez continued, "But you wouldn't believe the number of divorces caused by the strike. A lot of couples broke up, either the wife was inside and the husband was outside or the other way around."[15]

As amply documented in "Women at Farah," tensions among kin and friends took its toll, and, as the strike wore on, financial pressures mounted. Many families lost their homes, automobiles, and other possessions. Although the union had an emergency strike fund and distributed groceries and clothing, many Farah activists found themselves in severe economic straits. One woman explained, "A lot of people lost their homes, cars—you name it, they lost it." Such circumstances fueled marital tensions, but 85 percent of the strikers were women, and they sought ways to balance picket and family duties.[16]

Children have taken their place on the picket line throughout modern Chicano labor history, as early as the 1930s. As an example, during the 1933 Los Angeles Dressmakers Strike, ILGWU representative Rose Pesotta organized 300 children in costume for an impromptu Halloween parade in front of the factories where their mothers were picketing.[17] While perhaps mothers initially brought their children to the line because they had little choice, the youngsters began to prove themselves useful in distributing leaflets outside stores. Adults were less likely to make abusive comments toward a child.[18] In the words of Farah activist Julia Aguilar, "Now, we just bring our children to our meetings, and we bring them to the picket lines. Sometimes they ask, 'Are we going to the picket line today, mommy?'" Aguilar continued, "It's kind of hard with kids. But I'm willing to sacrifice myself and I think my husband is beginning to understand."[19]

The settlement of the Farah Strike in March 1974 had, for many women, come at great personal cost. Few activists would enjoy the benefits because many of the most vocal were fired after a few months, ostensibly for failing to meet inflated production quotas; union representatives blithely refused to generate any grievance procedures to protect and retain these women.[20] Mexican women have not fared well in their affiliation with mainstream labor unions even though they have contributed much of the people power, perseverance, and activism necessary for successful organization. As in the case of Farah, they typically have been denied any meaningful voice in the affairs of the local they had labored so valiantly to build.

Yet the Farah strikers had created community with one another and asserted their claims for social justice. As Coyle, Hershatter, and Honig wrote, "The Chicanas who comprise the majority of the strikers learned that they could speak and act on their own behalf as women and as workers, lessons they will not forget."[21] Elsa Chávez represents one of the women activists who have sought to merge personal and community empowerment. After she was fired, Chávez began to work at another clothing factory, but came to the realization that she wanted—and could achieve—a college education. I first met Ms. Chávez when she was a student in my Chicano history class at the University of Texas at El Paso; two former strikers had enrolled in the class, a fact I discovered as I lectured on the Farah strike and noticed the two reentry women, both bilingual education majors, sitting in the front row winking and giggling to each other. "Oh, we're sorry, Dr. Ruiz," they said, "but we were there." A bit nonplused, I turned the class over to them. Elsa Chávez dreamed of opening up a school for "slow learners" and had begun to organize a group of Mexican American women in her education classes for this school.[22]

Labor struggles can also be centered on the involvement of the entire family. The United Farm Workers provides the most well-known example. Drawing on his experience with the Community Service Organization (CSO), Cesar Chávez began to organize farm workers in the San Joaquin Valley in 1962. During the grape boycotts of the late 1960s and 1970s, Chávez and his United Farm Workers Organizing Committee (later the UFW) utilized tactics such as the secondary boycott, national support committees, and identification with the Catholic Church. A charismatic leader preaching social justice and nonviolence, Chávez became the most prominent advocate for the rights of Mexicans in the United States. By 1973, the UFW "had contracts with 80% of the grape growers in the San Joaquin Valley" and "at its height the union had 100,000 members."[23]

UFW organizers, many of whom grew up as farm workers themselves, recognized that the family formed the unit of production in agriculture and consequently focused on the involvement of every family member. Referring to *campesinas*, Cesar Chávez related, "We can't be free ourselves if we can't free our women."[24] Signing union membership cards has always been a monumental decision for most farm workers because they risk not one job but the livelihood of the entire family. While the husband might be the first to sign the card, he often does so at the insistence of his wife. Former UFW legal department volunteer Graciela Martinez Moreno (1983) explained to me:

> At the beginning, women were more afraid of the union. But once they got the information about the benefits their children would receive, the women became good supporters. The biggest problem was getting through the initial fear, but if you got to the wife, the husband was sure to follow. The quiet, subtle pressure of the wife was very effective.[25]

But there is more to the story than this, for Mexican women have been well represented at the leadership and service levels of the United Farm Workers. Women, to a large extent, operate the service centers, health clinics, day nurseries, and legal departments.[26] Founding the first UFW Service Center in the Midwest in concert with her husband, María Elena Lucas offered a realistic portrayal of exhaustion:

> And I worked such long hours, during the nights and on the weekends . . . but I just didn't know how to say no to people. I got very skinny. Sometimes I'd have thirteen or fourteen people waiting for me to do different things for them. It was just impossible. . . . Cesar had told me, "It's not good to play Santa Claus to the people. It'll be neverending" and I started getting to the point where I understood . . . I was burning out.[27]

Frustrated by the UFW's reluctance to organize migrant laborers in Illinois and exhausted from her job as a union social worker, Lucas became an organizer in 1985 with the Farm Labor Organizing Committee (FLOC) led by Baldemar Velásquez. Joined by four of her compañeras, including her own daughter, and their children (Gloria Chiquita had six kids), Lucas helped organize over 5,000 Midwestern farmworkers and orchestrated a successful union election and contract. María Elena Lucas and her friend Gloria Chiquita both became vice-presidents in FLOC, although Lucas expressed a feeling of powerlessness concerning decision making within the union board. She also recognized the difference in support systems between men and women organizers. Referring to men, she remarked, "They have the support of their wives and families, but most of us women have to work against our husbands and all of the services they expect."[28]

Fran Leeper Buss's oral history of María Elena Lucas, *Forged under the Sun/Forjada bajo el sol*, provides the most nuanced portrait of a woman rank-and-file organizer. What emerges most vividly from Buss's skillful editing of Lucas's life story is the strength and comfort migrant women find in their friendships with one another. Lucas gives unvarnished testimony to the oppression and abuse women face in the fields and at times in the home and the union hall.[29]

In her path-breaking dissertation, "Women in the United Farm Workers," Margaret Rose documents women's networks in the *campesino* centers, ranch committees, and boycott campaigns. Rose divides UFW women into two typologies—"nontraditional" (UFW vice-president Dolores Huerta) and "traditional" (Helen Chávez, Cesar's widow). Although Rose portrays Huerta as someone fitting her union nickname of "Adelita" (the symbolic *soldadera* of the Mexican Revolution), she notes how even the "nontraditional" Huerta relied on extended kin and women friends in the union (the "union family") to care for her eleven children during her frequent absences. Although criticized for putting la causa first, Dolores Huerta has had few regrets. As she informed Rose, "But now that I've seen how good they [my children] turned out, I don't feel so guilty."[30]

Dolores Huerta is a fearless fighter for social justice. In 1962, she taught school in Stockton, California, while being a political activist with the CSO and a mother of six with a seventh on the way. "When I left my teaching job to go start organizing farm workers, a lot of people thought I had just gone completely bananas."[31] A tough, savvy negotiator, Huerta skillfully manipulated her positionality as a mother at the bargaining table.

> When I had my younger children and I was still negotiating, I would take nursing breaks . . .

everybody would have to wait while the baby ate. Then I would come back to the table and start negotiating again . . .

I think it made employers sensitive to the fact that when we're talking about benefits and the terms of a contract, we're talking about families, and we're talking about children.[32]

Although they contributed in different ways, Dolores Huerta more public and Helen Chávez more private—there was no separation of home and union. For Helen Chávez, the UFW became an extension of her familial responsibilities. She worked in the fields while her husband organized, took care of the children and household, and participated in the social service end of the union. In a rare interview, Helen Chávez offered a glimpse of daily family life: "I hadn't worked for a while, because at the time of the year you could only pick up a day's or a week's worth of work. . . .You just made a few hampers [of peas] and that was it.[33] She further recalled winning a supermarket contest:

> Every time you went to Safeway, they would give you a little coupon. . . . Every time we went to the store we saved these. . . . So when we got one of those little tags, I told the checker, "This is going to be my winner," and he laughed. I was just joking with him. I gave the tag to the kids. . . . I think it was one of the girls who put saliva on it, and came in yelling, "Mom, Mom, you got the flag! You won!" . . . I rushed back to Safeway. I was really excited. I had won $100 and, oh boy, what a lot of food for the kids! After I got my check, I told Cesar, "Look, we can get some things." And he said, "I'm sorry, but this is going to our gas bill." He said he was about to lose his gasoline credit card because he owed $180. I was so disappointed, I sat and cried. I made so many plans for that $100![34]

As the union grew, Helen Chávez left the fields and became the manager of the credit union. Her integration of family, work, and activism exemplifies the "political familialism" described by sociologist Maxine Baca Zinn. Many women, like Helen Chávez, preferred to work behind the scenes, and, as Margaret Rose remarked, "Their contribution remains vital, but largely unrecognized."[35]

As Barbara Kingsolver's *Holding the Line* demonstrates,

distinctions between traditional/nontraditional, striker/sup-porter, and Mexican/Euro-American can become blurred. Her study of the 1983 Phelps Dodge copper strike in Arizona piv-ots on workers' identities as longtime residents of the mining towns of Clifton and Morenci. There existed a mingling of fami-lies—Euro-American, Mexican, and Euro-American/Mexi-can—whose genealogies were as much part of the mines as the shafts. While not to minimize the historical legacies of eth-nic tension, the strikers of 1983 perceived themselves more along the lines of a class-based mining community. Arizona copper miners had a long history of labor activism and, after World War II, viable union representation. According to Kingsolver, the women "had grown up with the union, a tool as familiar to them as a can opener or a stove."[36] Yet she also argues that, although these women had knowledge of and some direct experience in labor disputes and a few had worked in the mines themselves, this strike changed their conscious-ness. Although they faced tear gas, arrests, and grave finan-cial hardships, these women blocked traffic, took charge of the picket lines, and organized mass demonstrations. They kept their vigil for months. One law enforcement officer dis-ingenuously remarked, "If we could just get rid of those broads, we'd have it made." Furthermore, many had gone to work for the first time and recorded feeling confident and independent as the result of outside employment. "I think there are a lot of feminists around here," Jessie Tellez informed Kingsolver. "There are some strong women here who won't ever go back to the way things were."[37] Cleo Robeledo put it this way: "Be-fore, I was just a housewife. Now I am a partner." In *Chang-ing Woman*, historian Karen Anderson argues that these small-town Arizona women acted out of an "attachment to their community" and "used the managerial and interpersonal skills they had developed as homemakers in order to organize . . . and mediate." Reminiscent of the shift in consciousness among the miners' wives of *Salt of the Earth*, this strike stands as another example of the fusion of the private and public spheres for collective goals. However, as both Rudy Acuña and Karen Anderson have pointed out, the strike did not have a rosy ending. The NLRB ordered an election in which only the scabs could vote, and the union was decertified.[38]

Wages, benefits, safer working conditions, seniority, and union recognition are not the only reasons women will go out on strike. Regarding women's labor activism, modes of consumption can be as important as modes of production. In 1973, Tejana pecan shellers employed by McCrea and Son in Yancy, Texas, went out on strike for equal pay for equal work and for more sanitary conditions but also because they resented "being coerced into buying 'Avon' products from the employer's wife."[39] Activism among Mexican women workers takes many forms, and the contours of their individual and collective agency shift in response to work environment, familial roles, and personal subjectivities.

In analyzing the rich history of labor activism among Mexican women in the United States, the transformation of women's consciousness, whether explicitly "feminist" or not, must be problematized through the shifting interplay of gender, race, class, culture, generation, and region. It is easier to celebrate the ways in which Mexican women have exercised control over their work lives than to examine the costs involved. In *Women's Work and Chicano Families*, anthropologist Patricia Zavella reveals the intricate sets of negotiations, networks, and decisions made by Mexican cannery workers in the Santa Clara Valley as they strove to build a rank-and-file caucus within the Teamsters' Union. Constructing a lucid, engaging narrative, she brings out the patriarchal infrastructures as well as attitudes on three levels—on the shop floor, in the union hall, and at home.[40] Zavella recognizes that family, neighborhood, the ethnic/racial community, or union membership cannot guarantee a comfortable "community."

In *Sunbelt Working Mothers*, Zavella, with coauthors Louise Lamphere, Felipe Gonzales, and Peter Evans, continues this discussion of work, family, and unions, with an emphasis on women's multiple networks. Focusing on Hispana and Euro-American factory workers in Albuquerque, the authors accentuate the importance of class and social location in building networks. "Our approach to ethnic and racial difference," they write, "focuses on behavioral strategies in response to material conditions, rather than exclusively on a cultural construction of ethnic identity."[41] However, these authors, among others, note that in the 1980s and 1990s, the transformation of women's work networks into effective union representation seems more elusive than ever. In recent years, runaway shops, antilabor campaigns, high-priced union-busting consultants, participative management styles, police harassment, mechanization, unemployment, and even the NLRB have stymied labor activism.[42]

While labor organizing, in general, has waned, union campaigns among service workers in Los Angeles show a remarkable vitality in building communities of resistance. Both "Justice for Janitors" (affiliated with the Service Employees International Union) and the Hotel and Restaurant Employees Union, Local 11, demonstrate the power of grassroots organizing among the most politically and economically vulnerable sectors of the labor force—custodians, housekeepers, and food service workers, many of whom are undocumented Latino and Latina immigrants. In Los Angeles, those without union representation earn from $4.25 to $5.35 per hour—wages low enough for citizens "to qualify for food stamps."[43] Local 11's president María Elena Durazo is a college-educated Chicana for whom the idea of "going back to your community with your education" (a predominant theme of the Chicano student movement) was never empty rhetoric. Referring to immigrants as "the future of LA," Durazo eloquently stated, "I hope people will see unions as a tool for change and I hope we in the unions can respond to the challenge."[44]

With drive and conviction, Durazo leads a union that cannot be ignored. According to scholar/activist Mike Davis, Local 11 rewrites the book when it comes to organizing. "There will be no formal strike nor stationary picket line. . . . Across the city there will be leafleting, human billboards, flying pickets, delegations to city officials, and inevitably mass civil disobedience" (*Los Angeles Times*, 20 March 1994). Seeking a living wage, the members of Local 11 "speak of building not just a union, but a social movement like those of the 1930s and 1960s."[45]

As a labor historian, I will try to resist the temptation of privileging the workplace as the locus for claiming public space. Mexican women have relied on other institutions as well, including, historically, the Roman Catholic Church. In *Hoyt Street*, her autobiography of growing up in Pacoima, Mary Helen Ponce portrays the local parish as the heart of her neighborhood, in which time is recorded according to holidays and sacraments. In the barrios of the Southwest, Mexican women have been the stalwart volunteers for church fundraisers. At *jamaicas*, they sell tamales and *cascarones*, operate the cake walk, serve punch, organize the raffle, and help aspiring young anglers at the "go fish" booth. As feminist theologian Yolanda Tarango has argued, church activities were for many Latinas "the only arena in which they could legitimately, if indirectly, engage in developing themselves."[46]

Over the last twenty-five years, the Catholic Church, as both an institutional funding source (e.g., the Campaign for Human Development) and as a community center, began to support grassroots organizing campaigns among Mexican Americans. The best known is the Alinsky-based Communities Organized for Public Service (COPS) in San Antonio, Texas. In 1973, with the support of local parishes, especially parish women, Ernie Cortés Jr., began to organize neighbor by neighbor in San Antonio's Westside. He asked residents about their needs and concerns. This grassroots approach has permeated the infrastructure of COPS, with leadership emerging from local networks. Women's voluntary parish labor now became channeled for civic improvement and, indeed, several Tejanas have been elected president of the organization.[47]

Drainage problems and unpaved streets became their first order of business. Heavy rains made "peanut butter" of Westside roads; along with mud gushing into area homes and businesses, at times children died in "flash floods on their way to and from school."[48] Calling a public meeting with the city manager at the local high school in August 1974, COPS representatives caught him off guard with their numbers (over 500 people attended), their research, and their polite, yet firm queries. As former COPS president Beatrice Gallegos stated, "I sir'ed him to death." Through the use of demonstrations, political mobilization, research, and negotiation, COPS has significantly improved the material conditions of Westside and Southside neighborhoods. Focusing on municipal issues and boards, members of the twenty-five chapters of COPS ensure that developers, planners, school administrators, city officials, and Northside politicians do not ride roughshod over their communities. COPS has decisively influenced the distribution of Community Development Block Grants (CDBG); "56 percent of the CDBG money allotted to San Antonio has gone to COPS-endorsed projects." They have also been active in local utility and environmental issues and opposed the funneling of over one million dollars of federal urban renewal funds into a suburban country club. COPS also engaged in voter registration drives and, while not endorsing candidates, its members closely monitored the positions taken by local politicians.[49]

The film *Adelante Mujeres* credits COPS with the 1981 election of Henry Cisneros as mayor of San Antonio, the first Tejano to hold the position since Juan Seguin in 1841. Yet, the connection is not as clear as it may first appear. COPS may have generated a level of political consciousness or civic engagement among Mexican Americans; Cisneros, who had significant crossover appeal among Euro-Americans, may have reaped the benefits of this heightened politicization.[50]

Unlike other community-based organizations in which leverage seems to rise and ebb, COPS is a respected grassroots confederation with considerable municipal power. Scholars with divergent political perspectives have also recognized its importance as a model for community empowerment. Political scientist Peter Skerry praises COPS for the deftness with which the organization currently deals with development issues—relying on negotiation rather than confrontation. In defending Alinsky-style groups, such as COPS, from leftist criticism, historian/activist Rudy Acuña notes that without these groups, "Many middle-class and poor Latinos would not be involved in social change programs." Or as political scientist Joseph Sekul put it, "COPS has taken giant steps toward raising the quality of life in older neighborhoods, some of which may now become places where people can stay if they choose, rather than leave because they must."[51]

Along with issues of family and neighborhood, COPS has cultivated the leadership of women. In the words of former COPS president Beatrice Cortez, "Women have community ties. We knew that to make things happen in the community, you have to talk to people. It was a matter of tapping our networks."[52] Unfortunately, Peter Skerry fails to appreciate the importance of women's civic labor as he impugns weakness in leadership to the organization's reliance on "housewives." Referring to what he considers "the authoritative role of organizers," he writes:

> Because organizers expend considerable time . . . working with them, leaders tend to find their involvement . . . quite stimulating. Unaccustomed to the sort of attention they receive, leaders typically experience marked personal growth . . . But at the same time, these leaders . . . must be willing to put up with the organizers' demanding, sometimes harsh treatment. . . . For those who have a lot to learn, the bargain may seem a reasonable one. But for those with broader horizons and opportunities, it may not. As a result, the leaders . . . have been, with few exceptions, working- and lower-middle-class Mexican-American housewives with limited career

prospects. These organizations have a much tougher time attracting college-educated Mexican Americans, especially well-educated men.[53]

Such condescension hardly merits elaboration. Skerry misses the significance of Mexican women's histories of community responsibility, education, and action. Or, as Ernie Cortés simply stated, "COPS is like a university where people come to learn about public policy, public discourse, and public life."[54]

Feminist historian Sara Evans contextualizes Tejana participation in COPS within U.S. women's history. Bridging the public and private spheres, Evans argues that "women created a new public terrain through voluntary associations that became areas where citizenship could take on continuing and vital meanings, personal problems could be translated into social concerns, and democratic experiments could flourish."[55] While I agree with this supposition, I would also hasten to add that Mexican women's civic labor is neither recent in nature nor emulative in content. Examples of such activism can be located throughout the history of Mexican women in the United States. *Mutualistas*, like La Asociación HispanoAmericana; parish organizations, such as Hijas de María; middle-class auxiliaries, like the "ladies" of LULAC; and labor unions, such as UCAPAWA, provide strong evidence of women claiming public space for their community, their kin, and themselves.

With COPS as the model, similar organizations have emerged throughout the Southwest. Although beyond the scope of this study, Los Angeles alone has at least three recognized and vital Alinsky-style community confederations: United Neighborhood Organization (UNO), South Central Organizing Committee (SCOC), and East Valleys Organization (EVO).[56] Recently, members of SCOC tried to get Food 4 Less to build on a neighborhood lot owned by the discount grocery firm and the Community Redevelopment Agency. In the words of activist Orinio Ospinaldo:

> But having seen no progress at the Vermont site for many years, we were forced to take a dramatic step. . . . SCOC launched an action against Food 4 Less. We 65 adults and children went by bus to the Claremont [an upscale college community] office of Food 4 Less chairman, Ron Berkel. His office was

closed, so we distributed flyers outside. The leaflets
compared the price of his home to the price of opening a new grocery store.[57]

Such direct action brought Berkel to meetings with the SCOC
and Los Angeles Mayor Richard Riordan, and according to
Ospinaldo, "Suddenly, things look promising." A single parent of three, Ospinaldo linked both family and community in
the following remarks:

> No matter where you live, that's your community and
> you have to fight to claim it. . . . But don't do it alone.
> You need the strength of people . . . [united] for a
> common good. . . . Second, try to involve your
> children. I've found an activity that is fulfilling and
> that acts as an example for my children.[58]

Despite these articulated goals, the regional Catholic hierarchy has not always supported Latino and Latino/African
American community endeavors even when initiated by members of its own religious orders. *Calpulli* in San Bernardino
provides such an example.

For over twenty years, Sister Rosa Marta Zarate and Father Patricio Guillen have pursued a vision of a dynamic
mesitizaje of Latin American theology, MesoAmerican traditions, and community development projects. Forming
Communidades Ecclesiales de Base (CEBS) in San Bernardino,
Ontario, Riverside, San Diego, and the Imperial Valley, *calpulli*
(the Aztec equivalent of neighborhood) fosters self-sufficient
economic cooperatives. Unlike COPS, which works within the
system, CEBs seek to build financially sustainable communities outside the arena of municipal politics. In some respects,
calpulli represents an indigenous settlement house, offering
classes in English, vocational education, and other commonly
defined immigrant services. In addition, it closely resembles
economic cooperatives found in Nicaragua, El Salvador, and
other parts of Latin America. For example, calpulli's projects
"include a travel agency, tax and legal counseling, book store,
gardening and landscaping service, clothing manufacturing,
and food service."[59] Scholars Gilbert Cadena and Lara Medina
summarize Zarate and Guillen's efforts as follows:

> Today, they and a team of lay people successfully
> apply the tenets of liberation theology by creating a
> system of profit and nonprofit cooperatives employing
> residents from the local community. Their goal is to

create economically self-sufficient organizations that operate based on the principles of shared profit, shared responsibility, and shared power.[60]

Calpulli's successes have not gone unnoticed by church officials in Los Angeles. Several have looked askance at what they perceive as unorthodox community organizing. Indeed, Sister Rosa Marta Zarate received an ultimatum—return to Mexico or leave her order. She chose calpulli over the convent.

Zarate and Guillen also seek to make connections with southern California Native Americans and to educate project members in Meso-American history. Sister Rosa Marta Zarate reinterprets Aztec society from popular conceptions of feathered warriors and flamboyant sacrifices to understanding the economic cooperation that girded Aztec neighborhoods as well as an appreciation for their gendered spiritual values (e.g., recognizing Tonantzín, the earth mother). Preserving a historical memory also applies to contemporary activism. Calpulli has inaugurated an oral history project.[61] *El Plan de Acción de Calpulli* encapsulates its mission as "an organization inspired by the cultures of our people, our history, our projects, and our destiny." Or as Lara Medina relates, "The underlying theme is living out their faith in a God who wants justice and humanity." She continues, "This faith motivates them to develop projects that will empower the personal and communal lives of la gente."[62]

Contemporary women's activism, however, does not necessarily revolve around the church. The work of sociologist Mary Pardo, for example, clearly delineates the networks of neighborhood organization among Mexican women in East Los Angeles. Founded in 1984, the Mothers of East Los Angeles arose out of Resurrection Parish [no pun intended] to halt the construction of a prison in their community. This group of concerned women attracted 3,000 supporters as it staged demonstrations and engaged in political lobbying. Juana Gutiérrez summed up her involvement as follows, "I don't consider myself political. I'm just someone looking out for the community, for the youth . . . on the side of justice."[63]

State Assemblywoman Gloria Molina fervently supported their cause. She pointed out that the new prison would be built "within a four mile radius" of four correctional facilities and "within two miles" of twenty-six schools. Believing that enough is enough, Molina asked the rhetorical question:

> Do you think this could happen to Woodland Hills
> or Torrance? LA is supposed to have a prison,
> consequently, our community must bear the burden
> because we don't have the political strength to
> oppose it.[64]

However, Mothers of East Los Angeles would forge that political strength.

While Peter Skerry characterized the women as housewives "led by a parish priest," Mary Pardo delineates Mexican women's organizing strategies that evolved independently of the Catholic Church. In her dissertation "Identity and Resistance: Mexican American Women and Grassroots Activism in Two Los Angeles Communities," Pardo offers compelling portraits of women as neighborhood activists, women who contextualize their civic labor as an extension of familial responsibilities. Although considered "political novices," the Mothers of East Los Angeles took on Governor George Deukmejian and the Department of Corrections and won. The prison was never built.[65]

Almost from its inception, the Mothers of East Los Angeles have dedicated themselves to environmental issues. Their activities have ranged from leading the fight against a proposed incinerator to distributing free toilets to neighborhood residents. The Mothers of East Los Angeles has also raised money for scholarships and organized graffiti clean-up teams. The fusion of family and community resonates in the voices of these women. "The mother is the soul of the family; but the child is the heartbeat," Aurora Castillo, one of the Mothers of East Los Angeles' 's founders, explained. "We must fight to keep the heart of our community beating. Not just for our children, but for everyone's children."[66] Like Dolores Huerta and the women of the United Farm Workers, the Mothers of East Los Angeles have has drawn on familial motifs for community and personal empowerment.

Mexican women's community activism is not limited to city streets. In his photojournal, *Organizing for Our Lives: New Voices from Rural Communities*, Richard Street poignantly documents the struggles of Mexican and Southeast Asian farm workers against toxic waste, pesticides, labor abuses, and discrimination in housing and education. Highlighting the activism among women, Street profiles several grassroots associations represented by California Rural Legal Assistance. In chronicling organized protests against the building of an incinerator by Chem Waste in Kettleman City, Street photographs a young Mexican girl dressed in her frilly Sunday best. The Mexicanita is holding a large sign featuring Bart Simpson with the balloon caption, "DON'T HAVE AN INCINERATOR, MAN!"[67] This appropriation of an icon of U.S. popular culture represents a bifurcation of consciousness where the boundaries blur to the point that cultural codes converge in this subversion of the image.

In 1988, Mujeres Mexicanas, a campesina organization, was formed in the Coachella Valley. This group has participated in voter registration drives and electoral politics. Richard Street credits its members for the election of three Chicano city council candidates as well as the initiation of AIDS education in the valley. "They provided pamphlets, condoms, and bleach to disinfect needles. No local government or health agency in Coachella Valley was attempting anything like it."[68]

Many of the mujeres also belong to the United Farm Workers, in which Millie Treviño-Sauceda has been a rank-and-file organizer. In explaining the mission of Mujeres Mexicanas, Treviño-Sauceda revealed:

> Since the beginning we all agreed that our role was to promote the socio-political and psychological empowerment of campesinas. We also agreed that professional women-the ones with college educations—could only be advisors, not active members, because professionals tend to take over the leadership of the group. We wanted campesinas to be in control .[69]

The testimonies of the campesinas give witness to the power of women's collective action. In the words of María "Cuca" Carmona, "We have found our place within our community and even within our homes."[70]

Sustaining community space can be as important as finding it. For some areas, economic survival is resistance. In northern New Mexico, former SNCC volunteer and Chicano movement activist María Varela has helped create and foster viable economic cooperatives among impoverished Hispano farmers, shepherds, and weavers. Los Ganados del Valle, which was founded in 1983, "operates on $150,000 annual budget and has 50 families as members" (*Chronicle of Philanthropy*, 24 July 1990). The cooperatives market yarns, quilts, clothing, and rugs; in 1990, its Tierra Wools subsidiary reached annual sales of $250,000. Los Ganados del Valle has also organized around local environmental issues concerning grazing rights. A recipient of a MacArthur foundation fellowship, Varela astutely contends, "I learned . . . that it is not enough to pray over an injustice or protest it or research it to death, but that you have to take concrete action to solve it."[71] "Concrete action" resonates in the voices presented throughout this volume. In examining women's activism, I am struck by the threads of continuity, the intertwining of community, family, and self. For some women, their involvement remains couched in familial ideology, while others articulate feelings of personal empowerment or contextualize their actions within a framework of community-based feminism. Whether or not they proclaim feminist identities, their actions privilege collective politics over personal politics. Claiming public space, furthermore, can sustain, not subordinate, women's personal needs. Struggles for social justice cannot be boiled down to a dialectic of accommodation and resistance but should be placed within the centrifuge of negotiation, subversion, and consciousness. Building community is both a legacy and a responsibility. As a storyteller, listener, recorder, and amateur theorist, I am reminded of a passage in Eudora Welty's *One Writer's Beginnings*:

> Each of us is moving, changing, and with respect to others. As we discover, we remember; remembering, we discover; and most intensely do we experience this when our separate journeys converge.[72]

Feminist theorist Chela Sandoval has adroitly distilled "the differential mode of oppositional consciousness" that underlies "concrete action." In her words: "The differential mode of oppositional consciousness depends upon the ability to read the current situation of power and of self-consciously choosing and adopting the ideological form best suited to push against its configurations."[73] In reflecting on her positionality in the hegemonic racial and economic structures of El Paso, Farah striker Estela Gomez addressed her grievances in a courageous letter to the editor:

> A lot of people in the El Paso community ask quite often, with all of these good benefits Willie Farah provides at his factory, why did these people walk on strike? . . . These benefits were only there for the good of the company, not for the worker. . . . All these

benefits put together could never make up for the only thing we are now struggling for and that is human dignity.

What good was the vaccuum [sic] cleaner he gave us for Christmas, when a lot of us didn't even earn enough to afford a carpet. . . . And the turkey for Thanksgiving—was it to make up for the time your supervisor made you cry because he wanted more production from you, as if you were a machine and not a human being? . . .

Be grateful to Farah they say, for all this man has done for you. I say Farah should be grateful to us, the Mexican-American, who from our sweat have [sic] worked hard to make the pants that have built his empire.[74]

Mexicana/Mexican American/Chicana activists, with determination, creativity, acumen, and dignity, have strived to exercise some control over their lives in relation to material realities and individual subjectivities as forged within both the spatial and affinitive bonds of community. Their courage comes forth out of the shadows.

Notes

1. Elsa Chávez [pseudonym], interview by author, 19 April 1983. See also Laurie Coyle, Gail Hershatter, and Emily Honig, "Women at Farah: An Unfinished Story," in *Mexican Women in the United States: Struggles Past and Present* (Los Angeles: UCLA Chicano Studies Research Center Publications, 1980), 117, 119; San Francisco Bay Area Farah Strike Support Committee, "Chicanos Strike at Farah [pamphlet]," (January 1974), 2–3, 6–7; Sidney Metzger, Bishop of El Paso, to the Bishop of Rochester, 31 October 1972, letter reprinted in *Viva La Huelga: Farah Strike Bulletin no. 15* (ACW newsletter).

2. Coyle, Hershatter, and Honig, "Women at Farah," 135.

3. Allen Pusey, "Clothes Made the Man," *Texas Monthly* (June 1977), 133, 136–37; "A Boycott to Aid Garment Workers," *Business Week* (26 August 1972): 53–54; *Lubbock Avalanche Journal*, (26 November 1972); *El Paso Times* (6 June 1983); San Francisco Bay Area Farah Strike Support Committee, "Chicanos Strike at Farah," 9; John Rebchook, "El Paso Is a Minimum Wage Town," *Special Report: The Border* (El Paso: El Paso Herald Post, Summer 1983), 74. Note that

in 1983, the El Paso Chamber of Commerce honored Willie Farah as its "Manufacturer of the Year," an "award bestowed on a business-man who has excelled in the advancement of his career while dem-onstrating an exceptional measure of concern for the community" (*El Paso Times*, 6 June 1983).

4. See San Francisco Bay Area Farah Strike Support Commit-tee, "Chicanos Strike at Farah," 4, 7; Coyle, Hershatter, and Honig, "Women at Farah," 127, 128–30; *Viva La Huelga: Farah Strike Bulle-tin no. 1; Washington Post* (28 September 1972); *Business Week* (26 August 1972).

5. See *Viva La Huelga: Farah Strike Bulletin, no. 6; Washington Post* (28 September 1972).

6. See *El Paso Times* (29 November 1973, 22 February 1974); *El Paso Herald Post* (27 June 1973, 7 January 1974, 11 January 1974); Paul Newton Poling, "For the Defense of the Farah Workers" (pamphlet published by Farah Manufacturing, ca. 1973); Chávez in-terview; Coyle, Hershatter, and Honig, "Women at Farah," 128–30. "The headline "Farah Workers Group Diverts Yule Donation from Church" was a typical headline in El Paso papers (*El Paso Herald Post*, 22 December 1972).

7. *Guardian* (6 March 1974).

8. Quote is taken from the *El Paso Herald Post* (15 December 1973). Examples of such letters can be found in the *El Paso Herald Post* (23 November 1973, 28 January 1974, 15 February 1974), *El Paso Times* (15 December 1973, 14 January 1974, 25 January 1974).

9. Quote is taken from the *El Paso Herald Post* (23 January 1974). Examples of letters supporting the strikers can be found in the *El Paso Times* (14 January 1974, 27 January 1974, 2 February 1974).

10. *The Washington Post* (28 September 1972).

11. Ibid. See *The Advance* [ACW National Newspaper] (January 1973), 5–16; Deborah DeWitt Malley, "How the Union Beat Willie Farah," *Fortune* (August 1974): 167, 238; *Viva La Huelga, Farah Strike Bulletin, no. 1* (1972); *Viva La Huelga, Farah Strike Bulletin, no. 1* (1972), no. 4 (1972), no. 8 (1972), no. 10 (1972); *El Paso Times* (12 September 1972); *El Paso Herald Post* (2 February 1973). Please note that Senator Gaylord Nelson (D-Wisconsin) chaired the Citizens' Committee for Justice for Farah Workers and the legendary African American labor leader A. Philip Randolph served as honorary chair. National figures who publicly joined the committee included Senator Edward Kennedy, Carey McWilliams, Joanne Woodward, Vernon Jordan, Archibald MacLeish, Ramsey Clark, Clark Kerr, and Arthur Schlesinger, Jr. (*Viva La Huelga, Farah Strike Bulletin, no 4, 1972*). Furthermore, the *El Paso Herald Post*, in announcing the arrival of Democratic vice-presidential candidate Sergeant Shriver, mentions Shriver's "advance man" Bill Clinton (*El Paso Herald Post* (12 Sep-tember 1972). The headline reads: "Democrats Plan Big Love-In."

12. *Texas Monthly* (June 1977): 137.

13. Coyle, Hershatter, and Honig, "Women at Farah," 134. See also p. 135, 141.

14. Chávez interview. In 1972, Farah employed from 9,000 to 10,000 workers. Farah strike-support publications and the classic scholarly study "Women at Farah" place the number of strikers at 4,000. The anti-union piece "For the Defense of the Farah Workers" and an article in *Fortune* magazine underestimate their numbers by half, or 2,000 strikers. *The Washington Post* judges the strikers at 3,000 out of 8,500 workers. See Coyle, Hershatter, and Honig, "Women at Farah," 117; San Francisco Bay Area Farah Strike Support Committee, "Chicanos Strike," 1; Poling, "For the Defense of the Farah Workers," 5, 13; *Fortune* (August 1974): 165, 167; *The Washington Post* (28 September 1972).

15. Chávez interview.

16. See Coyle, Hershatter, and Honig, "Women at Farah," 117, 129, 131–34; Chávez interview; Portland [Oregon] Strike Support Committee, "Farah Strike: Our Struggle, Too [pamphlet]" (1973), 7, 12.

17. Rose Pesotta, *Bread upon the Waters* (New York: Dodd, Mead, and Company, 1944), 50–51. During the 1959–1961 Tex-Son garment strike in San Antonio, Mexican-American children passed out balloons to children entering local department stores imprinted with the message "Don't Buy Tex-Son Children's Clothes." See the Tex-Son strike photographs, George Lambert Collection Archives, University of Texas, Arlington, Arlington, Texas. For more information on these strikes, see Clementina Durón, "Mexican Women and Labor Conflict in Los Angeles: The ILGWU Dressmakers Strike of 1933," *Aztlán* 15, no. 1 (1984): 145–61; Irene Ledesma, "Texas Newspapers and Chicana Workers' Activism: 1919–1972," *Western Historical Quarterly* 26, no. 3 (autumn 1995): 309–331.

18. Hershatter, and Honig, "Women at Farah," 133–34.

19. San Francisco Bay Area Farah Strike Support Committee, "Chicanos Strike at Farah," 16.

20. Chávez interview; Coyle, Hershatter, and Honig, "Women at Farah," 117, 138–42.

21. Coyle, Hershatter, and Honig, "Women at Farah," 143.

22. Chávez interview.

23. Jacques Levy, *Cesar Chávez: Autobiography of La Causa* (New York: W. W. Norton, 1975) provides a comprehensive and intimate portrait of Cesar Chávez and the birth of the United Farm Workers (UFW). See especially Book 4, titled "The Birth of Union," 149–218, and Book 5, "Victory in the Vineyards," 219–325. An outstanding scholarly monograph on the UFW is Linda C. Majka and Theo J. Majka, *Farm Workers, Agribusiness, and the State* (Philadelphia:

Temple University Press, 1982). Figures on union membership are taken from the *Los Angeles Times* (27 March 1994).

24. Quote is from Levy, *Cesar Chávez*, 160. See also Barbara Baer and Glenda Matthews, "Women of the Boycott," in *America's Working Women: A Documentary History—1600 to the Present*, eds. Rosalyn Baxandall and Susan Reverby (New York: Vintage Books, 1976), 363–72; Graciela Martínez Moreno, interview by author, 10 January 1983; Ernest Moreno, interview by author, 10 January 1983; María del Carmen Romero, interview by author, 8 January 1983. The best historical survey on women's involvement in the United Farm Workers is Margaret Eleanor Rose's "Women in the United Farm Workers: A Study of Chicana and Mexicana Participation in a Labor Union, 1950 to 1980" (Ph.D. dissertation, University of California, Los Angeles, 1988). For further details on family involvement, see Chapter 6 of this dissertation.

25. Martínez Moreno interview. See also Moreno interview and Romero interview.

26. Martínez Moreno interview; Rose, "Women in the United Farm Workers," 9, 150–151, 243–89.

27. Fran Leeper Buss, ed., *Forged under the Sun/Forjada bajo del Sol: The Life of María Elena Lucas* (Ann Arbor: University of Michigan Press, 1993), 216–17. See also 195.

28. Buss, *Forged under the Sun*, 258. See also 220–21, 225–31.

29. With regard to sexism within the union, María Elena Lucas stated, "There's been times as a woman with the FLOC that I've felt swatted like a fly, and as a woman, I think that's wrong" (Buss, *Forged under the Sun*, p. 258). In a recent scholarly study of the Farm Labor Organizing Committee, the authors make no mention of the contributions of María Elena Lucas, referring to her briefly as a victim of pesticide poisoning. "Usually a bright and cheerful woman, she told her story of pesticide poisoning . . . with tears on her face," states W. K. Barger and Ernesto M. Reza, *The Farm Labor Movement in the Midwest* (Austin: University of Texas Press, 1994), 31. It is a strictly male-centered narrative that erases women's roles as leaders and rank-and file-activists:

30. Rose, "Women in the United Farm Workers," 101. See also x, 7–10, 46, 68–80, 96–103. An excellent portrait of Dolores Huerta can be seen in "Act One: Work and Family," in the TBS series *A Century of Women* (1994). Noted Chicana filmmaker Sylvia Morales produced this segment.

31. Rudolfo Acuña, *Occupied America : A History of Chicanos*, 3rd. ed. (New York: Harper Collins, 1988), 269. See also Alan Covey, ed., *A Century of Women* (Atlanta: TBS Books, 1994), 46. [This is the companion volume to the TBS series of the same name, cf. n. 30.]

32. Covey, *A Century of Women*, 47.

33. Levy, *Cesar Chávez*, 168.

34. Ibid., 168–69.

35. Rose, "Women in the United Farm Workers," 150. See also 117, 134–37, 140, 144–51. Rose refers to "political familialism" in n. 45, p. 160. See Maxine Baca Zinn, "Political Familialism: Toward Sex Role Equality in Chicano Families," *Aztlán* 8, no. 1 (1975): 13–26.

36. Barbara Kingsolver, *Holding the Line: Women in the Great Arizona Mining Strike of 1983* (Ithaca: ICR Press, 1989), 17. See also 1–21. For historical background on Arizona mining, see James W. Byrkit, *Forging the Copper Collar* (Tucson: University of Arizona Press, 1982) and "Los Mineros," a PBS American Experience series, produced by Hector Galán (1991). (The historical consultant for "Los Mineros," Christine Marín, a doctoral student and archivist at Arizona State University, is writing on the history of Mexican mining families in Arizona.) A breath-taking new study is Linda Gordon, *The Great Arizona Oprhan Abduction* (Cambridge: Harvard University Press, 1999).

37. Kingsolver, *Holding the Line*, 15, 186. See also 15, 31–33, 146–49, 157–62, 176–90.

38. Karen Anderson, *Changing Woman: A History of Racial Ethnic Women in Modern America* (New York: Oxford University Press, 1996), 147–48. See also Acuña, *Occupied America*, 448.

39. Marta P. Cotera, *Diosa y Hembra: The History and Heritage of Chicanas in the U.S.* (Austin: Information Systems Development, 1976), 179.

40. Patricia Zavella, *Women's Work and Chicano Families: Cannery Workers of the Santa Clara Valley* (Ithaca: Cornell University Press, 1987).

41. Louise Lamphere, Patricia Zavella, Felipe Gonzales with Peter B. Evans, *Sunbelt Working Mothers: Reconciling Family and Factory* (Ithaca: Cornell University Press, 1993), 285. Note: *Hispana* is a common term of self-identification for Mexican-American women in New Mexico and Colorado.

42. Lamphere, et al., *Sunbelt Working Mothers*, 290–91. Lamphere's Chapter 5, "Management Ideology and Practice in Participatory Plants" (138–82), seems particularly enlightening. For more examples of the structural difficulties in organizing women in southwestern industries, see Vicki L. Ruiz, "'And Miles to go . . .': Mexican Women and Work, 1930–1985," in *Western Women, Their Land, Their Lives*, eds. Lillian Schlissel, Vicki L. Ruiz, and Janice Monk (Albuquerque: University of New Mexico Press, 1988): 117–36.

43. *Los Angeles Times* (6 September 1993); see also (12 August 1992) and (20 March 1994).

44. *Los Angeles Times* (27 September 1992).

45. *Los Angeles Times* (20 March 1994).

46. Mary Helen Ponce, *Hoyt Street: An Autobiography* (Albuquerque: University of New Mexico Press, 1993); Personal observations by the author; Yolanda Tarango, "The Hispanic Woman and Her Role

in the Church," *New Theology View*, Vol. 3 (November 1990): 58. Cascarones are eggshells filled with confetti.

47. Joseph D. Sekul, "Communities Organized for Public Service: Citizen Power and Public Policy in San Antonio," in *The Politics of San Antonio: Community, Progress, and Power*, eds. David R. Johnson, John A. Booth, and Richard J. Harris (Lincoln: University of Nebraska Press, 1983), 176–77; Sara M. Evans, *Born for Liberty: A History of Women in America* (New York: The Free Press, 1989), 309.

48. Peter Skerry, *Mexican Americans: The Ambivalent Minority* (New York: The Free Press, 1993), 177–78.

49. Sekul, "Communities Organized for Public Service," 175, 181. See also 175–90; Skerry, *Mexican Americans*, 176–80; Sidney Plotkin, "Democratic Change in the Urban Political Economy: San Antonio's Edwards Aquifer Controversy," in *The Politics of San Antonio*, 167–71; Acuña, *Occupied America*, 433–34; John A. Booth, "Political Change in San Antonio, 1970–82: Toward Decay or Democracy," *in The Politics of San Antonio*, 195–96, 200.

50. See "Adelante Mujeres," video produced by the National Women's History Project (1992); Arnoldo De León, *Mexican Americans in Texas: A Brief History* (Arlington Heights, Ill.: Harlan Davidson, Inc., 1993), 37, 139; Booth, "Political Change in San Antonio," 200, 202, 204.

51. Skerry, *Mexican Americans*, 176–80; Acuña, Occupied America, 436; Sekul, "Communities Organized for Public Service," 190.

52. Evans, *Born for Liberty*, 309.

53. Skerry, *Mexican Americans*, 149.

54. Evans, *Born for Liberty*, 309.

55. Ibid., 313.

56. For differing views of contemporary Alinksy-based groups in Los Angeles, contrast Acuña, *Occupied America*, with Skerry, *Mexican Americans*.

57. *Los Angeles Times* (2 May 1994).

58. Ibid.

59. Lara Medina, "*Calpulli*: A Chicano Self-Help Organization," *La Gente* (1990). See also Gilbert Cadena and Lara Medina, "Liberation Theology and Social Change: Chicanas and Chicanos in the Catholic Church" (unpublished manuscript), 12–17. Gracias a Lara Medina for this news clipping and for our conversations on Latino liberation theology.

60. Cadena and Medina, "Liberation Theology and Social Change," 13.

61. Cadena and Medina, "Liberation Theology and Social Change," 14–16. I gave an oral history workshop for *calpulli* in January 1994. During the workshop, Sister Rosa Martha Zarate articulated the need to make links with local Native Americans and recognize the significance of Mesoamerican indigenous traditions.

62. Medina, "*Calpulli*: A Chicano Self-Help Organization."

63. *Los Angeles Herald Examiner* (28 September 1986). See also Mary Pardo, "Identity and Resistance: Mexican American Women and Grassroots Activism in Two Los Angeles Communities" (Ph.D. dissertation, University of California, Los Angeles, 1990); Acuña, *Occupied America*, 424. Gracias a Howard Shorr for sending me this clipping.

64. Tom Chorneau, "Molina Lays Siege to Prison," *Los Angeles Downtown News* (ca. June 1986), p. 6.). News clipping courtesy of Howard Shorr.

65. *Los Angeles Herald Examiner* (28 September 1986). See also Skerry, *Mexican Americans*, 181; Pardo, "Identity and Resistance."

66. Schuyler, "LA Moms," loc. cit. See also *Chicago Tribune* (20 March 1995); *Los Angeles Times* (7 September 1995); Nina Schuyler, "LA Moms Fight Back," *Progressive* 56, no. 8 (August 1992): 13. Gracias a Betsy Jameson for sharing these clippings with me.

67. Richard Steven Street, *Organizing for Our Lives: New Voices from Rural Communities* (Portland, Or: Newsage Press and California Rural Legal Assistance, 1992), 29. Gracias a Richard Street for sending me a copy of this important book.

68. Street, *Organizing for Our Lives*, 69–70. See also 66–81.

69. Ibid., 68.

70. Ibid., 75.

71. *Chronicle of Philanthropy* (24 July 1990); *New York Times* (20 August 1990). Gracias a the National Women's History Project for sending me these news clippings. With regard to Los Ganados del Valle's efforts to secure cooperative grazing rights, see Laura Pulido, *Environmentalism and Economic Justice: Two Chicano Struggles in the Southwest* (Tucson: University of Arizona Press, 1996).

72. Eudora Welty, *One Writer's Beginnings* (Cambridge: Harvard University Press, 1983), 102.

73. Chela Sandoval, "U.S. Third World Feminism: The Theory and Method of Oppositional Consciousness in the Postmodern World," *Genders* 4 (1991): 15.

74. *El Paso Times* (6 February 1974).

"She Has Served Others in More Intimate Ways": The Domestic Servant Reform in Yucatán, 1915–1918

Emma Pérez

In May 1916, Nicolasa Gutiérrez filed a complaint against her employer, Alvino Manzanilla Canto. Manzanilla, who owned the plantation San Francisco, responded to the complaint that Gutiérrez had filed with the Mexican government's justice department by refusing to comply with her demands. Señora Gutiérrez had requested that her employer pay fifteen dollars for her trip home to Veracruz. The employee maintained that the *hacendado* (plantation owner) brought her to his plantation, where she remained *enganchada*, or "hooked," as a contract laborer. She served as a domestic in his house for eighteen months. Manzanilla protested her request for payment of the trip and insisted that he hired only male laborers. The owner alleged that she had worked eight days on his plantation and then had assisted in his home where she had received a good salary. Manzanilla Canto schemed to discredit the servant by inferring that she was immoral and disloyal, traits that did not become a woman and certainly not a house servant (Canto 1916).

That Nicolasa Gutiérrez could file a grievance at all was unusual, given that servants, with or without a contract, had few rights. Prior to 1916, domestic servants like Gutiérrez kept their complaints to themselves. Gutiérrez was able to sue her employer, a wealthy, influential plantation owner, because the arrival of a socialist general from the interior of Mexico had

41

changed the lives of domestic servants in Yucatán, setting aside a system in which they had no recourse within a rigid class society that offered women few rights.

A trusted ally of Venustiano Carranza, General Salvador Alvarado had marched on Mérida, the capital of Yucatán, on 19 March 1915 to revolutionize the remote peninsula (Alvarado 1915). Because Yucatán was located in the southeastern corner of the country, far from the interior where battles raged, the state had been largely unaffected by the Mexican Revolution. When Carranza declared himself the leader of the revolution, he was forced to take refuge in Veracruz from 1914 to 1917, when he assumed the presidency. By then, his policies had shaped Alvarado's, Carranza's appointee as governor of Yucatán.[1]

The new governor immediately generated reforms that had far-reaching effects. Just a month after his inauguration, he introduced Decree Number Five to improve working conditions for domestic servants (Alvarado 1915). The decree empowered women at the bottom of the social scale by providing them with legal recourse against unjust employers. Alvarado was fully aware that 57 percent of the female population in Yucatán earned their living as domestics; in Mérida alone, 61 percent cleaned and cooked for people other than their families.

Furthermore, Yucatán's dependence upon henequen, its monocrop, hindered the state's potential for real changes. Indeed, it was this dependence that thwarted a Yucatecan reform movement. Henequen, a sisal plant of hard fiber used to make binder twine, was introduced to the region in 1838 (Joseph 1982, 22–29). It bolstered Yucatán's prosperity initially but then created a boom-and-bust plantation economy that fluctuated at the whim of world market prices, a situation that further intensified exploitative relations between hacendados and workers (Wells 1982, 233–242). Plantation workers were exploited through debt peonage, a system that tied them to a plantation through enforced debt. This was the Yucatán that Governor Alvarado faced in 1915.

This essay has three goals: to offer a glimpse into domestic servants' lives through their own words; to show that the revolution ignored gender issues; and to examine how sociosexual-racial relations are linked to a job like domestic service where deference and harassment characterize the occupation. I employ the term *sociosexual-racial relations* to show the juncture between class, gender, and race, but more specifically to criticize how this fusion places working-class women of color in a position of powerlessness that they must struggle against constantly in a society that ideologically exploits them because of their economic status, their sociosexual relations with men, and their racial relations with white people. Hence, the discussion of sociosexual-racial relations points out that poor women of color are perceived as powerless and therefore easily exploited. Finally, I hope that a case study on Mexican women will yield answers to contemporary puzzles about feminism, socialism, class, gender, and race relations.

Accounts by working-class women are usually unavailable to historians. Though not a definitive study of domestic service in Yucatán, this essay offers a window into women's lives through government documents that reflect the personal testimonies of women. Although government officials or family relatives sometimes wrote the servant's complaint, it was nevertheless recorded in her own words. Naturally, the official might have misinterpreted or misunderstood the testimonies, a factor that demands consideration. Because the grievance was between the employer and the employee, the employer's perception of domestics can also be gleaned from the documents.

In her comparative study on domestic servants in England and France, Theresa McBride attributes the "rise of a servant class to the growth of a middle class" during the Industrial Revolution (1976, 11). Rural to urban migration placed these women in available service positions. While there seems little comparison between an industrializing Europe and a developing Yucatán, McBride does provide useful insights.

McBride noted that the census defined a domestic servant as either a household employee or a hired agricultural worker (1976, 139). In Yucatán, where large landholding families hired domestic servants who probably moved back and forth between the house and the fields, such a definition seems applicable. Nicolasa Gutiérrez's case, for example, indicated that she had worked in both arenas (Manzanilla Canto 1916). The Mexican census of 1910 reported an exorbitant number of women as domestic servants yet practically none as agricultural workers. Because the duties overlapped, the census placed them only in the one category. Unfortunately, it is impossible to determine how many women actually worked in the henequen fields. Considering that henequen was the backbone of the region's economy, it seems reasonable to assume that a substantial number of women worked in the fields.

Lourdes Arizpe's study of women in the informal labor sector confirms further the overlapping worlds of field- and housework. Arizpe points out that in Mexico and in other Latin American developing nations, women's labor in rural areas has been recorded incorrectly. She argues that women are "classed as housewives," and therefore, "economically inactive" because they only perform "agricultural tasks" like "seeding and weeding during harvest time." When the seasonal work is over, they return to the household where many work as domestics (Arizpe 1977, 30).

Domestic service in Latin America has dominated women's occupations since the early twentieth century, especially in urban areas. Tracing women's rural to urban migration can determine how many women ended up in service work when they arrived in the cities. In Yucatán, plantations provided employment for women, and thus many worked in the rural areas, serving in the home and laboring in the fields.

Reform or Revolution

Reform and revolution are hardly compatible when the socioeconomic system under reform resembles capitalism. While bourgeois socialists have argued for the gradual evolution of capitalism to socialism through reforms, Marxists point out that capitalism must be absolutely replaced to achieve the final result: an egalitarian, communist society (Harrison 1978, 11–23).[2] Socialist-feminists also criticize "reforming" a capitalist-patriarchal society that claims to offer women equal rights yet by definition defies such privileges.[3] While Marxists explain the workers' oppressive conditions in the labor market, whether women or men, they fail to discern the subtle nuances of gender oppression that move beyond the market place. Class analyses are detectable because one can observe surplus value. But, "the value over and which is necessary to cover a worker's means of subsistence" (Sweezy 1970, 56–66)[4] says nothing of sexual exploitation.

In analyses of oppression, a class analysis often subsumes gender precisely because of the social relations that create and are created by gender ideology. Socialization, then, constructs gender identity (MacKinnon 1982, 531).[5] Gender ideology decodes how a society keeps women in their place and how they, too, keep themselves in their place and sustain a patriarchal, capitalist society that oppresses them (Barrett 1980).[6]

Yucatán's bourgeois revolution did not provide the possibility for a refined class analysis. Instead, the revolution showed how gender ideology aided the cause to the detriment of women's real progress. The governor, however, turned to reform. The domestic service decree represented a bourgeois reform that imposed a temporary solution to a deeper, more complex problem—that of an economy that served an elite population. Alvarado attempted to rectify injustices by reforming a society that primarily aided wealthy landowners. The revolutionary party's governor did not overthrow an economic system that kept domestics in an exploited position, nor did he offer alternatives. Instead, Decree Number Five addressed race, class, and gender inequalities in a job held by a majority of the female population. Some of the inequities were resolved, some were not. More than anything, the reform allowed servants to complain, thus exposing race, class, and gender relations during the revolution. Perhaps the Governor hoped to win the political endorsement of these women. How much their support could possibly help him, however, was indeed questionable, because women held no political entitlement.

Domestic service exploits intimacy and boundaries. The servant and the family she served often created familial ties. The domestic serves the family who employs her as if she were a mother to the children, a mistress to the husband, and a confidante to the wife of the household. The family being served crosses boundaries and creates a false notion of intimacy with the household servant. The servant, on the other hand, masks herself in order to be employed, feigns loyalty to survive, and also tries to establish boundaries to sustain self-dignity. To survive their employment, women deferred to employers absolutely, in all matters. Employment pertained to "serving" a privileged family in a household where the servants, especially Maya, were expected to be "loyal," "respectful," "grateful" and "moral." Decree Number Five helped female household servants begin to establish boundaries between themselves and privileged employers.

Historically, one's gender, race, and class determined whether one would enter domestic service. While young men often acted as house servants, their numbers did not compare with those of the young women who did so, nor did young men endure the frequent sexual and social harassment that women suffered. As historian Gerda Lerner points out, "the practice of using slave women as servants and sex objects became the standard for the class dominance over women in all historic periods." Hence, slavery, domestic service, and sex became inextricably enmeshed. Domestic service originated from slavery as young women became part of the booty when conquerors raided villages (Lerner 1986, 88).

While the sexual exploitation of the women in the cases cited in this study does not seem obvious, women from a low economic status, and often distinctly Maya, were abused by employers who took advantage of them. Their gender, their race, and their class placed them in a social category where men, middle-class women, and non-Indians could exploit them. So while the job depended upon intimate, familial relations, sociosexual-racial exploitation was also inherent (Rollins 1985, 155–203).[7]

In Mérida, the female population reached 41,924 in 1910 (Secretaría de Agricultura y Fomento 1918, 1307). Of these women, 25,669 worked as domestic servants. For rural Yucatán the numbers were comparable. Of the state's 171,588 females, 98,162 secured employment as domestics (1806–1807). Women employed as laundresses accounted for only 1,728, the second largest number of Mérida's wage-earning women. There were 684 listed as seamstresses, making sewing the third most popular occupation. Teaching formed the fourth highest with 312 of the city's women working in this profession (1806–1807). Overall, these statistics demonstrate that women worked as domestic servants more than in any other occupation in Mérida and in the state of Yucatán.

Decree Number Five changed the lives of domestic servants. From 1916 to 1918, a series of complaints like Nicolasa Gutiérrez's were filed with the Department of Labor and the Department of Justice. These complaints establish that the ordinance changed women's lives, if only minimally. Through these documents, one can discern who some of these women were, who they worked for, and what conditions they faced at work. How much did they earn? How were they paid and how often? Why did they file grievances, and who usually won, the employee or the employer? Did they live with the families who employed them? If they had children, did the children live with them?

The law had seven articles, however, and Articles Two, Three, and Four summarized the most common abuses against domestic workers by their employers. Article Two mandated that domestics receive a salary, while Article Three outlawed paying servants with clothes or food in lieu of a salary. Article Four prohibited employers from forcing employees to profess the employer's religion. Evidently, employers sought to enforce Catholicism over Maya religious practices (Alvarado 1915). Governor Alvarado signed the decree on 24 April 1915.

Grievances Filed by Domestic Servants

Nicolasa Gutiérrez caused an uproar on the hacienda San Francisco when she used Decree Number Five against her employer. She testified that hacendado Alvino Manzanilla forcibly detained her with a contract that kept her enganchada.[8] The entire Manzanilla family tried to disprove the servant Gutiérrez's claim. Family members protested by painting her as a "wretched beggar with syphilis" (Manzanilla 1916).

The landowner refused to pay the fifteen-dollar passage to send her home because he assumed the case would set a precedent requiring him to do the same for workers from Spain, China, or Korea. He argued, "I should not be obligated to pay for her passage because she only worked for me for eighteen months." He further protested, "the cost of her passage should be distributed among all those she served in Yucatán and she has served others in more intimate ways" (Manzanilla Canto 1916). He accused her of disloyalty to him and his family, but more important, he accused her of sexual promiscuity, dishonorable behavior for any woman and unacceptable from his servant.

Manzanilla implied that Gutiérrez was not a respectable woman, but his wife, señora María C. M. de Manzanilla, described Gutiérrez even more harshly in a letter to her son, José. Curiously, the letter is dated 26 May 1916, the same date on which señor Manzanilla filed a protest rebutting the employee's grievance. In the letter, señora Manzanilla reported that she had met the woman on the holy holiday of San Francisco in December 1914. She found her on the streets of Mérida begging and ill with syphilis. She took her to a doctor and paid a considerable sum of money for medication and health care. Then, in March, señora Manzanilla took Gutiérrez to the nearby seaport of Progreso hoping that the ocean breezes would help cure her. In Progreso, Gutiérrez escaped with a carpenter, Manuel Sosa, seizing the linen clothing that the señora lent her during her illness. The señora noted that when she found the servant, her only clothing was "a single black skirt which had a very bad odor, (yet) that is the way those unfortunate people from the interior carry themselves." She further bemoaned, "They are going to give us ladies a hard heart." Señora Manzanilla also blamed herself for having concealed from her husband facts about this "shameless woman." Shortly before taking Gutiérrez to Progreso, the servant "had relations with a Chinese man who gave her a valuable ring." According to María Manzanilla, the "unfortunate Chinese man came here to claim a large sum of money for the ring" after Gutiérrez had fled. The planter's wife explained that within fifteen days of her escape, Gutiérrez became the concubine of Progreso's police chief, Aurelio Bagundo (Manzanilla 1916).

Alberto Rincón, the Manzanilla family's legal representative, used the señora's letter as testimony before the governor. On 29 May 1916, Rincón protested the sentence handed down by the inspector of police against his client. He pointed out that Nicolasa Gutiérrez could not possibly have had a contract with Manzanilla's company because "the company only made contracts with the patriarch of the family and single male workers." He insisted that unless the company made a contract with this woman's husband or unless "she secretly allied herself with one of the contracted families," she could not have been on contract. Gutiérrez was unmarried, however, and employed families who knew her could not be located (Rincón 1916). Lorenzo Manzanilla, the son who handled contracts, alleged that he had never seen Gutiérrez. The son's testimony was questionable, however. Lorenzo had a reputation for hiring agents who abducted children from their homes in Mexico City, forcing them to work on his plantation and secretly keeping them from their parents.[9]

When Rincón proceeded, he invoked the letter written by the "respectable" wife of señor Manzanilla. The correspondence discredited Nicolasa Gutiérrez and defamed her reputation. Not only was she syphilitic but she also engaged in sexual relations with a Chinese man, as well as the police chief of Progreso. When señora Manzanilla found the beggar, she was "filthy, sick and smelly." After helping her, clothing her, and taking her to the doctor and finally to the seashore to be cured, Nicolasa repaid the "respectable" wife by "escaping" (Rincón 1916).

The testimonies by the plantation owner Alvino, his wife María, and their two sons, José and Lorenzo, painted an unfavorable case for Nicolasa. That the inspector general of police decided the grievance in her favor seems surprising considering the family's corroboration. Perhaps the government official reasoned that Nicolasa's fifteen-dollar request was not worth quibbling over. The Manzanilla family, however, conspired to defend their rights as plantation owners. The wife's letter to her son, José, is engaging because she implied so much about herself and her servant. Señora Manzanilla depicts herself as a charitable, religious woman with a Christian responsibility to "rescue" Gutiérrez from the street. As the wife of an elite man, she exemplifies how their society held Indian women as inferior.

The language used to describe Nicolasa is also worth noting. They characterized her as an immoral, filthy concubine. They suggested that the Indian woman from the interior practiced poor hygiene. Terms such as "enganchada" and "escape" denote debt peonage or servitude. In other words, Gutiérrez was more than just a hired domestic servant. Whether or not she had a contract remains unclear, but the family insisted that she was indebted to them and had no right to escape. The clothes that señora Manzanilla insisted she stole could have been payment for her services, a practice outlawed by the decree in 1915 (Alvarado 1915).

Gutiérrez worked outside in the fields as an agricultural worker and inside the house as a domestic servant. She performed dual duties and yet earned only the title of domestic. Curiously, señora Manzanilla's letter makes no reference to the quality of Gutiérrez's work. Instead, she accented her immorality. The family built the case around the employee's moral character, a harsh allegation considering that the domestic worker only requested a modest sum of money for her trip back home. The point, however, is that a poor, indigenous woman worked in an occupation that gave her no rights, and when she tried to claim her due, her sexual practices became the focus—as if they had anything to do with requesting fifteen dollars to go home. Patriarchal power, after all, relies upon disputing women's rights by focusing on their sexual conduct.

In January 1916, a lengthy, complicated complaint came before the governor. The Maya Hilaria Canul and her two daughters, Guadalupe Chan and Mercedes Millán, sought retribution from Adoralido Olivera, a sacristan. Canul had been a servant for her employer, señora Carolina Moreno de Cervera, since the age of seven. When Canul got older, she married a house servant, Julián Chan, and they had two daughters. The family of four spent decades "being loyal" to their employers, Carolina Moreno de Cervera and her husband, Ignacio Cervera (Canul, Chan, and Millán 1916).[10]

After señor Cervera died, Carolina Moreno sold their plantation and purchased a house in Mérida for Hilaria as a gift or compensation because Hilaria had devoted her life to dutifully serving her employer. Subsequently, two clerics and Olivera met señora de Cervera, took advantage of her "Catholic fanaticism," urged her to sell her furniture to him, and also requested that the remaining valuables be split among the servants. When Carolina Moreno died, Olivera moved quickly. He ousted the servants from their home, then sold it with the furniture. According to the daughter, Mercedes Millán, he sold everything because he was anxious to leave for La Habana, Cuba.

Dated 14 January 1916, the document was addressed to Governor Alvarado and signed by Mercedes Millán. Speaking on behalf of herself, her sister, and her mother, Millán stated in the opening paragraph, "we are indigenous people, we cannot explain ourselves with clarity." She proceeded, "we are here to denounce the robbery of our inheritance by the sacristan Adoralido Olivera." Mercedes appealed to the Governor to investigate the matter and hold Olivera responsible for his misdeeds.

In her own testimony, Hilaria Canul testified before Juan Pablo Reyes, the secretary general of war assigned to hear the complaint. Decree Number Five allowed military officials to hear domestic servants's complaints. Canul reported to the official:

> About fifty years ago, more or less (my ignorance keeps me from remembering the exact date), my mother died and so my father, Agustín Canul, delivered me to the house of Ignacio Cervera where I was a servant.
>
> I was seven years old when I became señor Cervera's servant. Five years later, I married one of the house servants and from that marriage had two daughters.
>
> But I must say that as a faithful servant of the house, that I and my family were treated with care. After nineteen years of working in the house,

suddenly, señor Ignacio Cervera died from a
pernicious illness and left his wife Carolina Moreno
as owner of his property.

Señora de Cervera had no children. She devoted herself
to Catholicism, and her servant called her "fanatic" about religion. After selling her hacienda, "Panaba," she bought a
house in Mérida, which she willed to Hilaria and her two
daughters. In that house, she sheltered poor families, built a
chapel, bought costly religious statues, and received three
priests who lived there. The priests began holding mass on
Sunday, and Hilaria Canul reported that "at that time, a new
guest arrived to live in the home."

He was señor Adoralido Olivera, the sacristan of the ca-
thedral in this city. He came from the town of Calkini. Olivera
was very poor; and, despite his hypocritical and effeminate
character, he made señora Cervera admire him, and gradually she gave him her confidence and her money.

The servant complained that Olivera knew that the dying
woman had no descendants, and she made her last requests
to Olivera. Hilaria Canul noted that señora de Cervera "wanted
the jewelry split equally among us," and she also willed the
title of the house to the Indian women. Canul, then, recalled
señora Cervera's torment and Olivera's impudence:

> There are some images in life that remain in one's
> memory like a photograph. I remember during the
> final hours of señora de Cervera's life, she suffered
> an attack and she appeared to have died. When
> Adoralido was notified, he came quickly and took
> down the hammock where her body lay but the
> extreme shaking made the señora regain con-
> sciousness and Adoralido barely made time to hang
> the hammock and leave the house not to return until
> her death was positive.
>
> These notorious events are public, but the Cath-
> olicism that binds this society demands that we
> forget the event.

Two weeks after her death, the sacristan moved quickly.
He threw Canul and her daughters out of the house and subsequently sold it for 90,000 pesos to the state government.
Canul reported, "To suppress our complaints when we reminded
him of the señora's requests, he gave us 40 pesos which he later

51

lowered to 30." The document is signed by Juan Pablo Reyes, who wrote Hilaria Canul's testimony as she spoke.

In her own words, Canul revealed working and living conditions for domestics. Turned over to the Cerveras at age seven by her father, Hilaria married another house servant when she was still a child of twelve. She referred to herself and her daughters as indigenous people, or Maya. Hilaria explained that she and her family were paid for their services with food and clothing, a custom outlawed by Decree Number Five. The servant's opinion of the Catholic Church is also worth noting. Twice she assailed señora de Cervera's religious fanaticism, and throughout the record Hilaria blamed the sacristan Olivera for her employer's overzealous Catholicism. Although she made no reference to her religion, she seemed to voice an antagonism between her Maya culture and the Church which further confirmed her disdain for Olivera.

José Adoralido Olivera defended himself against Canul's accusations in twenty-six handwritten legal pages, where he explained his relationship to señora de Cervera. Born in 1862 in the neighboring city of Campeche, he left to work in the small, rural town of Calkini in Yucatán. At age twenty-one, he arrived in Mérida with 8,000 pesos, prepared to study in the seminary. Through hard work, he became the resident archivist, major sacristan, and treasurer. He earned 200 to 300 pesos monthly. Olivera worked so hard that "since living in the city, I am not familiar with the theater, films, or any public events, nor do I remember spending a single penny on transportation for my own recreation . . ." (Adoralido Olivera 1916). He rose daily at 4:00 A.M. to fulfill his responsibilities and could not begin his studies until 7:00 P.M.

He reported that on 2 March 1883, while walking through a neighborhood, he heard cries from a house. "I had the high honor of meeting the señora Carolina Moreno de Cervera, who grieved her widowhood. I served her in all that I possibly could during those critical moments" (Adoralido Olivera 1916). Olivera visited señora de Cervera's home so frequently that he began to pay her two pesos daily for breakfast and lunch.

Through the years, Olivera made himself indispensable to señora de Cervera. The sacristan discovered that the lady had incurred many debts. To help her, he purchased furniture, jewelry, and other objects that she sold to him for 500 pesos. On 30 March 1901, both parties signed a legal agreement stating the sale of the property with the stipulation that Olivera could not possess the items until after señora de Cervera's death (Adoralido Olivera and de Cervera 1901).

A month later, Olivera wrote his will. He declared that he owned his home, and he owned furniture and objects at señora de Cervera's home. That property, he noted, would not be in his possession during her lifetime. Olivera willed 6,000 pesos each to two young men, Alfredo de Cámara and Adolfo Espejo Solís; he set aside 2,000 pesos for his funeral; and he left property to his sister, Concepción Olivera (Adoralido Olivera 1901). Olivera did not identify the young men as members of his family, nor did he say whether or not they were affiliated with the Church. One can only assume that they must have been close friends to be included in his will. Why Olivera wrote his will only a month after he bought property from señora de Cervera seems unclear. Perhaps he wanted to ensure beyond doubt, through another document, that he owned many items in her house.

Olivera became señora de Cervera's financial adviser, and she also entrusted the house and all her finances to him. He reported in his lengthy testimony that señora de Cervera owed money when she died. Because he handled her finances, he was held legally responsible for her debts. He argued that he did not have any money to pay her debts and that after her death she still owed a mortgage on the house that Hilaria Canul claimed belonged to her and her daughters (Adoralido Olivera 1916).

At señora Canul's request, Secretary General Reyes did question a few witnesses about Carolina Moreno de Cervera's death. Unfortunately, the witnesses did not agree with each other about the cause of death. One said she died of pneumonia; another thought she had a heart attack, and yet another was unsure. All of the witnesses supported Olivera's claim to señora de Cervera's house (Reyes R. 1916).

After hearing testimony from more witnesses, Reyes decided that neither Hilaria Canul nor her daughters had recourse against Olivera. Ultimately, Carolina Moreno de Cervera had left Olivera in charge of her property, finances, and will (Reyes R. 1916). Because he was responsible for her debts, he defied her will. Legally, the domestic servants could do nothing more, but they did make attempts through one more avenue. They asked the notary, Escalante Pinto, to attest to señora de Cervera's deposition. Once again, they met resistance from Olivera, who blatantly opposed the conditions of señora de Cervera's will (Avila and Canul 1916).

Hilaria Canul and her two daughters, Mercedes Millán and Guadalupe Chan, were forced out of the house that señora de Cervera offered for their lifetime of service. Olivera gave them 35 pesos to divide among themselves while his own wealth probably doubled despite the debts he said señora de Cervera left behind (Canul, Chan, and Millán 1916).

Sacristan Olivera began to woo señora de Cervera the day he entered the widow's home to console her. He initiated a relationship that lasted thirty years until her death. The energetic, organized, and diligent twenty-one-year-old who appeared so dedicated to the Catholic Church must have seemed like a godsend to the fifty-three-year-old woman who had just lost her husband.

An upper-class planter's wife who had never worked, señora de Cervera was financially secure when her husband died. However, she relied on him in both business and household affairs. The documents indicate that during his lifetime señor Cervera looked after his wife, their money, their business, and their property. Indeed, he had hired the servant Hilaria Canul when her father brought the seven-year-old to Cervera's plantation. As she grieved for her husband, the widow might also have been grieving for herself because she was ill-prepared to take over the responsibilities of the household and the plantation. She turned to a young man who not only gave her comfort but also organized her financial chores. Perhaps he restored her faith.

In any case, the ambitious young man probably saw an opportunity to help an influential member of the religious community and perhaps advance his own career. From the very beginning, Hilaria Canul and her two daughters distrusted the sacristan who took their employer into his confidence. Hilaria joined her employers in 1866 and had worked in their home for seventeen years when Olivera began to frequent the residence she knew so well. As Mayas, she and her daughters shunned Catholicism. The testimony reveals that Hilaria denigrated señora de Cervera's Catholicism. Canul also indicted Olivera's haste when he attended to the unconscious señora de Cervera, leaving her side when she regained consciousness. He returned to the house only when he was positive that the señora had indeed died. The servant, incensed over the insensitivity of a devout Catholic, resolved that "the Catholicism which binds this society demands that we forget the event." She refused to forget how Olivera mistreated a dying woman whose property he inherited. She also refused to forget that a Catholic betrayed her. In a sense, she blamed the Church for the robbery of her inheritance. Given that Governor Alvarado believed that clerics corrupted the revolution's goals, his administrators might have used this case as an opportunity to solidify their influence. That they did not do so proves the Church's continuing power.

Hilaria Canul, to her credit, used a reform instituted by leaders of the revolution to eradicate injustice against her. In this case, Decree Number Five did not benefit the Maya. Instead, a member of the Church reaffirmed his authority, even if indirectly. The sociosexual-racial exploitation of Maya women deprived them of their rights against a man who was more than likely mestizo and capable of upward mobility. Unfortunately, the revolution could not resolve the differences that allowed him privileges over the women's basic rights. Social deference was expected of these servants, especially to a man of the cloth. Despite their loyalty to their employer, they were not rewarded as they had expected. Even when domestics acted according to their station, that is, "loyal" and "devoted," they were not compensated.

In August 1918, Josefa Tamayo filed a complaint against her employer, Juana Euan, in their home town of Motul. At age fifteen, Tamayo's mother sent her to work for señora Euan. From 1907 to 1909, the young girl worked for an allowance of four pesos a month paid to her mother. Euan claimed to shower Josefa with gifts of gold jewelry to "show affection." According to Euan, her servant behaved disrespectfully one day and left suddenly, never to return. Eleven years later, Tamayo sought restitution. She asked for 1,000 pesos as payment for her domestic services (González 1918).

The military commander assigned to hear the complaint in Motul adjudicated in Tamayo's favor. Señora Euan appealed the decision and filed her own grievance against Josefa Tamayo in Mérida. Euan, the employer, contested that not even a cook in a restaurant earned the generous fees that Tamayo charged. Tamayo appealed for more than thirty pesos monthly, which to Euan's mind would rob her own children of their food. Señora Euan also chastised the military commander in Motul who tried the case, dubbing him a shyster who intended to claim half of Tamayo's money. The grievance was signed "for my sister who cannot sign her name, Carlos Euan" (Euan 1918).

The department officials in Mérida refuted the decision when they heard the appeal. They argued, "Señora Euan is not a capitalist; she is a barefoot mestiza, widowed, with children." They also stated that she owned a house and a bakery (González 1918). Based on Euan's testimony, the officials overturned the judgment and declared that Tamayo wrongfully accused Euan. Then they criticized Tamayo, harshly judging her "type." "In the minds of these people, they believe that the Revolution was meant to give money to the poor. They assume this is the justice of the Revolution" (González 1918).

Eleven years passed before Tamayo sought to remedy the injustice against her, but until Decree Number Five she had no legal recourse. Tamayo sued for the higher wages that she could not demand at age fifteen. Unfortunately, she petitioned for an unreasonable salary. While four pesos monthly seemed extremely low, Tamayo sued for over thirty pesos monthly of retroactive pay for three years of service. In 1918, domestics averaged twenty pesos monthly.[11] When she worked for Euan, however, servants made less than four pesos monthly. Perhaps a request within that range would have won the dispute. Instead, she gambled and lost.

In this example, the government's agenda excluded redistributing wealth to Tamayo's "kind." When they described her employer as a "barefoot mestiza," not a capitalist, they placed both women in the same category. Therefore, the revolution did not owe more to one than to the other. To the administrators, a lower-income widow who owned only a house and a bakery did not owe anything to a destitute woman like Tamayo who had treated her employer "disrespectfully." Once again, a servant's behavior was on trial. Tamayo, the servant, had not been sufficiently deferential to merit reward.

In four other complaints filed in 1918, the domestic servants won their cases. They solicited and won paltry sums compared to the compensation Hilaria Canul and Josefa Tamayo expected. Elvira Argaez Gil, for example, appealed for less than a month's salary. She accused Dr. N. B. Breckenridge of failing to pay her during the month he employed her. From the nearby city of Campeche, Elvira explained that she traveled to Mérida after Mr. José MacGregor, an agent for the Wattermier Oil Company, told her that he knew someone in Mérida who needed a cook. Emeterio T. Boot told her he would pay for her passage and her daughter's if she came to the city where he would employ her. When she arrived in Mérida, the employee discovered she would be working for not Boot, but instead for Dr. Breckenridge. Elvira also learned that he expected not only a cook but also a servant who would perform all of his household chores for thirty pesos monthly. In less than a month, the doctor fired Elvira. "[He] screamed at me and threw me out of the house," she testified.

Señora Argaez petitioned the Department of Labor for her wages. The domestic servant, Elvira Argaez Gil, was deceived by non-Mexican men who urged her to come to Mérida. These men, MacGregor, Breckenridge, and probably Boot, were more than likely middle-class, single, and white. Their income and race afforded them privileges in a region where mestizos and Mayas experienced socioeconomic exploitation. The way they negotiated with Elvira, a mestiza, a servant, and a single mother, reveals the power relations between the men and this domestic servant. Inconsistent and dishonest, they betrayed Elvira until the Department of Labor intervened. Dr. Breckenridge did not pay the servant her wages without first attempting to discredit her before Director López. The department collected the servant's wages from the doctor without much difficulty, however; the sum was small and hardly threatened the sociosexual-racial system that the revolution upheld.

The Department of Labor ruled favorably for yet another domestic servant who applied for a modest sum of money. When María Antonia Canul indicted her employer, señor José María Cortázar, charging him for five years of domestic service, Cortázar counterclaimed. For those five years she had received no income. He compensated the employee and her two young children with food and clothing and paid for her children's education. When Canul and her son, Nicano, became ill, their employer professed that he paid 300 pesos for a doctor and medication. Cortázar protested that he supported her sons while they lived in his household; therefore, he deserved reimbursement at one peso daily for each of them, amounting to 1,800 pesos for five years. The employer also conceded to paying his servant six pesos monthly for her years of service, totaling 370 pesos, but only if she consented to reimburse him.

In her grievance, señora Canul notified the Department of Labor that she expected the payment due her, but she also wanted a rosary that Cortázar had kept. Cortázar replied that he had given her a chain in return, but she was obviously displeased with the exchange (Lopez 1918).

After considering Cortázar's counterclaim and Canul's testimony, the director of the department, Plácido López, ordered Cortázar to pay Canul 370 pesos for five years of domestic service. If Canul wanted her rosary, she had to return his chain; and, finally, Cortázar could not expect the servant to pay him for supporting her sons because "she worked day and night for him" (Lopez 1918a). Director López ordered Cortázar to pay Canul the full amount within four days. He acquiesced, and the servant won her grievance (Lopez 1918b).

The domestic servant may have succeeded, but not without resistance from her employer, despite his blatant violation of Decree Number Five. For five years, Cortázar withheld Canul's salary and paid her by supporting her children and supplying them all with food and clothing. Cortázar practiced only what many other employers engaged in before Governor Alvarado's law prohibited the practice. Believing himself guiltless, the employer countered the grievance with his own, conveniently forgetting that because he did not pay his servant, she had no means to support her sons. Obviously a single man, perhaps Cortázar believed that he was the patriarch of this family made up of a servant who worked for him day and night and her two young sons who attended school. He may have felt betrayed by his "family" when María Canul filed a complaint to collect her salary. Señor Cortázar seemed to be from a lower- to middle-income status group. He lived in his own home and supported a live-in domestic and her children. The case verifies the exploitative social relations between an employer and employee as well as between a middle-class man and a penniless native woman. The revolution's leaders may not have consciously decided this case based on Canul's background, but the favorable outcome eased this Indian woman's life.

In another grievance, the domestic servant won, but not without a battle against the family who employed her. When Manuela Velázquez reported to her employer on 10 July 1918, she expected to receive her salary for the month. Her employer, María Natividad Navarrete, informed her, "Manuela, we don't have any money today, so we cannot pay your salary until later." Manuela was subsequently discharged without pay, hence her grievance entailed retrieving her due wages. Within a few days, the department judged that there were enough discrepancies in the employer's testimony to merit granting the employee her demands (Caceras 1918).

The Velázquez dispute unveils the process by which poor women confronted their employers. The testimony verifies how the family collaborated to discredit the domestic servant. After each made charges and counter-charges and each called the other a liar, Director López believed the employee, who asked for only an inconsequential amount of money.

In a less complicated case, Marcelina Tun petitioned the Department of Labor for thirty-four pesos that señora María Luis Cantón de Franco owed her. Tun reported, "I asked for payment and Cantón told me to return on Sunday so she could pay me." On Sunday, the employer made no payment. When the employer implored the department for justice, the servant Tun enumerated the charges: one month's salary for twenty pesos; fifteen extra days of service for three pesos; for washing, eight pesos; and a loan to Señora Cantón for three pesos. The services amounted to thirty-four pesos (Tun 1918). Buenaventura Franco, the woman's husband, contested the amount and argued that he owed Tun only twenty-eight pesos (Franco 1918). Tun, perhaps eager to settle the case, accepted his terms (Rubio 1918).

Conclusion

Decree Number Five benefited domestic servants during this governor's administration by allowing them to collect their salaries from employers who ordinarily ignored workers' pleas. In this cross-section of complaints, the servants won in five instances and lost twice. Perhaps it is no coincidence that the cases domestics won involved trivial sums of money. Nicolasa Gutiérrez, for example, only wanted fifteen dollars to go home to Veracruz. She won. Manuela Velázquez, Elvira Argaez, and Marcelina Tun each requested under forty pesos from their negligent employers, and all won their grievances. María Antonia Canul, who petitioned for 370 pesos, much more than the other three but still a modest amount, also won her case.

The two domestics who lost their cases pleaded for more than a few pesos. Josefa Tamayo sued for over 1,000 pesos of retroactive pay and subsequently lost her case before the Department of Labor. Another unsuccessful petition entailed a house that three indigenous women attempted to claim. The secretary general of war, Juan Pablo Reyes, ruled that Hilaria Canul and her two daughters could not take the property from sacristan Olivera. Canul, however, refuted more than a dead employer's will and more than the government's decision. She contested the Catholic Church when she indicted Olivera for the house she said belonged to her and her daughters. The Church's influence overruled the objections of three Maya domestics, despite their appeal to a Governor who disdained priests and their religion.

Principally, the decree responded to class tensions that had been brewing before Alvarado brought his revolution to Yucatán. The tensions were not absolutely resolved, but the law permitted poor native women to win compensation from employers who had exploited them for weeks, months, and even years. The domestic servant's complaints expose inequalities that divided the working Maya and their employers. By enforcing the domestic service law, the new administrators kept the Revolution's promises to aid a highly oppressed group of women through general reforms. The extraordinary reform may not have opened up opportunities for women, but it did acknowledge that a significant percentage of the female population worked in a highly exploitative occupation.

As with any bourgeois revolution imposing bourgeois reforms, this one also had its limitations and contradictions. This sample of cases evinces how the Revolution was restricted from without by the landed elite and by the new middle class that Alvarado addressed. The majority of servants won their cases, but not without a battle and only when remuneration was modest. This calls into question the range and intent of reform. On the one hand, Alvarado helped servants with Decree Number Five; on the other, he was bound by an ideology that only allowed humble measures to change Yucatán society.

Although women won financial remuneration, Decree Number Five did not address the sociosexual-racial status endemic to domestic service, nor did the revolution seek to resolve such contradictions. When women fought to win their cases before the revolution's government, they also fought for rights denied them based upon a sociosexual-racial hierarchy that placed them at the bottom. But they also fought to restore their dignity. In almost every case, employers accused the women of immorality, as in Gutiérrez's case, or of disrespect, as in Tamayo's case. Elvira Gil, for example, refused to defer to the whims of three white men who could not decide who would employ her. María Canul's employer, Cortázar, was outraged when she dared to request a salary from him because he had cared for her sons as if they were his own. He and other employers accused their employees of stealing. Although the domestic servants appealed for their wages, they also appealed for honor, respect, and dignity—rights that the revolution did not guarantee.

For Nicolasa Gutiérrez, "serving others in more intimate ways" was not the question. That a society of landed elite defamed her morals was the concrete issue. The revolution failed to address women's ideological oppression because it could not transcend its own limited ideology, which subsumed gender. With its bourgeois class foundation, the revolution subsumed gender at the expense of women's true advancement. Leaders were ill-prepared to eradicate domestic service, which by its nature exploited women socially, sexually, and racially. The occupation, after all, expected female servants to serve in intimate ways.

Notes

1. For details about the Mexican Revolution and its leaders during the violent phase, see Ruiz 1980, who devotes a chapter to each of these prominent leaders.

2. Harrison's superb little book outlines Karl Marx's theories. He makes an argument against reformism in his introduction and shows that Marx spent the latter part of his life convincing "bourgeois socialists" that reforming capitalism would not end its inherent exploitation of workers. See also Luxemburg 1970. In 1898 theorist and activist Luxemburg published essays in which she criticized Eduard Berstein and his theory of social democracy. His theory gave bourgeois socialists the idea that reforms, not revolution, could improve upon an oppressive capitalist system. Luxemburg, with an acute understanding of Marx's critique of the economy, knew that the working class could not tolerate a socioeconomic system that forced them to work for the capitalist who grew wealthy from the profits of their labor.

3. Many socialist-feminist theoreticians have developed criticism of capitalism, patriarchy, and gender ideology in the last two decades. For an overview, refer to the essays in Eisenstein 1979. Also, Sargent 1981 helped define socialist-feminism and advance an important debate.

4. Sweezy 1970 outlines Marx's theory of surplus value, the core of profit for the capitalist.

5. MacKinnon 1982 argues, "Gender socialization is the process through which women come to identify themselves as sexual beings, beings that exist for men."

6. Barrett 1980 advances the notion of gender ideology in her book. Based on much of Barrett's analysis, I discuss gender ideology at length in my essay, "A La Mujer."

7. Rollins 1985 discusses the detrimental impact of "deference and maternalism" for Black female domestics in her study. She argues that domestic service goes beyond economic exploitation, because the job involves a "personal relationship between employer and employee" that allows for "psychological exploitation unknown in other occupations" (155–56).

8. Joseph 1982 found such cases of contract laborers who were "enganchados" (73).

9. In his dissertation, Chacón 1983 identifies Lorenzo Manzanilla as the manager of the family hacienda and company, the Alvino Manzanilla Canto Company. He also provides evidence to show how Lorenzo Manzanilla colluded with men who abducted children from urban areas such as Mexico City and turned them over to plantation managers for a fee (416–19).

10. All references to the statements of Hilaria Canul, Guadalupe Chan, and Mercedes Millán are from their letter to General Salvador Alvarado, 14 January 1916, AGEY.

11. These cases show that domestic servants averaged twenty to twenty-five pesos monthly.

Bibliography

Adoralido Olivera, José. 1901. Document to the Justice Department, 15 April. Archivo General del Estado de Yucatán.

———. 1916. Letter to Juan Pablo Reyes R., Secretary General of the Department of War, 26 January. Archivo General del Estado de Yucatán.

Adoralido Olivera, José, and Carolina Moreno de Cervera. 1901. Document to the Department of Justice regarding property, 30 March.

Alvarado, Salvador. 1915. Decree Number Five. 24 April. Archivo General del Estado de Yucatán.

Argaez Gil, Elvira. 1918. Letter to Plácido López, the Director of the Department of Labor, 31 August. Archivo General del Estado de Yucatán.

Arizpe, Lourdes. 1977. "Women in the Informal Labor Sector: The Case of Mexico City." *Signs* 3 (fall): 30.

Avila, Adela, and Hilaria Canul. 1916. Letter to Juan Reyes R., Secretary General of the Department of War, 15 February. Archivo General del Estado de Yucatán.

Barrett, Michele. 1980. *Women's Oppression Today.* London: Verso Editions and NLB.

Caceras, Fernando. 1918. Document for Manuela Velázquez to the Department of Labor, 17 September. Archivo General del Estado de Yucatán.

Canul, Hilaria. 1916. Testimony to Juan Pablo Reyes R., the Secretary General of the Department of War, 18 January. Archivo General del Estado de Yucatán.

Canul, Hilaria, Guadalupe Chan, and Mercedes Millán. 1916. Letter to General Salvador Alvarado, 14 January. Archivo General del Estado de Yucatán.

Chacón, Ramón. 1983. "Yucatán and the Mexican Revolution: The Pre-Constitutionalist Years, 1910–1918." Ph.D. dissertation, Stanford University.

Eisenstein, Zillah, ed. 1979. *Capitalist Patriarchy and the Case for Socialist-Feminism.* New York: Monthly Review Press.

Euan, Carlos. 1918. Letter to Governor Salvador Alvarado, 23 August. Archivo General del Estado de Yucatán.

Franco, Buenaventura. 1918. Document to Plácido López, Director of the Department of Labor, 27 September. Archivo General del Estado de Yucatán.

González, C. A. 1918. Letter to Governor Salvador Alvarado, 14 October. Archivo General del Estado de Yucatán.

Harrison, John. 1978. *Marxist Economics for Socialists: A Critique of Reformism.* London: Pluto Press.

Joseph, G. M. 1982. *Revolution from Without: Yucatan, Mexico, and the United States, 1880–1924.* New York: Cambridge University Press.

Lerner, Gerda. 1986. *The Creation of the Patriarchy.* New York: Oxford University Press.

López, Plácido, Director of the Department of Labor. 1918a. Document to Governor Salvador Alvarado regarding María Antonia Canul against José María Cortázar, 24 August. Archivo General del Estado de Yucatán.

———. 1918b. 14 September. Archivo General del Estado de Yucatán.

Luxemburg, Rosa. 1970 [1898]. *Reform or Revolution.* New York: Pathfinder Press.

MacKinnon, Catherine A. 1982. "Feminism, Marxism, Method, and the State: An Agenda for Theory." *Signs* 7 (spring): 531.

Manzanilla Canto, Alvino. 1916, 26 May. Document to the Department of Justice, in Departamento Legal, *Archivo General del Estado de Yucatán.*

Manzanilla, María C. M. de. 1916. Letter to José A. Manzanilla, 26 May.

McBride, Theresa. 1976. *The Domestic Revolution: The Modernization of Household Servants in England and France, 1820–1920.* New York: Holmes and Meir Publishers.

Pérez, Emma. 1990. "A La Mujer: A Critique of the Mexican Liberal Party's Gender Ideology." In *Between Borders,* ed. Adelaida R. Del Castillo. Los Angeles: Floricanto Press.

Reyes R., Juan Pablo, Secretary General of the Department of War. 1916. Document regarding testimonies by Andrés de Saenz Santa María and José Castro López, 22 January. Archivo General del Estado de Yucatán.

Rincón, Alberto. 1916. Testimony to the Governor and Military Commander of the State, 29 May. Archivo General del Estado de Yucatán.

Rollins, Judith. 1985. *Between Women: Domestics and Their Employers.* Philadelphia: Temple University Press.

Rubio, Jorge Peniche. 1918. Document for Marcelina Tun to the Department of Labor, 27 September. Archivo General del Estado de Yucatán.

Ruiz, Ramón. 1980. *The Great Rebellion.* New York: W.W. Norton and Co.

Sargent, Lydia, ed. 1981. *Women and Revolution.* Boston: South End Press.

Secretaría de Agricultura y Fomento. 1918. *Tercer censo de poblacin de los Estados Unidos verificados el 27 de octubre de 1910,* 2 vols. México: *Oficina Impresora de la Secretaría de Hacienda.*

Sweezy, Paul M. 1970. *The Theory of Capitalist Development.* New York: Monthly Review Press.

Tun, Marcelina. 1918. Document to Plácido López, Director of the Department of Labor, 23 September. Archivo General del Estado de Yucatán.

Wells, Allen. 1982. "Family Elites in a Boom-and-Bust Economy: The Molinas and Peons of Porfirian Yucatan." *Hispanic American Historical Review* 62, no. 2: 233–42.

"Woman Sterilized As Gives Birth": Forced Sterilization and Chicana Resistance in the 1970s

Virginia Espino

On 20 August 1973 Guadalupe Acosta arrived at the University of Southern California–Los Angeles County Medical Center past due by several weeks and uncertain about the fate of her child. When Ms. Acosta first discovered she was pregnant, she made a conscious effort not to go to the University of Southern California–Los Angeles County Medical Center because rumors that prevailed in her community warned that county personnel "didn't treat you right . . . they made the women suffer" (Dreifus 1975, 13). Instead, she sought obstetrical care from a private doctor, whom she believed would offer better services than the county hospital provided. However, when Ms. Acosta reached her ninth month, her doctor informed her that her baby suffered from a grave deformity that would complicate delivery (*Madrigal v. Quilligan* 1978, 43). Because his facility could not accommodate her special needs, he advised Ms. Acosta "to go to the County hospital because they had better equipment" (Dreifus 1975).

When Ms. Acosta began to experience severe labor pains she reluctantly became admitted to the county hospital. Once in the delivery room, she quickly understood why many warned her against having her child at that facility.

> When I was being examined, they pushed very hard on the stomach. Very, very hard. With their hands. One doctor would have one leg open. The other doctor would have the other leg open. And then, there were two doctors just pushing on my stomach

> and I couldn't . . . I couldn't stand it. I pushed the
> doctor because I couldn't stand the pain. When he
> came back, he hit me in the stomach and said, "Now
> lady, let us do what we have to." I felt sick . . . I kept
> telling them to do something to bring the baby . . .
> They kept me in that condition from six o'clock in
> the evening till three o'clock in the morning. That
> was the last time I saw the clock—the last time I
> remember anything. (Dreifus 1975, 14)

During the period that Ms. Acosta lay unconscious, the physicians performed a cesarean section and delivered a stillborn baby. Without hesitation they carried out the next of their perceived duties, an unauthorized tubal ligation (*Madrigal v. Quilligan* 1978, 66–67). In the many hours that Ms. Acosta lay strapped to the delivery bed, not one nurse or doctor approached her about the possibility of undergoing any surgical operation. She only recalled being moved from one room to another, being touched and poked by several doctors, and then being put to sleep.

Ms. Acosta's experience at the county hospital represents just one example of the many women sterilized without their knowledge or informed consent at the Los Angeles County Medical Center during the 1970s.[1] Women came to the facility to give birth, and while they were "under the duress of labor, drugged, and confined" the doctors cut their fallopian tubes (Hernandez 1976, 9).

Because scholars of eugenic sterilization focus their research on forced sterilizations at mental and penal institutions, they have overlooked an important trend which Ms. Acosta's experience illustrates: the sterilization of women and men in apparently legal and voluntary procedures, where consent was obtained through coercion or not at all. Although this paper addresses the experience of only ten Mexican immigrant women named in a lawsuit against the facility where they were forcibly sterilized, the forced sterilization of Native American, African American, and Puerto Rican women reached epidemic proportions in the 1970s. The precise number of women who were forcibly sterilized in this manner remains an area for scholarly investigation.

While forced sterilizations in the United States date back to the late nineteenth century, the sterilizations explored in this paper took place against the backdrop of an era when the United States experienced "a flowering of movements on a wide variety of issues" (Freeman 1983, xiv). As Terry Anderson illustrates in *The Movement and the Sixties*, the 1960s and early 1970s represented an "endless pageant of political and cultural protests" (x). Chicanos, Asian Americans, gays and lesbians, African Americans, Native Americans, students, and women created organized movements to protest what they viewed as governmental, social, and economic abuses against their communities. During this period of protest, Chicana activists introduced the issue of forced sterilization into the public discourse through grassroots organizing and an unprecedented class-action lawsuit against the director of obstetrics, University of Southern California–Los Angeles County Medical Center; "certain John Doe doctors"; and other state and federal officials (*Madrigal v. Quilligan* 1978). A reconstruction of their activism articulates the race, class, and gender tensions of the period and marks a shift in the public response to violations against the body. This essay uses the forced sterilization of Mexican women as a vehicle to explore the emergence of a distinct Chicana ideology, an ideology that reflected needs apart from the agendas of the women's rights movement and the Chicano movement.

Part of the Chicana resistance to forced sterilization emanated out of a reaction to what Chicanas viewed as racist medical practices on the part of the doctors. Antonia Hernandez, one of the lawyers who represented the women, observed that "all of the victims . . . belonged to a racial minority, were poor, and could not readily understand the English language" (Hernandez 1976, 9). Chicana activists believed that the victim's status—poor, Mexican, and immigrant—motivated the doctors to prescribe care according to their eugenic ideology rather than the physical needs of the patient.[2] Dr. Bernard Rosenfeld, a physician-researcher working undercover at the County hospital, witnessed women being "cajoled, pressured and sometimes coerced into consenting to surgical sterilization." In his research, Dr. Rosenfeld found "a myriad of attitudinal 'hang-ups' among a significant minority of the resident and intern staffs" at the hospital. He concluded that some of doctors "held deep-seated personal beliefs about overpopulation, [while] others . . . held strong views about class prejudice [and] others simply believed all persons on welfare should have their tubes tied" (Kistler 1974).

The eugenics movement originated in the nineteenth century and waned somewhat after Nazi Germany stunned the world with its eugenic practices. The sterilization abuse in the *Madrigal v. Quilligan* case indicates that decades after the eugenic movement reached its apogee, eugenic thinking pervaded the minds of some medical professionals. The English scientist Francis Galton coined the term *eugenics* in 1883. A cousin of Charles Darwin and follower of his theory of evolution, Galton developed a theory of human heredity based on his belief that one could improve the human stock by giving the "more suitable races or strains of blood a better chance of prevailing speedily over the less suitable" (Kevles 1985, x). Galton held a firm conviction that "there was a natural hierarchy of the human races that placed Anglo-Saxons above all others" (Larson 1995, 17). He therefore founded a movement that took hold in Europe and North America, based on the premise that one could "build a better civilization for man [if they encouraged the] propagation by those with desirable traits [while] restricting propagation by those with undesirable traits" (Haller 1984, 3–4).

In the United States the eugenics movement took hold in the early twentieth century primarily among the superintendents of asylums for the so-called feebleminded, insane, and alcoholic and among prison wardens, prison physicians, sociologists, and social workers. Here, eugenicists translated European beliefs through the rhetoric of the progressive reform era. Many social reformers believed that society had a dual responsibility: to care for the delinquent and dependent and to ensure that the people in their care did not propagate and thus "contaminate the generations to come" (Haller 1984, 5). Although historian Philip Reilly argues that during the 1950s and 1960s the United States experienced the passing of a eugenic theses—what he terms the "quiet years"—the events at the county hospital illustrate that eugenics was alive and well. Some hospital staff accepted the practice of forced sterilization of Mexican women because they did not fit the doctors' standards of who is fit to propagate. One staff doctor at the county hospital gave these instructions to the new interns: "I want you to ask every one of these girls if they want their tubes tied. I don't care how old they are, remember every one you get to get her tubes tied means less work for some poor son of a bitch next year" (Kistler 1974).

Linda Gordon, in her seminal work *Woman's Body, Woman's Right: Birth Control in America*, asserts that a lack of free choice existed among the recipients of sterilization surgery. She argues that the operations were performed "in a strongly eugenic fashion, since the victims were primarily poor, black, Hispanic, and especially Native American women." She notes that the number of suits against physicians charging coerced sterilization grew dramatically around 1973, and that virtually none of the victims were white middle-class women (Gordon 1990, 433). And more indicative of the pervasive attitude that poor women were considered unfit to procreate, Gordon asserts that, "in the 1970s, the federal government paid 90 per cent of the cost of most sterilizations, under Medicaid, while offering almost no financial support for abortions (432).

Chicanas confronted the forced sterilization issue at a time when they began "calling attention to her . . . oppression as a Chicano and as a woman" (Nieto-Gomez 1974, 34). At the same time that Mexican women fell victim to eugenic sterilization, the cultural nationalism of the Chicano movement and the universalist ideology of the women's rights movement subsumed Chicanas into nonpersons. Chicano "nationalism's preferred male subject is imbued with a masculine, patriarchal ideology" that offered no room for a Chicana presence (Chabram-Dernersesian 1992, 84). The Women's rights movement wanted to erase race and class differences and unite women "under the banner of woman," which reduced the meaning of woman to the experience of white middle-class women (Nieto 1974, 36). In the Chicano movement, Chicanas were expected to develop an identity through men, and in the women's movement they were expected to identify with issues unrelated to their experience. In response to their race, class, and gender oppression, Chicanas gave birth to a political movement that offered their community new ideas about sexuality, womanhood, and reproductive choice, ideas that articulated their difference from Chicanos and white women.

Alma Garcia asserts that a Chicana feminist consciousness "emerged from a struggle for equality with Chicano men and from a reassessment of the role of the family as a means of resistance to oppressive societal conditions" (Garcia 1989, 219). In redefining their role in the Chicano family, the Chicana feminist wanted to include discussions of sexuality and a woman's right to choose into the discourse of Chicano liberation.[3] According to Anna Nieto-Gomez, a Chicana feminist and civil rights activist, "sterilization reinforced that this bullshit about community and the whole family was just a bunch of bull."

While the Chicano movement focused its fight on discrimination in the work place, school, and political arena, forced sterilization indicated to Chicanas that as women they were "out there vulnerable [and] unprotected" (Nieto-Gomez 1994).

By 1970, Chicanas realized that their lack of reproductive rights played a central role in their oppression, both inside and outside their community (Nieto-Gomez 1976, 10). Francisca Flores, founding member of Comisión Femenil, recognized that "Chicanas are fighting for their own identity" (1971, 6). They experienced sexism within the movement and therefore needed an organization that would establish a "platform for women to use for thinking out their problems [and] to deal with issues not customarily taken up in regular organizations" (Flores 1971). The Comisión Femenil emerged out of the Mexican American National Issues Conference in Sacramento. Yolanda Nava, an early member of Comisión Femenil, recalled that the "men [at the conference] didn't want to acknowledge that women's issues were important and should be part of the resolutions that they made."[4] Although initially Comisión Femenil focused on employment, job training, and child care, they also wanted to establish an organization that provided women with a nonthreatening environment to discuss reproductive rights issues, such as abortion, "without having to first discuss the emotional question of moral issue" (Flores 1971, 6). Comisión Femenil members believed that "Abortion is a fact of life . . . [and] . . . a personal decision" (Flores 1971).

Other Chicana feminists addressed sexuality issues in community newspapers. In a provocative article that articulates the gender tension within movement, Sylvia Delgado asked this question of the Chicano movement: "Are we going to go down as saying intercourse is to make babies while in our heads we are glad that in the past lays we had, there was no pregnancy?" (1971, 3). Sylvia Delgado warned Chicanas to ignore "La Raza's cry" to fight genocide by increasing the population and instead advised Chicanas thinking about intercourse to "start planning for either birth control or parenthood." In contrast, prominent activists like César Chavez urged Chicanos to use reproduction as a tool for liberation. He argued that "smaller families would only diminish the numerical power of the poor . . . The only solution is to make the minority much less a minority and make the race multiply and progress" (Littlewood 1977, 85).

Rather than focus on reproductive rights, many male activists within the Chicano movement viewed the forced sterilizations of Mexican immigrant women as a race issue. It supported their theory that they represented an internal colony within the United States where white Anglo-Saxons maintained a system that kept them socially, culturally, and economically subordinated (Gutiérrez 1993, 46). Despite such rhetoric, Anna Nieto-Gomez remembers that the "sterilization case did not get a whole lot of PR from . . . the Chicano movement." She states that they were "if anything, quiet" about the abuse. For the Chicanos that Anna Nieto-Gomez (1994) came in contact with, job opportunities for men served as a panacea for all the problems facing the Chicano community.

Furthermore, the Chicano movement adopted Aztec imagery that "emphasized the virility of warriors and the exercise of brute force" (Gutiérrez 1993, 45). Within most movement organizations, men took on the leadership roles; and while at times placing Chicanas on a pedestal for adoration and protection, Chicanos also relegated them to housework, child care, and secretarial roles.[5] The song, "The Female of Aztlán," articulates the traditional role expected of Chicanas espoused by the Chicano movement: "Your responsibility is to love, work, pray, and help . . . the male is leader, he is iron, not mush." Chicano pride asked men to stand up for their rights and it asked women to "stand by her man" (Sosa Riddell 1974, 156). The Chicano activist did not view reproductive rights as an issue worthy of organizational time. Most male organizations viewed women's concerns in relation to their own ability to provide and protect them rather than seeing Chicanas as a viable constituency with concerns and demands of their own.[6]

As historian Vicki L. Ruiz writes, "from the early days of the student movement, women were not always satisfied with the rhetoric and praxis of the their compañeros," and the emergence of Comisión Femenil indicates that some Chicanas who participated in Chicano movement activities selected to move out of Chicano organizations in order to address their specific needs as women (1998, 108). Contrary to the assertion made by scholars Denise A. Segura and Beatriz M. Pesquera that "Chicana activists . . . usually rejected the ideology of separatism and tried to find ways of integrating their concerns within Chicano Movement organizations" (1992, 70), Yolanda Nava remembers that the impetus to organize

Comisión Femenil came from a "need to have our own program." Realizing that they "weren't going to get anywhere in a traditionally male run organization," some women abandoned these organizations at the same time keeping the concerns of the Chicano movement a primary objective (Nava 1996). Comisión Femenil members embraced the Chicano movement "because [they] worked hard" for it. But they refused to be "relegated to the back" and instead demand equal partnership with other movement organizations (Molina 1996).

Although Chicanas shared some of the same concerns of the "left" or women's liberation branch of the women's movement—education, child care, and reproductive rights—Chicanas realized that race difference and class position shaped their experience (Segura and Pescara 1992). For Anna Nieto-Gomez, women's health issues illustrated the differing needs of Chicana and white women. She argued that, "Anglo women contend with the cruel prejudice doctors have towards women patients [while] Chicanas must also contend with doctors' racism, insensitivity to the Chicano culture, and the lack of bilingual medical staff. . ." Furthermore, she asserted that, "economics limit her choice of medical facilities to state and county health clinics which usually have inadequate health services" (1974, 40).

The incidence of forced sterilization against Mexican immigrant women illustrated the sharp difference between the two communities of Chicana and white feminists. From white women's perspective, sterilization was a right a male-dominated society tried to deny them (Gordon 1990, 431–36). Chicanas, however, saw sterilization being imposed upon the more vulnerable members of their community. Esther Talavera warned the Chicana community in 1977 that "sterilization is not an alternative in family planning." She argued that Chicanas "have not had the privilege" to choose sterilization over other forms of birth control (1977, 8). Gordon asserts that the "women's liberation movement . . . in the early 1970s, had to be taught about sterilization abuse by black and other minority movements" (Gordon 1990, 433).

The experience of Rebecca Figueroa, one of the plaintiffs in the lawsuit, illustrates the circumstances under which some of the sterilization surgeries were authorized. Ms. Figueroa arrived by ambulance to the county hospital in April of 1971 suffering from severe hemorrhaging. While in the labor room awaiting a cesarean delivery, she was "approached several times regarding whether or not she desired to have her tubes tied." Initially, Ms. Figueroa rejected the offer of tubal ligation surgery (*Madrigal v. Quilligan* 1978, 66–67). Yet, "after several hours of labor and pressuring," she agreed to the surgery.

The issue of forced sterilization surfaced in the late 1960s, through the organizing efforts of Alicia Escalante, founding member of the Chicana Welfare Rights Organization (CWRO) and herself a recipient of public assistance. The CWRO set up a location where women could take action on the issues that affected them politically, economically, and socially. They focused on the "problems women suffered as women, especially the poor woman, the low income woman, the woman on assistance, the single woman" (Escalante 1994). Alicia Escalante created a nonthreatening environment at the CWRO offices where women felt comfortable enough to talk about the private issues one only revealed with family members or *comadres*. She recalls that the ongoing sterilizations were exposed in one of the organizations meetings.

> Some of these women were poor women . . . and were utilizing the General Hospital for the birth of their children. I remember one in particular. She came to the organization. She was a member and she supported the activities that we did in the organization. And in discussion she said, "Look, I had a baby and now I don't take care of myself [use birth control] but I don't get pregnant anymore. No more children come. Before [my husband] just had to look at me [and I would get pregnant]." (Escalante 1994)[7]

The CWRO monitored government agencies funded to serve the poor for possible abuses. Alicia Escalante wanted the organization to advocate for "Chicana women . . . [who were] so vulnerable and had very little voice on their personal life including their own bodies" (1994). Facilities like the county hospital received government funds to treat the poor, yet with a lack of government monitoring, some employees allowed their beliefs about poor immigrant women to dictate their medical practice. To many doctors at the county hospital, a brown woman meant a population dependent on welfare. They saw it as their responsibility as well as their duty to prevent that population from increasing. Anna Nieto-Gomez, a Chicana feminist and civil rights activist, remembers reading the physician's notes regarding the sterilizations they performed:

> They thought they were throwing in a benefit,
> throwing in a free service. They saw themselves as
> agents of the public, saving the taxpayers money.
> After all [the doctors thought] these people are just
> going to breed and be dependent on welfare. (1994)

A staff doctor told Jovita Rivera that she should have her tubes tied because her children were a burden to the government. In an effort to convince Georgina Hernandez to authorize sterilization, the physicians told her that her Mexican birth and poverty would make it unlikely she could provide the proper care and education of future children. The hospital staff accused Laura Dominguez of burdening the taxpayers with her children (Hernandez 1976, 5–8). Some of the doctors believed that the "more tubes you tie, the fewer kids you have to support on welfare later" (Hernandez 1974).

The situation under which the sterilizations occurred left many of the women unaware of the fact that they had been victimized. The case of Dolores Madrigal illuminates the circumstances under which some authorizations for sterilization surgery were obtained without the patient's knowledge of the consequences of the procedure. Ms. Madrigal arrived at the county hospital on 12 October 1973, under the physical and emotional trauma of labor. Soon after her arrival a staff doctor and nurse approached her with the surgical sterilization consent forms in hand. Uncertain about the procedure and unable to read the consent forms written in English, she sought the assurance of the hospital staff that the operation could be reversed. Once she secured a verbal guarantee, she signed her authorization for a tubal ligation. Only after the surgery did the hospital staff inform her that she would never again conceive a child.

The circumstances around the sterilization of Maria Hurtado and Ms. Acosta testify to the fact that in some cases the hospital staff did not seek the patient's authorization prior to performing the sterilization surgery. While Ms. Hurtado lay unconscious in the county hospital delivery room, the attending doctors surgically sterilized her. She found out about this abuse six weeks later when she returned to the hospital for a routine postnatal checkup. Ms. Acosta did not learn of her sterilization until she returned to the county hospital two months later to request birth control pills (Hernandez 1976, 5–7).

The CWRO lacked the kind of funding that would pay for a legal battle against a county facility, but a new generation of Chicano lawyers, professionals, and grassroots organizers came forward to support the women's cause (Rizk 1977, 13). Alicia Escalante remembers hearing stories about the sterilizations from the time the CWRO opened in 1968, but it didn't become a legal battle until Antonia Hernandez from the Model Cites Center for Law and Justice and Gloria Molina from Comisión Femenil took interest (Nava 1994). The CWRO and Comisión Femenil differed in their approach to Chicana activism. Where the CWRO advocated for the rights of welfare mothers, Comisión Femenil wanted to address the needs of "working" women. Comisión Femenil first set out to focus on employment issues; the decision later to take on the forced sterilization of unemployed Mexican women suggests that the gender and race issues connected with forced sterilization transcended class differences among Chicanas. To Comisión Femenil members Chicanas did not make up a homogeneous group: They were stay-at-home mothers, working women, students, and also activists (Molina 1994).

Antonia Hernandez and Gloria Molina dedicated many hours to the legal battle and the battle for public opinion. They created diverse contacts and networks in the Los Angeles community of political and legal activists. Their political savvy, education, and commitment to the issue made a legal battle possible. Comisión Femenil's initial project, The Chicana Service Action Center, provided a base from which to work. It was a meeting place equipped with phones and typewriters. Through this agency they raised funds for the class-action lawsuit, organized demonstrations, and produced press releases to inform the larger community. Antonia Hernandez, a recent graduate from University of California, Los Angeles, law school, acted as both principal attorney and community activist for the women's cause.

Hernandez, along with Richard Navarette, filed a class-action civil rights suit on behalf of the women sterilized. They sought both monetary compensation and a change in federal guidelines that would create a barrier to forced sterilizations, as well as sterilizations performed on the basis of uninformed consent (Ring 1975, 20).[8] They organized their case around the testimony of the women, Dr. Rosenfeld, and other expert witnesses. However, the judge in the case, U.S. District Court Judge Jesse W. Curtis, based his ruling solely on the testimony of one of the expert witnesses when he made his final ruling.

In an effort to strengthen their case, the lawyers had sought the professional consultation of Carlos Vélez-Ibáñez, professor of anthropology at the University of California, Los Angeles. They believed that his assessment of the case would present scientific data to the court to substantiate the women's own testimony as to the social and cultural ramifications of their sterilizations. Carlos Vélez-Ibáñez conducted an anthropological field study on the women involved in the lawsuit. Primarily utilizing oral interviews with the women and their families, he compared the social and cultural system of the women before and after their sterilization. Carlos Vélez-Ibáñez concluded that due to their place of origin—nine out of the ten women came from rural Mexican villages—they had developed the high value for childbearing that most Mexican rural communities maintain. His research indicated that, because of the sterilization, the women "had gone through a process of social disengagement" in every aspect of their lives: as mothers, wives, daughters, sisters, and friends (Vélez-Ibáñez 1980, 241). Judge Curtis, however, used Carlos Vélez-Ibáñez's argument to rule in favor of the defendants. He surmised from the anthropologist's testimony that the "cultural background of these particular women . . . contributed to the problem in a significant way" rather than any malice on the part of the doctors and the hospital. The judge's opinion indicated that he viewed the language barrier a problem, but not the fault of the doctors involved. He stated that he sympathized with the women for their "inability to communicate clearly" but insisted that "one can hardly blame the doctors for relying on these indicia of consent which appeared to be unequivocal on their face and which are in constant use in the Medical Center" (Vélez-Ibáñez).

Although Chicano activists lost the lawsuit, they did not lose the fight against forced sterilizations. Antonia Hernandez argued that in addition to monetary compensation for the unauthorized sterilizations, "For Chicanas, the critical issue is the assurance that their right to procreate is respected and safeguarded" (Hernandez 1976, 35). Chicana resistance around the issue alerted the Chicano community to the abuses Chicana and Mexican women experienced at the county hospital. One can gain a sense of the community's mistrust of the county hospital in the wake of the lawsuit from a statement Dr. Quilligan, the director of obstetrics at the county hospital, made to *The Progressive* magazine: "the adverse publicity has affected our patients . . . They come in great fear, feeling that we're going to grab them and sterilize them—which is the furthest thing from our mind" (Dreifus 1975).

The resistance movement also forced the *Los Angeles Times* to explore the issue through several stories that revealed to the larger public the racial and class bias of the doctors at the county hospital. One week after activists staged a demonstration to protest the sterilization, the *Los Angeles Times* carried a front-page story outlining Dr. Rosenfeld's findings of forced sterilization at the county hospital. The paper stated that, "While such implications may startle the outsider, some physicians who are willing to talk about the situation privately say the 'push' for doing the maximum number of sterilizations possible . . . is not uncommon" (Kistler 1974). They also carried a story detailing their own findings of the doctors' disregard for the federal guidelines established to protect women from sterilization abuse.

On a national level, the lawsuit connected California to the other, more publicized cases of sterilization abuse that occurred in Alabama and New York. The federal government was forced to look at this abuse as a national trend in public hospitals, rather than as isolated incidents. Based on the Los Angeles episode, the California Department of Health re-evaluated its sterilization guidelines to ensure the right of informed consent and issued an informational booklet, in both English and Spanish, that discussed sterilization and its consequences. The booklet warned the reader of possible misunderstandings in terminology, asserting that, "some people call sterilization tying the tubes. But don't think the tubes can be untied! They can't." It reminds the reader that "only YOU can make up your mind to be sterilized" and alerts them not to "let anyone push you into it" (California State Department of Health n.d.).

This period remains a very sensitive one for those directly involved in the lawsuit, because their commitment came from a passion to find justice for the victims. Losing the lawsuit meant that the entire community remained a victim to an established order the Chicano movement attempted to reshape. Yet, despite this severe blow, one cannot ignore the more subtle, but quite profound victories Chicanas gained from their resistance. As Antonia Hernandez so eloquently states, "I lost the case in court, but I won the case of public opinion" (1998). They educated an entire community about the particular issues around reproductive rights that they faced. Despite their own desire to postpone childbearing, they understood that for their community reproductive rights also meant the right to reproduce. Moreover, they forced the State of California to reevaluate its guidelines in order to safeguard informed consent. As a result, University of Southern California–Los Angeles County Medical Center and other hospitals like it had no choice but to end the use of coercive tactics and respect a woman's right to chose.

Notes

1. Antonia Hernandez (1976) discusses the issue of "informed consent" relating to Chicanas. She asserts that medical personnel did not "satisfactorily inform the patients of the consequences attendant to such surgery" because no guidelines regulate their procedures. Informed consent would assure that both the consent forms and the information about sterilization surgery would be in the primary language of the patient. If the patient is illiterate, they would be provided with oral explanations of the procedure and its consequences. Furthermore, the language would be accessible to non-medical individuals whether it is explained in oral or written form.

2. In her oral interview, Anna Nieto-Gomez uses the term *eugenic* to describe the ideology that led to the forced sterilization of Mexican women at the County hospital (Nieto-Gomez 1994).

3. At the National Chicana Conference held in Houston, Texas, in 1971, the topics dealt with addressed marriage, the role of Chicanas in the family, child care, sex, and the Catholic Church. Nieto-Gomez asserts that at this conference "the femenista spoke about changing her role in the *familia* and creating a new role through the movement" (Nieto-Gomez 1974, 38).

4. Yolanda marks the year of this conference in either 1970 or 1971. Marta Cotera (1970) dates the event to 10 October 1970. I found no mention of this conference in Acuña 1988, Camarillo 1984, or Quiñones 1990.

5. See "*El Movimiento* and the Chicana" (1971, 40-42); Rincon (1971, 15-17); also, "*El Mundo Femenil Mexicana*" (1971, 1). Vicki L. Ruiz (1998, 109) discusses the "queen for a day or maid for a week" syndrome.

6. Gloria Molina, past president of Comisión Femenil, recounted to the author a story about a preparation meeting to develop an agenda to present to Senator Tunney. The men and women disagreed

about what should be the priority issues. The men, who controlled the meeting, sought preference for economic development. The women of Comisión Femenil demanded that child care be given priority since their "opportunity for employment and economic development" depended on it. The men countered, "Child care is not an issue."

7. "Ella vino a la organización era miembra y soportaba las actividades que nosotros nos hacíamos en la organización. Y en plactica dice, 'pues fíjese que yo tuve un niño, pero ahora ya ni me cuido. Ya no tengo criatura, ya no viene niños. Pero antes con puro verme'" (translation by the author).

8. This article dates the lawsuit to 18 June 1975.

Bibliography

Acuña, Rudy. 1988. *Occupied America: A History of Chicanos.* New York: Harper & Row.

Anderson, Terry H. 1995. *The Movement and the Sixties: Protest in America from Greensboro to Wounded Knee.* New York: Oxford University Press.

California State Department of Health, Office of Family Planning. 1977. *What About Sterilization? Patients' Information on Female Sterilization.* Sacramento, Calif.: CSDH.

Camarillo, Albert. 1984. *Chicanos in California: A History of Mexican Americans in California.* San Francisco: Boyd & Fraser Publishing Company.

Chabram-Dernersesian, Angie. 1992. "I Throw Punches for My Race, but I Don't Want to Be a Man: Writing Us-Chica-nos (Girl, Us)/ Chicanas into the Movement Script." In *Cultural Studies,* eds. Lawrence Grossberg et al. New York: Routledge.

Cotera, Marta. 1980. "Feminism: The Chicana and Anglo Versions." In *Twice a Minority: Mexican American Women,* ed. Margarita Melville. St. Louis, Mo.: C. V. Mosby Co.

Delgado, Sylvia. 1971. "Chicana: The Forgotten Woman." *Regeneración* 2, no. 1.

Dreifus, Claudia. 1975. "Sterilizing the Poor." *The Progressive* (December 1975).

Escalante, Alicia. 1994. Interview with author. 22 April.

Flores, Francisca. 1971. "Comisión Femenil Mexicana." *Regeneración* 2, no. 2.

Freeman, Jo. 1983. *Social Movements of the Sixties and Seventies.* New York: Longman.

Garcia, Alma M. 1989. "The Development of Chicana Feminist Discourse, 1970–1980." *Gender & Society* 3, no. 2 (June).

Gordon, Linda. 1990. *Women's Body, Women's Right: Birth Control in America*. New York, Penguin Books.

Gutiérrez, Ramón. 1971. "*El Movimiento* and the Chicana." *La Raza* 1, no. 6 (December).

———. 1993. "Community, Patriarchy and Individualism: The Politics of Chicano History and the Dream of Equality." *American Quarterly* 45, no. 1 (March).

Haller, Mark. 1984. *Eugenics: Hereditarian Attitudes in American Thought*. New Brunswick, New Jersey: Rutgers University Press.

Hernandez, Antonia. 1976. "Chicanas and the Issue of Involuntary Sterilization: Reforms Needed to Protect Informed Consent." *Chicano Law Review* 3, no. 3.

———. 1998. Interview with author. 24 March.

Hernandez, Mariana. 1974. "L.A. Women Protest Forced Sterilizations." *The Militant* (20 December).

Kevles, Daniel J. 1985. *In the Name of Eugenics: Genetics and Uses of Human Heredity*. New York: Alfred A. Knopf.

Kistler, Robert. 1974. "Women Pushed into Sterilization, Doctor Charges." *Los Angeles Times* (2 December).

Larson, Edward J. 1995. *Sex, Race, and Science: Eugenics in the Deep South*. Baltimore: The John Hopkins University Press.

Littlewood, Thomas B. 1977. *The Politics of Population Control*. South Bend, Indiana: University of Notre Dame Press.

Madrigal v. Quilligan. 1978. United States District Court. No. CV 74-2057-JWC. May 30.

Molina, Gloria. 1996. Interview with author. 24 October.

Nava, Yolanda. 1996. Interview with author. 24 February.

Nieto, Consuelo. 1974. "The Chicana and the Women's Rights Movement." *Civil Rights Digest* 3, no. 7 (Spring).

Nieto-Gomez, Anna. 1974. "La Femenista." *Encuentro Femenil* 1, no. 1.

———. 1976. "Sexism in the Movimiento." *La Gente* 6, no. 4 (March).

———. 1994. Interview with author. 23 April.

Quiñones, Juan Gomez. 1990. *Chicano Politics: Reality and Promise, 1940–1990*. Albuquerque: University of New Mexico Press.

Rincon, Bernice. 1971a. "*La Chicana*: Her Role in the Past and Her Search for a New Role in the Future." *Regeneración* 1, no. 10.

———. 1971b. "*El Mundo Femenil Mexicana*." *Regeneración* 1, no. 10.

Ring, Harry. 1975. "Forced Sterilization: Chicanas Fight Back in Los Angeles." *The Militant* (August).

Rizk, Georgina Torres. 1977. "Sterilization Abuses Against Chicanas in Los Angeles." *La Raza* 3, no. 1 (Spring).

Ruiz, Vicki L. 1998. *From Out of the Shadows: Mexican Women in Twentieth-Century America*. New York: Oxford University Press.

Segura, Denise A. and Beatriz M. Pesquera. 1992. "Beyond Indifference and Antipathy: The Chicana Movement and Chicana Feminist Discourse." *Aztlan* 19, no. 2.

Sosa Riddell, Adaljiza. 1974. "Chicanas and *El Movimiento*." *Aztlan* 5, no. 1.

Talavera, Esther. 1977. "Sterilization Is Not an Alternative in Family Planning." *Agenda* 7, no. 6 (November–December).

Vélez-Ibáñez, Carlos. 1980. "The Non-Consenting Sterilization of Mexican Women in Los Angeles." In *Twice A Minority*, ed. Margarita Melville. St. Louis, Mo.: C. V. Mosby Co.

"We Lived and Breathed and Worked the Movement": The Contradictions and Rewards of Chicana/Mexicana Activism in el Centro de Acción Social Autónomo-Hermandad General de Trabajadores (CASA-HGT), Los Angeles, 1975–1978

Marisela R. Chávez

> There was a real emphasis on doing political work and being a political person and a de-emphasis on just the personal problems.
>
> —Gilda Rodríguez, CASA member

> It has been said that the member must mold personal life according to the organization.
>
> —Isabel Chávez, 1976

In 1975, deciding to move the operations of their newspaper *Sin Fronteras* from San Antonio, Texas, to Los Angeles, California, the members of el Centro de Acción Social Autónomo–Hermandad General de Trabajadores (CASA-HGT) discussed the kinds of columns that should be incorporated into their newspaper. During the discussion, they agreed that columns on the labor movement, economics, political issues, and social conditions in Mexico would be "indispensable" and that there should be a political commentary and an editorial in each issue. The members also decided that a column on "La Mujer en Lucha" (The Woman in Struggle), though important, "could not merit such a priority of space and it was agreed that the subject could be dealt with adequately in the column on cultural themes and general education."

The integration of women's issues into the "cultural themes and general education" section of the newspaper epitomizes the ideology concerning the status of women in this organization. CASA members did not see the need to treat women or women's issues as a separate category in their class struggle, and this stance proved difficult for women in the organization. For while CASA theoretically dealt with the issue of the "woman question," CASA never addressed the practical applications of women's equality within the organization. As such, women worked for the emancipation of the working class from capitalist exploitation but never for the emancipation of women from traditional roles, nor even for practices that would ease their equal participation in the organization, such as child care.

CASA came into existence during the Chicano movement of the 1960s and 1970s, which consequently must be considered in light of the rise of student movements within these same years. As historian Edward J. Escobar states, "While the Chicano movement developed in response to a historically unique set of grievances, it emerged within and benefited from the broader currents of social protest that existed in the sixties" (1993, 1486). Within the Chicano movement, CASA existed as somewhat of an anomaly in that, unlike most Chicano movement organizations, CASA did not totally embrace the idea of cultural nationalism. Instead, CASA espoused an openly Marxist political line. As such, CASA situated itself at the far left of the Chicano movement political ideology spectrum. When CASA came into existence as a Marxist organization in 1975, the Chicano movement burned brightly on college campuses. As historian Juan Gómez-Quiñones (1990) posits, the Chicano movement began in a liberal reformist tradition that with time and experience tranformed into cultural nationalism and then to class-based politics. CASA members experienced this transition themselves, as members of other Chicano movement organizations prior to their involvement with CASA, and became influenced and informed by these experiences. Unlike other movement organizations such as La

Raza Unida Party or the Crusade for Justice, CASA members took the path of class liberation and third-world struggle.

The women in CASA thus existed as women and as Marxists in a movement dominated by cultural nationalist ideology. Cultural nationalists embraced Chicanismo as an identity based on their claim to the nation of Aztlán, the mythical homeland of the Aztecs, thought to be north of Mexico City. Ernesto Chávez defines cultural nationalism as a "culturally constructed ideological movement for the attainment and maintenance of autonomy, cohesion and individuality for an ethnic group deemed by its members to constitute an actual or potential nation" (Chavez 1994, 3–5).[1] Aztlán became the potential Chicano nation. While the methods for attaining the nation of Aztlán varied, cultural nationalists sought self-determination, defined what it meant to be Chicano, and held strong anti-American tenets. Chicano cultural nationalism also set forth an embrace of Mexican culture, extolling deep pride in Mexican history, and ultimately set in motion a great renaissance of Chicano artistic and literary expression.

Within this embrace of Mexican culture and history, nationalism took a male-identified course. Angie Chabram-Dernersesian discusses how Chicanas become subsumed in the literary expression produced in the Chicano movement, which therefore constitutes Chicanas' absence from the discourse surrounding movement literature and history. Chicano identity through "linguistic qualifiers" such as "o/os subsume the Chicana into a universal ethnic subject that speaks with the masculine instead of the feminine and embodies itself in a Chicano male." Because Chicano identity assumed a male role, it became a "masculine, patriarchal ideology." The term *macho* became synonymous with "Chicano" and, in turn, left out the women. Chabram-Dernersesian states, "With this gender objectification, the silenced Other, Chicanas/hembras, are thus removed from full-scale participation in the Chicano movement as fully embodied, fully empowered U.S. Mexican female subjects" (1992, 82–83).

CASA did not negate the cultural nationalism of the Chicano movement but incorporated nationalist ideas of self-determination, shared history and culture, and identity into its adopted Marxist stance. CASA thus became imbued with some of cultural nationalism's male identification, which partially informed CASA's vision of "the woman question." CASA did not view issues of gender as feminism or as a separate sphere of their worldview. Heidi Hartmann discusses the role of feminism within Marxist ideology (1991, 2–4). She argues that the "marriage" of Marxism and feminism does not produce an egalitarian relationship. Rather, Marxism—which she sees as "sex-blind"—subsumes feminism. Hartmann, however, does not espouse a total reliance on feminist theory, which she sees as not sufficiently materialist and "blind to history." She therefore proposes a union of the historical and materialist methods of Marxist analysis, with the identification of patriarchy as a social and historical structure of feminist analysis, to provide a more feasible assessment and analysis of history (2–4).

In CASA, therefore, "the woman question" contended not only with Marxism but with issues of Chicano nationalism and identity. CASA members, including women, saw women's issues as an equal part of the class struggle and did not see the need to separate them, like women in the feminist movement. However, a difference existed between the theoretical desire for the equal participation of women in all aspects of the organization and its actual practice. Women made up a vital portion of CASA's membership rolls and provided the work that basically ran the organization; but the concrete practices that would have allowed women to participate on more equal footing with men, such as childcare, did not exist. As a result, conflict and contradiction permeated these women's experiences. Although it seems that women in CASA could not count on much support within the organization, they dedicated almost their entire lives to it. Their participation in this organization allowed them to grow politically, intellectually, and socially. Through this growth, CASA helped shape the rest of their lives.

The women this study focuses on—Andrea Elizalde, Diane Factor, Jana Adkins, Teresa Rentería, Patricia Vellanoweth, Evelina Márquez, Evelina Fernández, Irma García, Isabel H. Rodríguez, Margarita Ramírez, Elsa Rivas, and Gilda Rodríguez—began to experience political, intellectual and social growth with the rise of the Chicano movement from 1966 to 1968. Most graduated from east side parochial and public schools in Los Angeles and entered college between 1966 and 1972. While Isabel H. Rodríguez and Patricia Vellanoweth began to participate peripherally in political protests in high school, like Andrea Elizalde, Margarita Ramírez, Evelina Márquez, Elsa Rivas, Evelina Fernández, and Gilda Rodríguez, their political involvement blossomed in college through groups like United Mexican American Students (UMAS), el Movimiento Estudiantil Chicano de Aztlán (MEChA), La Vida Nueva, and the Third World Women's Alliance. Isabel H. Rodríguez and Patricia Vellanoweth also became involved in community organizations like Casa Carnalismo in the housing projects in Boyle Heights. From Casa Carnalismo, Rodríguez and Vellanoweth joined the Committee to Free Los Tres (CTFLT), which ultimately led them to CASA. Others, like Jana Adkins and Diane Factor, two of the very few Euro-American members of CASA, joined CASA without directly experiencing the political evolution of Chicano movement politics but with experience in New Left organizations (Rodríguez 1996; Vellanoweth 1996; Reutería 1996).

Some women, such as Irma García, had very early ties to CASA. Patricia Vellanoweth had already worked with CASA since 1970 and with the CTFLT. She became exposed to CASA through Bert Corona, at the time one of her history professors at California State University, Los Angeles. Vellanoweth had already worked with organizations like the United Farmworkers, an organization called Casa Carnalismo, the Raza Unida Party, and campus organizations. She states, "All of that stuff was going on at that same time . . . And so it just grew" (1996). It seems that for women such as herself, political activity that started in late high school or in the college years continued to snowball.

Teresa Rentería seems to have been dually influenced to join CASA by her husband and, ironically, by *Maryknoll Magazine*, a Catholic missionary magazine subscribed to by her parents. She remembers first reading and hearing about CASA at her parents' home through their *Maryknoll Magazine,* which published reports on CASA because of the social services it provided immigrant members. Thus, Rentería thought CASA a benevolent society. Her husband Ricardo Rentería, however, who attended the University of California, Irvine, at the time, learned that CASA was a leftist organization dedicated to labor issues. Ricardo began to attend CASA forums, and eventually Teresa joined him. (Rentería 1996).

Other women, such as Margarita Ramírez and Evelina Márquez, joined CASA not in Los Angeles but in San Jose, California. Although Márquez had been involved in the movement in Los Angeles as a student at UCLA, she joined a propaganda collective in the bay area called Prensa Sembradora.

She had left Los Angeles with future CASA member Carlos Vásquez, when St. Mary's College in Orinda, California, hired Vásquez as a faculty member. They both joined Prensa Sembradora, and Vásquez played an influential role in recruiting other students from St. Mary's to Prensa Sembradora (Márquez 1997).

Margarita Ramírez's story reveals similar connections. During her time at St. Mary's College in northern California from 1971 to 1975, she, along with other students, staged demonstrations and protests to demand a Chicano studies program, participated in the formation of MEChA, and began to study the question of Chicana liberation. With fellow student María Elena Durazo and through the urging of Carlos Vásquez, Ramírez joined Prensa Sembradora in 1974. There, she began to work with Evelina Márquez and Magdalena Mora. During this time, Ramírez became exposed to class-based politics and ideology. She states, "He [Carlos Vasquez] got us involved very much in the work around class politics, Marxism-Leninism, study groups. We were reading Marx and Mao and different kinds of theories." The ideology stemmed from her involvement not only with Prensa Sembradora but with other students on her college campus. These different students exposed her to the situation of people in Mozambique and Angola. She states, "More the stronger influence were not even necessarily Chicanos. They were from other nationalities. They were foreign students . . . foreign exchange. Part of them grew up here but they came here . . . So they sort of all mingled somehow" (Ramírez 1996).

Influenced greatly by the Chicano movement of which they felt a part, these women joined CASA in one of the continuing stages of organizational and political activity on their part. CASA became the synthesis and provided a framework—Marxism—for the struggle they had previously waged. Through CASA, they hoped to forge ahead with a Mexicano/Chicano social justice agenda they had already begun and to solidify and strengthen the aims of the Chicano movement. But they also held a different view of their struggle. They no longer saw it as a liberation struggle for Chicanos, but for the Mexican working class as a whole, on both sides of the U.S.–Mexico border.

For some women, joining CASA had negative effects on their struggle for Chicana liberation. Ramírez and Márquez, along with Durazo and Mora, had studied issues of Chicana liberation extensively through their involvement with Prensa Sembradora. In addition, they studied women's struggles in the international realm. Ramírez states, "And so when you studied the origins of the women's oppression you find a pattern in terms of how it emerged and how it manifested itself throughout cultures in the world." In addition to analyzing the experiences of international peoples, Ramírez, with Durazo, Márquez and Mora, began to question and study the roles of women in revolutionary struggle. Through this study, these women came to believe that women's struggles were part of the revolution and were not a separate issue—an ideology that fit nicely into CASA's realm (Ramírez 1996; Márquez 1997).

In 1974, the members of PS decided to cease to exist as an organization to become part of CASA. A CASA chapter had formed in San Jose between 1972 and 1973 and addressed issues much like those in Los Angeles: undocumented immigrants and labor struggles of Chicanos/Mexicanos. As a member of CASA in San Jose and later Oakland, Ramírez experienced a politicization that challenged her to question her identity as a Chicana; she ceased to identify herself as "Chicana" and adopted the term "Mexicana." CASA's cultural transnationalist class-based ideology had struck a chord. She states, "Up to CASA I was very much a Chicana liberation feminist, adhering to the triple oppression, you know the whole theories of how we're just sidestepped and not given a chance" (Ramírez 1996).

Women's issues, however, seem to have gotten lost in the transition from PS to CASA. Ramírez made a conscious decision to join CASA and downplay her Chicana liberation feminism. She states, "And so it was hard. It was hard, because you felt that there were few orgnizations like CASA." Ramírez thus felt that no other organization in the Chicano movement addressed issues of a transnational class and solidarity with Mexico. In her embrace of Marxism-Leninism through CASA's male-identified leadership, she began to deal less with issues of Chicana liberation.

Although all the women hoped that CASA would "always continue," how long they would have remained members of CASA seems questionable because of the quality of their experience in this organization. These women, indeed, provided the backbone of the organization but clearly did not occupy the most visible or important roles. A sexual division of labor seems to have existed in CASA where men held the more visible leadership roles and women held largely silent roles as fundraisers, editors, photographers, newspaper writers, and administrative staff. Men therefore received the recognition as leaders. As one woman states, "women did the shitty work" ("The Woman Question" n.d., Vellanoweth 1996).

When analyzed, however, women performed vital work for the life and sustenance of the organization. After CASA ceased being a mutual aid organization, membership fell dramatically, and CASA could not count on the yearly membership dues of its approximately 4,000 members (Chávez 1994, 179). Thus, CASA had to rely extensively on different sources of funding. After CASA's merger with CTFLT, the organization relied on fundraisers, sales from *Sin Fronteras*, and monthly *cuotas* (dues) from its members, which ranged from $3.00 to $25.00 per person. Records from September 1975 to July 1976 show an average monthly *cuota* collection of $100.00. In addition, from February 1976 through May 1977, *Sin Fronteras* operated on a monthly average deficit of $97.76. While at times *Sin Fronteras* cleared a net income of as much as $460.09, from July through November 1976, CASA ran an average deficit of $470.17. Thus, CASA obviously needed to rely on more than just monthly dues and newspaper sales.[2]

Patricia Vellanoweth and Teresa Rentería worked extensively in fundraising for CASA. As head of the Finance Committee, Patricia Vellanoweth's main duty, along with the other women that made up the committee, became raising money. For example, evidence from CASA "Ticket Ledgers" reveals that in 1977, the duty of selling tickets to two fundraising events— a "Tardeada de CASA" (An Afternoon with CASA) and a "Baile Sin Fronteras" (*Sin Fronteras* Dance)—fell primarily to women (Ticket Ledger n.d.). While Vellanoweth and Rentería do not appear on these lists, they engaged in similar activities throughout their participation in CASA. As fundraisers these women had to be resourceful and ingenious in order to produce a profit. Solicitation of donations of food, materials, and locations proved to be one of the most successful strategies for producing profits. Teresa Rentería planned and organized *tardeadas* (afternoon get-togethers) for approximately fifty people in her own home with nothing but solicited donations from meat markets and meat packing plants for many years. CASA left fundraising to women, according to Vellanoweth, because "we were the best ones that knew how to fundraise" (Vellanoweth 1996; Rentaría 1996).

Fundraisers, in addition to providing much-needed financial support for CASA members, also became events to socialize and to have fun. Many fundraisers featured bands, a DJ, cocktails, films, poetry, and *teatro*. CASA also had a New Year's Eve fundraiser in 1977.[3] Thus, in the tradition of CASA's all-encompassing philosophy, the CASA fundraisers and parties served a dual purpose of entertainment and politicization. While CASA did not facilitate social connection on an organizational basis, members, due to their young age, oftentimes used CASA fundraisers as social events. They had fun—albeit in a politically conscious manner.

CASA members also enjoyed themselved while "pulling security" for CASA offices. As an organization that felt besieged by police surveillance and infiltration, each CASA member had a duty to oversee the office's security at night. Thus, CASA obligated males and females alike to "pull security" all night long, regardless of other obligations such as employment. While at times the gender balance between men and women "pulling security" proved equal, sometimes only women did the job, or only men. Thus, in physical terms, CASA seems to have taken women's equality to heart in assigning same gender security teams for the CASA offices.

Security, however, also proved a time for socializing and having fun. Most security lasted all night long and, at times, on the weekend nights. As member Andrea Elizalde recalls,

> Everybody did it. Everything was communal. It just went down the [line]. They just made a list of everybody and these were your hours. If you were a woman or not or whether—the big joke with me is I'd never been in a fight in my whole life. What was I going to do if somebody broke in? . . . It was a party in a way. I remember we would pull these securities and . . . in those days Whittier Boulevard was like the happening place for a lot of the community kids. You know they would cruise down Whittier Boulevard and our location was like in the heart . . . of this. So if we had to pull security on the weekends . . . we would just take our chairs out like going to the Rose Parade . . . And we would just sit out there and have a good old time. (Elizalde 1997)

91

In addition to fundraising and pulling security, women assumed important roles in *Sin Fronteras* as editors, writers, photographers, and layout designers, making up the majority of *Sin Fronteras* staff members. For example, Margarita Ramírez's role within CASA was as the "*encargada de distribución*" (distribution manager) for *Sin Fronteras*. As such, she took charge of the national distribution of the newspaper; she found places for its sale and oversaw its distribution to CASA chapters in El Paso, Chicago, Oakland, Santa Barbara, San Diego, Seattle, Colorado, and Los Angeles. In addition, Ramírez helped with researching, editing, and writing articles for the newspaper. Her name appears in the staff section of *Sin Fronteras* from November 1976 through January/ February 1978 as "business manager" (Ramírez 1996; *Sin Fronteras* 1976–1978).

From September 1975 through May 1976, Isabel H. Rodríguez, then known as Isabel Chávez, held the role of editor/director of the newspaper. As editor/director, she administered the work of the newspaper, which entailed overseeing the layout, distribution, writing, design, photography, and art sections of the newspaper. Together with the staff, the editor/director decided on which news stories to print, where the stories would be placed in the newspaper, and other related tasks. Rodríguez exercised much control over *Sin Fronteras*'s production and served on CASA's highest governing body in Los Angeles, the Political Commission (Rodriguez 1996; *Sin Fronteras* Feb. 1976 and June 1976; Chávez 1994, 188).

Between May and June 1976, Carlos Vásquez replaced Isabel H. Rodríguez as director of *Sin Fronteras*. Rodríguez, in turn, became editor, under Vásquez's leadership. Many factors contributed to Rodríguez's removal as director, including complaints by staff members of too many demands made upon them and Rodríguez's leadership style, cited as "authoritarian" and "dogmatic." However, power within CASA constituted another important issue. As editor/ director, Rodríguez served on the Political Commission, the governing body of CASA in Los Angeles, which historian Ernesto Chávez cites as "responsible for the political and ideological purity of CASA's members." The Political Commission therefore had the right to expel members who they suspected did not follow the correct politics or ideology (Chávez 1994, 191–92). As editor/director of *Sin Fronteras*, Rodríguez, at the time the only woman on the Political Commission, did not have a vote, because she had been appointed and not elected. As a consequence of being removed as chief leader of the newspaper, Rodríguez also lost her position on the Political Commission. Because Carlos Vásquez already held a position on the Political Commission as coordinator of information and propaganda, he easily assumed the role of director of the newspaper. The Political Commission, therefore, lost its only female voice (Internal Document 1975, 6–8; "Report of Resignations" n.d.; Rodríguez 1994).

The process employed to remove Rodríguez from chief leadership of the newspaper proved to be stressful and painful for her. A large membership meeting called her leadership of the newspaper into review, and she was criticized publicly. She states, "So there was a meeting, there were these general criticisms made, and I was exposed to everybody, how bad I was" (Rodríguez 1994). At the time, many, including Rodríguez herself, viewed her removal as just another order of business. She agreed somewhat with the criticisms made of her, explaining that she had no training in leadership nor in running or producing a newspaper. While she had assumed the job of editor/director, she did so without the proper skills. When members and the Political Commission found that she had not done what they expected, the all-male Political Commission decided to replace her as leader of the newspaper. There seems to have been no thought of how to help develop the leadership already in place. Thus, CASA did not provide Rodríguez with adequate training or, it seems, time to develop the kind of leadership they expected. Her work, however, proved necessary for the newspaper, and she remained as editor, although under the leadership of Carlos Vásquez. Therefore, she assumed the kind of work that most women in CASA assumed, that of the backbone (Rodríguez 1994).

While performing their duties as CASA members, women experienced or viewed situations that screamed of sexism. For example, some men in CASA used sexual or romantic relations with women in order to gain more members. Many men in the organization also pursued extramarital affairs (Rodríguez 1994; Elizalde 1997; García-Sinclair 1997; Ramírez 1996; Márquez 1997; and Factor 1997). The women of this study state that a general mood of sexism pervaded the organization, citing, for example, the sexual division of labor. Patricia Vellanoweth's experience, however, provides a concrete example. In 1975, the International Ladies' Garment Workers Union (ILGWU) hired

Vellanoweth as a labor organizer. She was proud to be part of the ILGWU as well as of CASA, and many lauded Vellanoweth for having opened the door for CASA in the union. Soon after acquiring her job, Vellanoweth learned she was pregnant. Upon hearing Vellanoweth's news, however, some members of CASA revealed feelings of regret and disappointment. Vellanoweth re-members a male CASA member telling her, "Look sister, how can you do that? How can you get pregnant? You're the first woman that was able to get into here, you're supposed to be organizing, how could you get pregnant?" (Vellanoweth 1996). Her husband, also a CASA member, escaped unscathed from such criticism. The idea that Vellanoweth had let the organi-zation down by getting pregnant exposes CASA's strong posi-tion of putting the organization before everything else—including family and children.

Due to CASA's revolutionary ideology and actions, CASA came under the surveillance of the FBI and the Los Angeles Police Department. This proved a frightening experience for some members, while others did not become fazed by it. The FBI and the Los Angeles Police Department visited most CASA members. Historian Ernesto Chávez acquired 660 pages of FBI documents on CASA through the Freedom of Information Act. These documents reveal that the FBI had infiltrated CASA and gathered information from April 1972 through August 1976 (Chávez 1994, 200). In the late 1970s and early 1980s, mem-bers of CASA, along with other organizations, became part of a class-action lawsuit against the Los Angeles Police Depart-ment for illegal surveillance and infiltration of their organiza-tion. The records of this lawsuit have been lost, but members such as Isabel H. Rodríguez received settlements of approxi-mately $8,000 for the LAPD's actions (Rodríguez 1996).

Police and FBI infiltration and surveillance was frighten-ing for all CASA members, but had an extra degree of inten-sity for women—especially single women living on their own. Elsa Rivas recalls her experience:

> And I remember this one time, I didn't have a phone in my apartment . . . And kind of the sun was starting to set and I walked down to Huntington Drive to use the phone 'cause that's where there was a phone booth. And a car followed me. It was an un-marked car. And I was really scared. I'll never for-get . . . So I kept walking, and he was just right

behind me just following. And it was getting dark. And I get to the phone booth . . . it was about a good quarter of a mile from my house. I get to the phone booth, and I don't even want to look back because I was scared . . . It was an old abandoned gas station where the phone booth was . . . And it's dark. I just remember I picked up the phone . . . and I just remember the headlights. The car pulls up like this, and it's facing me. And I'm inside the phone booth. And they took a picture. And the flash just lit up, it was like daytime. They had an incredible flash . . . It was real scary. And then he turned around. The guy split. He sat there for a while, and then he left . . . And for what? We weren't doing anything. I didn't feel I was doing anything that was illegal. You know, it was just to enlighten and educate. That was the scary part. (Rivas 1997)

As can be imagined, being under surveillance by police and having children must have proved especially frightening. CASA members knew of the clashes between groups such as the Black Panthers and the FBI and police departments. They did not doubt that relations between CASA and the police and FBI could escalate to the same extreme. As such, they feared for the welfare of their children when they saw unmarked police cars parked outside their homes and in front of CASA offices. Their belief in their cause, however, allowed them to remain involved amidst the fear (Vellanoweth 1996; Rodríguez 1994; Chávez 1997).

Those members who had children involved their entire families in CASA. While CASA expected its members to devote all of their free time and energy to the cause, extra provisions for those with children did not exist. When they did exist, those who had children of their own organized them, realizing the burden many parents in CASA carried. For example, CASA as an organization did not provide any child care. As the women of this study revealed, CASA left child care up to the parents, mainly the women, so that they could fulfill the expected duties of CASA membership. Most relied on their parents or parents-in-law for child care. But when this form of child care was not available, children roaming the CASA offices was a common sight.

Members of CASA lived a stressful, work-filled life. While many members worked full-time, part-time, or as students, they devoted almost all extra time to CASA. A document published by the local committee of Los Angeles in March 1976 summarized the membership experience as follows: "The schedule by day is maintained with constant practical work that has to be realized, and by night with external meetings, commission meetings, study circles, external work in coalitions, speaking engagements, theatrical performances, communal and factory work, etc." ("Concerning the Political Education" 1976). As women, though, CASA added extra burdens, for they were ultimately left with the responsibility of caring for their children. Those women who were married participated in CASA with their spouses and their children. As a testament to this statement, Patricia Vellanoweth (1996) states, "We'd work all day and then go to CASA, come home. Carlos worked in the law office . . . I worked part time. And then we'd come home, and we had between five and seven . . . We had to come home, make dinner, clean up, and go back to the meeting and come back at ten or eleven at night."

Isabel H. Rodríguez experienced a similar situation. She did not work an outside job during most of her involvement with CASA and worked at CASA full-time, relying on her husband's income. In February of 1976, Rodríguez resigned from her duties as editor/director of the newspaper and from the Political Commission. Her resignation stemmed from the conflict between constant devotion of her time to CASA and time devoted to her daughter. She wrote two letters of resignation in February of 1976. The second letter reveals the disturbing conflicts between parenting and the organization. She states,

> I am a member of the organization who is married and has a child. Consequently I have responsibilities to meet in the basic human needs of that child and her development as well as responsibilities in the house. The responsibilities I have ignored for the past two to three years . . . Flexibility in my opinion is thus applied in cases of comrades taking on jobs and inflexibility is applied when comrades with children request time to meet their responsibilities and insure the development, as much as possible considering we are in a capitalist country. . . the objective reality though is that it has to be done, the only other alternative being giving up kids for adoption, or eventually having neurotics or misguided and unconscious children who hate the struggle. (Chávez 1976)

For Rodríguez, as well as other mothers in the organization, CASA's neglect of parental duties went against the idea of a revolution. They decried the fact that CASA did not provide child care for its members with children even though the organization demanded so much time. For example, recalling her membership in CASA, Rodríguez described her typical day: "get up in the morning . . . drop off my child . . . go to the newspaper, and I'm there really late . . . working constantly, taking phone calls or editing . . . I don't recall eating . . . we would have meetings . . . stay there late into the night so I didn't see much of anything else. We worked on Saturday, we worked Sundays . . . I don't even remember who cleaned my house. I never did it." Inherent in CASA demands, therefore, lay a constant pressure upon those with families and children to neglect their parental responsibilities for the struggle (Rodríguez 1996; Chávez 1976a).[4]

Teresa Rentería believed that her entire family, including her children, should participate in CASA, and she and another woman member of CASA organized the Children's Brigade, which lasted approximately from 1975 to 1976. CASA members worked on Saturdays, obligated to go out and sell *Sin Fronteras*. Many times, when child care could not be procured, parents and their children would be out on the streets all day selling newspapers. As an educator, Rentería saw the need for some productive activity for the children of CASA. She states, "We had the Children's Brigade . . . we would pick everybody up on a Saturday, in two or three cars, so that the parents could go out and do political work . . . We had field trips so that the kids were exposed to cultural events and could play together and be together and form friendships together, and yet the parents could feel free that their kids were being taken care of and that they could do work" (Rentería 1996).

Within this tight schedule, women CASA members, due to their involvement in women's conferences, their Committee against Forced Sterilization, and their Marxist ideology, came into contact with women involved in the women's movement. For women of CASA, who based their ideology on the merger of cultural nationalism and Marxism, exposure and involvement with Euro American women was tension-filled. Most Euro-American feminists with whom women of CASA came in contact viewed their struggle in terms of sexual politics. For them, patriarchy represented the evil that needed to be eradicated. Most Euro-American feminists at the time therefore could not understand those women of color who rejected this stance and argued that race, class, and ethnicity were just as important, if not more important, for their situation. When Euro-American women tried to incorporate women of color into their agenda, the incorporation could be characterized as tokenism (Echols 1989, 291). Thus, while most of the women in CASA I interviewed did not relate or identify at all with the women's movement or have a definition of feminism, some took women's liberation to heart (Rentería 1996; Rodríguez 1996; Vellanoweth 1996).

For example, Irma García ardently believed in feminism. She joined CASA upon graduating from high school and through her involvement with a *teatro* (theater) group. In high school, García was called "Irma-lib." Influenced greatly by the first issue of *Ms.*, García clearly saw the sexism and double standards that existed in CASA. She states, "I think what was lacking was some kind of feminist awareness and classes for the men and women . . . I mean, I would see women come one day, stay for a month, and they'd be gone . . . any good-looking woman that came, there was ten guys competing to see who could get her in bed first" (García-Sinclair 1997).[5] Similarly, Andrea Elizalde (1997) states, "I think that men and even women, but men treated, they were so mouthy about supporting women in the organization . . . It was always women in the organization, your sisters, that you respected them and that you had to support them . . . In reality they treated their women very poorly, and I use the word *their women*, but that's how we were considered, you know, like women of the organization."

Thus, while some women clearly saw sexist practices in the organization, few ever voiced them like García and Elizalde. Other women, however, never saw women's liberation as having any effect on them. For example, Teresa Rentería saw it as "a lot of fluff," while Diane Factor considered the feminist movement too narrow. Some women, then, took women's liberation into the organization and relied on it for analysis of everyday goings on in CASA, while others dismissed it as irrelevant to their cause (García-Sinclair 1997; Elizalde 1997; Rentería 1996; Factor 1997).

Records and interviews reveal that two Euro-American women were members of CASA. Interviews also reveal that some members were not necessarily only Chicano or Mexicano. For many members of CASA, incorporating other nationalities into the organization fit within CASA's larger goal of a working-class revolution. While CASA saw itself as the vanguard for Mexicanos/Chicanos in the United States and Mexico, their class vision allowed them to form ties and allegiances with other people of color. It even allowed them to form allegiances with Euro-Americans committed to social change.

The incorporation of Euro-American women did not come without challenges. Jana Adkins became a member of CASA in Seattle through her work in the Chicano/Mexicano community there. After she moved to Los Angeles in 1976 to work on *Sin Fronteras*, some CASA members questioned her nomination to the Interim Political Commission because she was Euro-American. Others in CASA, however, supported her nomination and stated, "As progressive activists of all colors and nationalities, we try to understand that the nationalism of an oppressed nationality has a progressive character when it is directed against the source of national oppression. However, it loses that character when it becomes narrow, especially within an organization fighting racism and national oppression" ("History of CASA" n.d., 54). Adkins, however, does not recall any negative feedback due to her race but does recall consciously not seeking leadership and power because she did not feel it her place to do so (Adkins 1997).

In a similar manner, Diane Factor never aspired to hold a leadership role in CASA and, while she did adopt CASA's ideological stance of no borders, seems to have worked mostly with the labor-organizing aspect of CASA. As a member of the Teamsters and a school bus driver in Los Angeles, Factor was recruited by the CASA committee dedicated to trade union issues in hopes of gaining entry into the Teamsters union. Factor, who never actually recruited anyone to CASA, did gain from the experience of working with CASA in terms of training in trade union issues and in personal relationships. Like Adkins, Factor states, "As one of the few white people that was allowed in, it also let me be a part of a community that normally I wouldn't have gotten to be a part of. It was a great time in my life" (Factor 1997; Adkins 1997).

The great time had by so many, however, soon began to falter. From its inception as a Marxist organization, CASA experienced many problems, ranging from dissatisfaction among membership of their leaders, financial difficulties, factionalism, and criticism of specific CASA members. From 1975 to late 1977, these problems caused internal struggles, and tension filled the organization. In late 1977, Carlos

Vásquez, director of *Sin Fronteras* and member of the Political Commission, resigned from CASA, citing reasons of factionalism, nepotism, putschism, and a degree of other criticisms. Approximately one year later, thirteen members of CASA, men and women alike, resigned en masse citing many of the same reasons (Aguirre et al. 1978).

Although many CASA members resigned, the organization still survived. Those who remained sought to address the charges waged by Vásquez and "the thirteen." They thus wrote a seventy-page response to the two letters of resignation, which they titled, "History of CASA." This document stands as the most comprehensive analysis of CASA by its own members on its origins, direction, and eventual disintegration. While the remaining members struggled with their work, other factors, such as finances and families, began to impinge on their commitment to the organization. CASA folded at the end of 1978.

The women of this study viewed these struggles in light of their own experiences. They held largely secondary roles in comparison with men; they experienced sexism; and they became targets of power struggles. Teresa Rentería did not have such poignant experiences as Vellanoweth or Rodríguez but felt disillusioned with CASA, stating that the demands made upon members constituted a sound reason for the downfall of the organization in late 1978. In addition, after struggling for so long in the organization, some members burned out, while others gradually took on responsibilities commensurate with their age—raising families, working full-time, paying bills. As Andrea Elizalde stated, "Reality set in" (Elizade 1997).

Patricia Vellanoweth did not remain a member of CASA. She resigned from CASA in May 1976 for personal as well organizational reasons. Being involved within the organization, working, and being active politically proved extremely stressful, and she lost the baby she had previously been criticized for carrying. Due to this and the struggles she viewed in CASA and the evolvement of CASA into a cadre instead of a mass-based organization, Vellanoweth became extremely disillusioned and left. About the dissolution of CASA, she states, "Well, I feel less emotional about it. I think it was a very emotional time at the time. There were a lot of us that gave a lot. I mean, it was our whole life" (Vellanoweth 1996). Because CASA members devoted so much of their time to the organization, their social network also centered around CASA, engendering friendships and personal ties among members. When tensions started building throughout the organization, many friendships also dissolved, thus having an impact not only on members' political lives, but on their personal lives as well (Rodríguez 1996).

While the end of CASA disillusioned these women, their involvement shaped their future lives. Most of these women presently work as professionals serving the needs of the working-class and poor. Patricia Vellanoweth works as the primary administrator of a facility for Health Care Partners Medical Group. Isabel H. Rodríguez is an attorney with her own law practice—a partnership with her brother, also a former CASA member—and represents primarily Mexican workers in workers' compensation suits. Teresa Rentería is an educator with the Los Angeles Unified School District and is presently helping to develop the district's literacy program. Evelina Márquez works as the International Union Area Director for the American Federation of State, County, and Municipal Employees (AFSCME) in New Mexico. Diane Factor, an industrial hygienist, works with the UCLA labor center after previously being on the national staff of the AFL-CIO working in the health and safety department. Margarita Ramírez currently works as the main grants administrator for Liberty Hill Foundation, a grant foundation for grassroots organizing.

While some women do not work directly with the working-class, poor, or Latino community in their professions, CASA still has had a profound influence on their lives. Jana Adkins and Andrea Elizalde cite CASA as one of the most important influences in their lives today, leaving them with life-long friends and acquaintances and a network of socially conscious people. Irma García-Sinclair and Evelina Fernández, both actors, continue to work on projects beneficial to the Latino community. After leaving CASA, Fernández joined the stage production of Luis Valdez's "Zoot Suit" in Los Angeles, then joined the Teatro de la Esperanza in Santa Barbara, California. In 1984, she and her husband, José Luis Valenzuela, founded the Latino Theatre Lab, now the Latino Theatre Company, which has produced a number of plays and dramatic performances.

Vellanoweth, Rodríguez, and Fernández continue to work with community and political issues outside of their occupations. Fernández frequently speaks to young women at high schools, middle schools, and elementary schools about her profession. Vellanoweth works as a board member of the Dolores Mission, a community and church-based program in the Pico Gardens–Aliso Village housing projects in Boyle Heights. Dolores Mission, home to renowned gang intervention priest Father Gregory Boyle, also provides shelter to homeless families and, through the Women's Cooperative, offers women job training and operates a day care center. Isabel H. Rodríguez continues to work on political campaigns and presently is the chairperson of the Workers' Compensation Committee of the Mexican American Bar Association in Los Angeles (Fernández 1997; Vellanoweth 1996; Rodríguez 1996).

In retrospect, all women believe they owe their present-day development, political thought, and activity to their participation in CASA. Vellanoweth (1996) states, "I think it made me what I am today." Similarly, Rentería (1996) states, "I think it was a positive experience for my whole family, for all of us. It was a real period of growth . . . I mean leaps. I think it helped to shape all of our views." Finally, Rodríguez (1996) states, "I would say it gave me conviction and I still have that conviction . . . It gave me a real strong method of analysis. It's definitely made me more tolerant of people and in personal relationships. It's opened my eyes a lot."[6]

Although their experiences in CASA subsumed their roles as women into secondary roles due to the converging ideologies of cultural nationalism, Marxism, and traditional gender roles, these women still gained valuable experiences. Their disillusionment with CASA did not hinder their future participation in political activities or community issues. Due to their own initiative and conviction, these women remained in CASA amidst the sexism, power struggles, and in-fighting as a testament to their belief in the Mexicano/Chicano class struggle. These women lived, breathed, and worked the movement.

Notes

I would like to thank Vicki L. Ruiz for her comments on previous versions of this article and Edward J. Escobar and Susan Gray for their comments on the M.A. thesis from which this article stems. I would also like to thank the Graduate Research Support Program of the Associated Students of Arizona State University, the Graduate College, and the Vice President for Research for the grant that made the research for this article possible.

1. A primary document describing aspects of Chicanismo and cultural nationalism is Valdez and Steiner 1972 (402–406).

2. Financial information is taken from: "Internal Document, Comite Local, Los Angeles," 5 December 1975, pp. 9–11, CASA Papers; "Cuotas" September 1975 to July 1976, CASA Papers; "Financial Records: Sin Fronteras," February 1976 through May 1977, CASA Papers.

3. The CASA papers document these events with a number of flyers, including: "Festival Sin Fronteras," flyer, 20 November c. 1976, CASA Papers; "Una Tarde de Solidaridad con Sin Fronteras—Cocktail benefit," flyer, 15 May 1977, CASA Papers; "Tardeada de CASA," flyer, 24 October 1976, CASA Papers; "Noche Social Sin Fronteras," flyer, 25 September c. 1976, CASA Papers.

4. Other women with children also corroborated this fact: Vellanoweth 1996, Elizalde 1997, and Rentería 1996.

5. Information about women as sexual conquests also was corroborated by Ramírez 1996 and Rodríguez 1996.

6. The quotes cited here reflect the general consensus among women members of CASA in terms of its influence on their present-day lives.

Bibliography

Adkins, Jana. 1997. Interview by author. Tape recording. Los Angeles, California, 10 January.

Aguirre, Felipe, Kathy Ledesma, Juan Gutiérrez, Alfonso Rojas, Mario Vásquez, Fidel Gómez, Jose Jacques Medina, Evelina Márquez, María Elena Salazar, Susanna Martínez, Nicolas Pineda, Jose Luis Ramos, and Juan Mora. 1978. Letter to CASA. 1 October. Centro de Acción Social Autónomo–Hermandad General de Trabajadores (CASA–HGT) Records, 1963–1979. Palo Alto, Calif.: Department of Special Collections, Stanford University. (Hereafter cited as CASA Papers.)

Chabram-Dernersesian, Angie. 1992. "I Throw Punches for My Race, but I Don't Want to Be a Man: Writing Us—Chica-nos (Girl, Us)/ Chicanas—into the Movement Script." In *Cultural Studies*, eds. Lawrence Grossberg, Cary Nelson, and Paula Treichler. New York: Routledge.

Chávez, Carlos A. 1997. Interview by author. Tape recording. Alhambra, California, 5 February.

Chávez, Ernesto. 1994. "Creating Aztlán: The Chicano Movement in Los Angeles, 1966–1978." Ph.D. dissertation, University of California, Los Angeles.

Chávez, Isabel. 1976a. Letter to Political Commission, "Resignation letter." CASA Papers. 6 February.

———. 1976b. Letter to Political Commission, "Report Requested in Light of Resignation." CASA Papers. 18 February.

"Concerning the Political Education of CASA-HGT, Local Committee of Los Angeles." 1976. CASA Papers. March.

"Cuotas," September 1975 to July 1976, CASA Papers. December 5.

Echols, Alice. 1989. *Daring to Be Bad: Radical Feminism in America, 1967–1975*. Minneapolis: University of Minnesota Press.

Elizalde, Andrea. 1997. Interview by author. Tape recording. Whittier, California, 12 January.

Escobar, Edward J. 1993. "The Dialectics of Repression: The Los Angeles Police Department and the Chicano Movement, 1968–1971." *The Journal of American History* (March).

Factor, Diane. 1997. Interview by author. Tape recording. Los Angeles, California, 13 January.

Fernández, Evelina. 1997. Interview by author. Tape recording. Los Angeles, California, 9 January.

"*Festival Sin Fronteras.*" c. 1976. Flyer. CASA Papers. 20 November.

"Financial Records: *Sin Fronteras.*" February 1976 through May 1977. CASA Papers.

García-Sinclair, Irma. 1997. Interview by author. Tape recording. La Crescenta, California, 8 January.

Gómez-Quiñones, Juan. 1990. *Chicano Politics: Reality and Promise, 1940–1990*. Albuquerque: University of New Mexico Press.

Hartmann, Heidi. 1981. "The Unhappy Marriage of Marxism and Feminism: Towards a More Progressive Union." In *Women and Revolution*, ed. Lydia Sargent. Boston: South End Press.

"History of CASA." n.d. CASA Papers.

"Internal Document, *Comite Local*, Los Angeles." 1975. CASA Papers.

"Internal Document." 1975. CASA Papers. 5 December.

Márquez, Evelina. 1997. Interview by author. Tape recording. Santa Fe, New Mexico, 21 February.

"*Noche Social Sin Fronteras*," c. 1976. Flyer. CASA Papers. 25 September.

"Preliminary Report of the National Meeting of CASA, Which Took Place July 5 to July 12 in Los Angeles." 1975. CASA Papers. 23 July.

Ramírez, Margarita. 1996. Interview by author. Tape recording. Pico Rivera, California, 24 October.

Rentería, Teresa. 1996. Interview by author. Tape recording. San Gabriel, California, 13 March.

"Report of resignations of Carlos Chávez and Isabel Chávez from the National Political Commission." n.d. CASA Papers.

Rivas, Elsa. 1997. Interview by author. Tape recording. Los Angeles, California, 8 February.

Rodríguez, Isabel H. 1996. Interview by author. Tape recording. Los Angeles, California, 11 March, 17 March.

Sin Fronteras. 1975–1978.

"Tardeada de CASA." 1976. Flyer. CASA Papers. 24 October.

"Ticket Ledger," n.d. CASA Papers.

"Una Tarde de Solidaridad con Sin Fronteras—Cocktail benefit." 1977. Flyer. CASA Papers. 15 May.

Valdez, Luis, and Stan Steiner, eds. 1972. "El Plan Espiritual de Aztlán." In *Aztlán: An Anthology of Mexican American Literature*. New York: A. A. Knopf.

Vellanoweth, Patricia. 1996. Interview by author. Tape recording. Montebello, California, 12 March.

"The Woman Question," study guide, n.d. CASA Papers.

Creating Community: Mexican American Women in Eastside Los Angeles

Mary Pardo

> Resistance strategies employed in everyday life inform women's participation in those struggles traditionally recognized as resistance movements . . . it is about creating the conditions necessary for life and not intrinsically oppositional.
>
> —Bettina Aptheker, *Tapestries of Life*

How may Mexican American women's efforts to improve the quality of life in their communities be understood as work? No wages are earned, no profits reaped, nor commodities produced. However, the unpaid work that women do in meeting their socially assigned responsibilities extends beyond nurturing and reproducing families; it creates community and the conditions necessary for life. So, when we broaden our conception of work and take seriously women's unpaid community work, we advance a theory that may unify race, class and gender (Sacks 1989, 534–50).[1]

Nineteenth-century historical accounts of urban communities suggest that women's unpaid work often compensated for meager wages and inadequate public services. The working poor, particularly children and women, used the public streets to supplement their economic base; in the process, they also created social networks (Stansell 1990).[2] Today, the quality and quantity of public services such as recreation centers and schools in working-class communities continue to lag behind the needs of densely populated neighborhoods. For many working-class women, the community is both a living space and a work site. While most women desire amiable surroundings in which to meet their socially assigned responsibilities, not all know how to create them.

The life stories of Mexican American women who have developed successful strategies for community building provide the rich detail needed to explore how women link family concerns to a wider network of resources.[3] While their work influences conditions in their neighborhoods, their work outside the home can also change household arrangements. Women's community activism can either change the traditional domestic division of labor or reinforce traditional gender expectations.

As individual cases, the women's stories convey a sense of movement from household to neighborhood institutions. In the movement from one set of social relations to another, women often bridge the social distance that separates residents. The following discussion begins by presenting the eastside Los Angeles community context, focusing on the cases of women's community work that bridge social distance between Latino immigrants and established residents.[4] The discussion then creates links between state resources and inadequate community infrastructure and, finally, considers the relationship between women's community work and household organization.

Continuity and Change: Latino Immigrants and the Native Born

Eastside Los Angeles residents share ethnic origins (94 percent Latino); however, generation in the United States, language, home ownership, and income stratify residents. This differentiation means that integration of new immigrants may occur with some difficulty. One of the few community studies of immigrant and native-born social interaction suggests that immigrants and native-born Mexican Americans hold critical perceptions of each other. The study found no automatic incorporation of new immigrants into the Chicano community; instead, it found the absence of regular interaction between the two groups. Chicanos saw undocumented Mexicans as "rural and backward, rate-busters afraid to stand up for their rights"; Mexicanos perceived Chicanos as "not being hard workers who despite citizenship were not doing well materially and did not control their children properly."[5]

In eastside Los Angeles, school settings provide an instance where immigrants and the native born may experience daily observation, if not direct interaction. At Roosevelt High School, cliques of students habitually congregate in particular sections of the campus. English-speaking and Spanish-speaking students gather at opposite ends of the school grounds. The new immigrant students complain that the Mexican Americans call them pejorative names such as "wetbacks, *mojados*, 'TJs,' and *ranchos*."[6]

The interaction between immigrant and native-born adults is also fraught with some of the tensions observed among adolescents, and attitudes toward immigrants bear on how women establish community networks. The period between 1965 and 1980 marked one of the largest influxes of Latino immigrants into Los Angeles County; almost half of the over 800,000 Latino residents in the City of Los Angeles are not citizens (U.S. Census 1980). Residential patterns indicate that new immigrants (post-1965) seem more likely to reside next to older immigrants (pre-1965) than native-born residents (García 1985, 73–100).

As new immigrants cope with the economic and social demands of life in eastside Los Angeles, they often violate what established residents see as the neighborhood norm. Women active in the neighborhood expressed differing perceptions, ranging from annoyance to tolerance, about the living patterns of immigrants. While the native-born Mexicans reflect the second generation's immigrant past, *pochos* may represent a glimpse of the future for the children of native-born Mexicans. Mexicans call the second generation pochos, which means "faded" and, used colloquially, refers to assimilated Mexican Americans or "faded Mexicans." The social distance and familiarity between Mexican Americans and Mexican immigrants creates problems and possibilities for establishing neighborhood cohesiveness.

Mexicans American women became acquainted with many new immigrants when they perceived the need to inform them about neighborhood norms. For the last twenty years, Rosa Villaseñor, a fifty-one-year-old woman of Cuban and Puerto Rican descent, has rented a spacious three-bedroom apartment in a densely populated, privately owned 1950s housing tract called Wyvernwood.[7] Since 1970, she has observed the departure of most of the Anglo renters and second-generation

Mexican Americans and the arrival of new immigrant Latinos. Her neighbors refer to her as "Doña Rosa," indicating respect for her as an influential person in the complex.[8]

Recognized by her neighbors as frank and outspoken, Rosa sternly scolds those who transgress neighborhood norms— adults littering, youth writing graffiti on the walls, and young men racing cars through the small winding streets. Not one to mince her words, she says she thinks the new arrivals must be from "ranches," and she admonishes them until they stop the disruptive behavior. She shares with me her usual lecture to the unruly neighbors:

> When they race through here I tell them, "a car is not a horse and it is not a mule. Someday you are going to kill somebody, so you better stop." They say "Ay, Doña, don't talk to us that way!" But, they stop. I also threatened to make a citizen's arrest if I saw them in the street littering or doing worse things. But you know, I would never really have the heart to call the cops on them. But I tell them "really mean," so they think I am serious!

The assertion that someone is from the *rancho* or a *ranchito* suggests that a person is from a poor rural area and not fully accustomed to sophisticated metropolitan lifestyles. For established Mexican Americans, this helps explain behavioral differences between new immigrants and longtime residents. Rather than a matter of being Latino or Central American, differences are often linked to rural origins. In an alternative way, this attribute may be used to chastise a Latino, regardless of birthplace, who breaches etiquette.

Rosa balances the harshness of her scolding by sharing information on health clinics and "help hotlines" that offer rape and drug information. When the neighbors need to know how to reach public agencies or services, they call her. Rosa rather philosophically reflects on the activity just outside her doorway:

> See, in this community, you go out the door and you see everybody. Even if they are no good, they are out there! [laughter] I think I would miss that. Here there is something happening all the time—it keeps me going!

Her husband, Frank, agrees about the problems of Wyvernwood and notes that Rosa's activism has helped to improve conditions. Then he explains that he had "not taken the opportunity to move in 1970 when he could afford it." Now in his mid-fifties, he carefully considers the burden of a mortgage. To compensate for the declining quality of life in the apartment complex, Rosa and an established immigrant woman from El Salvador formed an informal partnership. The Hollenbeck Police Station's Neighborhood Watch Liaison, Sgt. Frank Hurtado, calls them "his best activists."[9]

Increasingly overcrowded within the last decade, the Wyvernwood Apartments have lost their reputation for being relatively free of gang violence. Immediately after the murder of a young boy by rival gang members, Rosa circulated petitions asking for more police foot patrols (Stein 1989, 1). She explains how she responded to the shock of the boy's murder:

> I never felt the need to get involved in this neighborhood because it was so peaceful. But after the shooting, I said I have to do something. So every night at 6:00, after I made dinner, I would go from apartment to apartment to get people to sign the petitions.

As a result of her activity, Rosa knows all her immediate neighbors and many people throughout the hundreds of apartments. Rosa clearly set up her signature-gathering schedule after she prepared dinner for her husband. She also set up our interview appointment and other visits that I made to Wyvernwood, as she put it, "at about 7:00 P.M., after everybody is taken care of." As Susser notes, working-class women take on activism as an "extra job" (Susser 1988).

Rosa describes the strategies she used to convince the largely immigrant residents to sign a petition to bring in police foot patrols. Her bilingual fluency made possible her success in obtaining two hundred signatures. As she explained:

> It would take me about half an hour just to explain to the people! First, I would ask if they would want me to speak Spanish or English. They were scared of the gangs, of the police, or maybe, I thought, because they were doing something wrong. So a lot didn't want to sign. If they didn't sign I would go back the next day and tell them, "Si firma esta nota, no va a pasar nada." [Nothing will happen if you sign.] I would tell them, "La persona que no firma, es porque tiene miedo, como está haciendo algo

malo." [The person who does not sign must be
afraid because he is doing something wrong.] Pero
él que no está haciendo nada malo no tiene miedo!"
[Laughing at her high-pressure tactics] See?
[Confirming that I saw her strategy]. And, they
would sign!

Rosa obtained the signatures by combining arguments in
a sequence that illustrates her perceptions of material conditions and social relations in the housing complex. She understands that immigrants have many fears: fear of deportation,
fear of becoming crime victims, and fear of family members
committing crimes. She addresses those fears by arguing that
collective action will help.

She has observed and confronted the teenage sons of some
residents in the act of removing the parts from stolen cars and
selling them to other residents. Using this information, she
reasoned with residents whose sons may have engaged in the
activity that signing the petition would bring less "trouble" or
"implication of wrongdoing" than refusing to sign.

Rosa's method represents a variation of how residents "manage" acts of violence and crime in their immediate neighborhood. In a Mexican community in Chicago, Horowitz found that
nongang community residents coexisted with gang youth by
avoiding contact with them. In a study of eastside Los Angeles,
Moore noted that the United Neighborhood Organization refused
to work with gangs and asked for stepped-up police patrols.
However, she states that community members were not hostile to gangs. In light of cutbacks in all community agency funding and the promotion of "law-and-order" solutions, requests
for increased policing seem one of the few options offered to
community residents (Horowitz 1987; Moore 1985).

Rosa speaks of the density of the housing and acknowledges that given the cost of living, she understands why two
and three families share one apartment. In some units she
knows three Latino families share the $650 monthly rent for
a two-bedroom unit. While she speaks with empathy about
their plight, she sees it as no excuse to neglect the upkeep of
gardens and apartments. She notes that the adjacent two-
bedroom apartment houses six adults and five children. She
also remarked that the neighbors made frequent trips across
the border for weddings, baptisms, birthdays, and other fam-
ily-related events, and that frequent absences from the apartment lead to poor upkeep.

The neighborhood across Olympic Boulevard, one block north of the Wyvernwood Housing Complex, differs in dwelling styles, upkeep, and density. Typical of Boyle Heights, small, neat, wood-framed, single-family homes line the street. The newer immigrants and established residents live side-by-side but in lower density than at Wyvernwood Housing Complex. The practices of some of the new immigrants invoke various reactions among the women.

With some exasperation in her voice, one woman expressed slight annoyance at what she sees as a hallmark of some of the more recent Latino immigrant neighbors:

> Some of these [new immigrants] think they are living on a ranch over here. Sometimes all of a sudden in the morning when you are asleep, you hear roosters crowing and then the roosters are always walking around the street. . . .

However, not all women felt annoyed by the crowing roosters. I asked some of the other women how they felt about the roosters that typically walk casually down the middle of the asphalt street. Angie Flores answered in a way that drew on her memories of the Mexican American and African American neighborhood of her youth:

> Well, some people say [about the new immigrants], *"tantos perros, tantos gatos!"* [so many dogs, so many cats!] The roosters walk around here all the time. But I remember on 41st and Long Beach, "El Hoyo," where I lived in the '40s, they had roosters too. So, I am used to that. As for the dogs, I don't need to have one because I can hear the dogs barking as someone walks down the street.

Unlike some of her neighbors, she considered the barking dogs an advantage; they alerted her to the exact location of strangers walking down the block.

Angie emphasized that she had never seen "so much poverty." Moved by what she saw, for one full year she assisted her parish priest in his efforts to counsel undocumented workers regarding the Immigration Reform and Control Act of 1986 (IRCA).[10] Angie tells of her work with immigrants:

> We started helping the people fill out forms. First it was only on Wednesdays from 8:00 to 12:00, then it was two days a week for about four months be-

113

> cause people would keep coming and coming. We
> would take their names, addresses, whether they
> were married and how many children. My comadre
> [child's godmother] lives across the street from the
> church, so she would keep the files in her house. In
> case someone gets picked up [by Immigration and
> Naturalization Service], he [the priest] would call my
> comadre and she could look up the card and vouch
> for them. Her husband just passed away, so she
> wants to keep active. Some would have only a place
> to pick up mail, and I thought maybe they didn't
> have homes. They were so afraid their families would
> be separated because some children were born here
> and some born over there [Mexico]. I felt so sorry for
> them that I wanted to do what I could for the
> "illegals" and for the community.

Angie's account illustrates a view of recent immigrants as the *pobrecitos* [unfortunate ones] that Rodríguez and Nuñez refer to in their study of Chicano perceptions of the undocumented. Her immediate block is occupied by single-family, owner-occupied homes similar to the one-story home she owns. Instead of simply blaming immigrants for the decline of city-sponsored services, such as a local post office, she links it to the influx of new Mexican immigrants, the exit of Jewish residents, and the lower socioeconomic status of new residents.

In largely immigrant communities, successful grassroots mobilization must overcome obstacles to communication. In some instances, longtime eastside residents share practical information about community resources and impart to immigrants the standards of community life in the neighborhood. Mexican American women say they have enhanced their Spanish fluency by communicating with new immigrants. Thus, women's bilingual skills as well as their understanding and perceptions of the immigrants' circumstances can either generate or hinder mobilization efforts.

Linking Community Needs with Community Resources

In addition to overcoming communication obstacles between immigrants and established residents, the women also bridged the difference between what they perceived as community needs and existing resources. The remainder of the essay discusses three cases illustrative of how women's collective work created additional community resources.

In the first case, women worked to supplement the needs—books and equipment—of the parochial schools their children attended. In the second and third cases, women identified and communicated community needs to state and city representatives who allocate resources for recreation centers. One case required community mobilization; the others demanded persistent requests, communication, and some volunteer effort to garner city funds and control over a local recreation center. A holistic reading of all three cases offers a portrait of how women's community work connects the public and private spheres.

Creating Resources: "Pillars of the Church."

In eastside Los Angeles, the parish boundaries may provide one of the spaces where community identity develops and associations flourish. Two general observations about the relationship between the Catholic Church and the Mexican community are appropriate at this point. First, the local parish pastor determines the degree of his community involvement. At the parish level, as Moore notes, "the church is not a monolith" (Moore 1966). Second, a distinction exists between the Catholic Church as a formal institution and the parish as the neighborhood base for many families. The Church may be the site of schooling and family counseling and a link with other institutions. Most of the women volunteered many years for parish fundraising. Some volunteer work centered on fundraising that generally benefited the local parish; other volunteer work directly benefited the parochial school children. Angie Flores also speaks of her forty years of volunteer work for the church:

> We helped for forty years to get the funds to build the church. Jamaica after jamaica [charity bazaar] . . . not just one jamaica, not two jamaicas, it was about three or four per year.

Angie's husband, Robert, who worked in construction, also donated his weekends to help build a garage and driveway for the church:

> My husband has been opening the church for twenty years. He also made the garage for the

115

school and the driveway. He got all these construction guys to go work there. After it was done,
the father asked how much is it going to be. My
husband told him, you don't owe anything;
everybody donated their work.

She commented that the priest calls her and her husband
the "pillars of the church" because of all the work they have
done. However, she says now they need to have time out. Her
husband, who now walks with the aid of a cane, experiences
some debilitation from arthritis. Angie thinks the arthritis resulted from standing in wet cement during the thirty years
of his working days. Her son, who moved a few doors away
from her, now assumes some of their former responsibilities
at the church.

Children's educational needs led almost all the women into
volunteer community work. Part of a mother's "traditional"
responsibility includes overseeing her child's progress in
school, interacting with school staff, and supporting school
activities. Based on mutual concern for the welfare of their
children, women met other mothers and developed a network
of acquaintances and friendships. All the women interviewed
had sent their children to parochial school.[11] Thus, their community activism was closely linked to the parish and often
began with the entry of their children into school.

During the 1950s, the Catholic Church began building
parochial schools attached to the parishes in eastside Los
Angeles. Pastors established Mothers' Clubs and called them
a "drawing card," noting that first-generation parents appeared
more attracted to the parents' group as opposed to other parish committees (McNamara 1957). Erlinda Robles, a Mexican
American woman residing in a house on the street where she
was born and raised, participated in the Mothers' Club
throughout the 1960s. She describes her volunteer work and
the tensions that existed among parents, priests, and nuns:

> I wanted my kids to go to Catholic school, and from
> the time my oldest one went there, I was there every
> day. I used to take my two little ones with me and I
> helped one way or another. I used to question things
> they did. And the other mothers would just watch
> me. Later, they would ask me, "Why do you do that?
> They are going to take it out on your kids." I'd say,
> "They'd better not." And before you knew it, we had
> a big group of mothers that were very involved.

My husband used to call us the "Tamaleras de Talpa" and the women would laugh. He called us that because once a week we would have a sale. Every Sunday we used to have a breakfast fundraiser with eggs, burritos [meat, beans, and chile wrapped in a flour tortilla], and tamales. We used to start about Wednesday making tamales. Some would clean beans, others would clean the hojas [dried corn husks used to wrap masa—corn meal dough—for tamales]. We had enough women doing it so it worked out okay.

Tamaleras, literally translated, means "tamale makers." In Mexico, women who earn a living making tamales occupy low status in the national occupational hierarchy, and they eke out a subsistence wage. So, when Valentín Robles jokingly labeled the women's work group tamaleras, he reflected the irony of continuity and change as Mexican American women in the United States produce tamales in order to create community resources, not individual or family subsistence.[12] As Erlinda described the traditional Mexican food women chose to prepare for the fundraisers, I asked her how they arrived at the selection of items. She said ethnic food sold the best. After mass in the morning, people who attended the church wanted "their Mexican food." When women tried selling "Anglo food," such as hot dogs or ham and eggs, sales decreased, and people complained. Breakfast in the parish hall after mass continues into the 1990s. Another woman confirmed that parishioners say they can easily make ham and eggs at home and prefer to purchase Mexican food.

Brown and Mussell argue that food choices express more than group preference; they also provide a way to "bind an individual to a group." As in other cities and other ethnic communities, second-generation ethnics may purchase ethnic food and avoid time-consuming preparation.[13] The preference for and preparation of Mexican food makes an identity statement about the common origins of immigrants and native-born Mexican Americans.

I commented that the preparation of food meant a lot of work and a very long work day. As Erlinda told the story, she had not stressed the labor that went into preparing the food for fundraisers. The implication of my question, from the perspective of a woman who has reluctantly prepared tamales on three occasions, contrasted with her reply. She reflected on the meaning of the collective activity beyond material benefit for the school:

> It was a lot of fun now that I think about it. I made good friends—some of us are still friends to this day. The priest would give us the money to get the ingredients. We would prepare some of it on Saturday. On Sunday morning, someone would go at 5:00 and start heating the tamales, so by the end of the 7:00 mass, the food would be warm. We would stay there until after 12:00 mass. Then we would stay until 2:30 and clean the kitchen.

The church kitchen became a place where Erlinda's husband, Valentín, then enlisted in the Navy and often stationed away from home, could be sure to find her. Thirty years later, Erlinda still meets with some of the other mothers from the Mothers' Club. The lasting friendships that she established through her participation in the collective work to create resources formed the "glue" that created a sense of community. So, women's unpaid work originated in their obligations as mothers and as members of a working-class, ethnic community.

Erlinda Robles volunteered for the Mothers' Club in the 1960s when the parish did not mandate women's participation. Erlinda reflects that a small group of women usually carried out the work that benefited many. By the late 1970s, the financial need of the parochial school increased, and the church mandated parent participation in fundraisers. The decreased participation of women may indicate the tensions between unpaid communitarian work and paid work as an increasing number of Mexican American women sought paid employment after 1970.

Although friendships continued to be established, the president of the now renamed Parents' Guild confronted increased difficulty in recruiting the volunteer labor needed to carry out weekly breakfasts. As president of the Parents' Guild, Rosa Villaseñor spoke of how she had to demand participation of a single mother at one of the meetings:

> She said she could not afford to pay or participate because she was a single parent going to night school and working. I told her that it was not fair for her to get away with having all the other mothers doing her work. She was doing things to better

herself, and that was fine for her. I told her either she paid or she should come on Sunday mornings at least for the *desayunos* [breakfasts]. I couldn't let her get away with it because then the other women would say, "Well, why should I do it?" She wasn't too happy about it, but she started helping on Sunday mornings.

I reacted with sympathy to the story of a single working mother seeking higher education. From an individualistic point of view, the single mother could have used the free time to study. But, from Rosa's position of responsibility for the collective, the woman's release from collective efforts would work to the detriment of a system of volunteer labor. It would sabotage group cohesiveness and commitment; quite literally, Rosa could not "let her get away with it."

"We Did All the Work and We Had a 'Say-so'!"

In the 1960s, parochial schools distinguished the positions to be held by priests and nuns. Nuns assumed the role of teachers and counselors, and the priests assumed the administrative positions.[14] The gendered division of labor among community women, priests, and nuns led women to perceptions of what was just and then to press for a right to decide on the distribution of the fruits of their fundraising efforts.

In one case, given the division of labor, some women thought nuns should be entitled to more authority in the parents' group. In another case, the women perceived that their volunteer work, which supplemented the costs of parochial schooling, justified their right to have a say-so about the use of funds. This meant they directly negotiated with the priest in charge of the school. Erlinda Robles speaks of her experiences working closely with a parochial school during the early 1960s:

> They [the priests] would invite the nuns who were the teachers only to the first meetings. So, the nuns didn't know anything about the mothers. They were left in the dark. Then we started insisting that the nuns start attending the meetings. They [the nuns] were so happy, you should have seen their faces. Then we wanted the fathers to attend too. That way they could feel they were part of it. So then they changed the name to the Parents' Club. After the nuns started attending, the priests knew when they

> were outnumbered. We had nuns who were ahead
> of their time. The nuns lived in the convent next to
> the school, and a lot of mothers would go to them
> for counseling. There were always kids and mothers
> going to the place they lived. The priests didn't like
> everyone going to see the nuns. But I told him, they
> are always available to the people; you are not. From
> 12:00 to 2:00 you take a nap and are not be
> disturbed! The nuns don't do that.

In many working-class communities, the church may be one of the few places immediately accessible and trusted for the everyday problems of the community.[15] It may also serve as a bridge to local secular institutions. Erlinda continued to differentiate the services provided by priests versus those provided by the nuns:

> They [the nuns] used to drive a lot of mothers and
> kids around, and they had an old station wagon. So
> we told the priests, we think the nuns deserve to get
> a new station wagon, and we will do the food sales
> to earn the money. The nuns didn't want the priest
> to think they put us up to the idea, so they tried to
> say no, they didn't need a new station wagon. But
> we insisted. And they got it after all.

Erlinda's description captures a complex set of social relations in the parish. The "patriarchal" character of the Catholic Church, reflected in the division of labor among priests and nuns, created a situation women questioned. Guided by their own observations and perceptions of equity and their practical concerns, the women carefully challenged existing decision-making practices, which excluded nuns. Similarly, the women used their volunteer work to enhance the effectiveness of the nun's activities by suggesting the purchase of a new station wagon.

Erlinda Robles also spoke of strategies they used to draw men as fathers and husbands into the enterprise:

> At the beginning, the priests used to say who the
> president of the Mothers' Club would be; they used
> to pick 'em. But, we wanted elections, so we got
> elections. Then we wanted the fathers to be involved,
> and the nuns suggested that a father should be
> president and a mother would be secretary or be
> involved there [at the school site].

Of course, this comment piqued my curiosity, because it seemed contradictory that women should want a man for president when women ran the guild. So, I asked if the mothers agreed with the nuns' suggestion. The answer was simple and instructive:

> At the time we thought it was a "natural" way to get the fathers involved because they weren't involved; it was just the mothers. Everybody [the women] agreed on them [the fathers] being president of the Parents' Guild because they worked all day and they couldn't be involved in a lot of daily activities like food sales and whatever. A mother was vice-president and took care of all the food sales. The president presided over all the meetings. During the week a steering committee of work used to make all the plans for the group and then meet with the president and let him know. One time the president did make a decision on his own to have a fundraiser that required the group to cook on Mother's Day. At the general meeting the group opposed him . . . because he didn't have the right to decide that. Nobody showed up that day to cook except him, his kids, and his wife. So he learned he wasn't going to get away with that. But now that I think about it, a woman could have been president and done the job just as well!

The group demonstrated dissatisfaction by boycotting the event and effectively conveyed the message that decisions needed collective approval. So, the 1990s gave Erlinda a new perspective on her 1960s perception of what was a "natural" order for men and women.

Women also got men into the group by giving them a position they could manage. The men may have held the title of "president," but they were not making day-to-day decisions about the work nor were they dictating the direction of the group. This should alert researchers against measuring power and influence by looking solely at those who hold titles.

Juana Gutiérrez, another community activist who worked with an adjacent parish school, complements Erlinda's accounts of the mothers' work to supplement the quality of education received by their children:

> I worked at Santa Isabelle. The first year when I was the vice-president, I did all the work for the president

too because he was a man and he worked [for wages]. I moved the people to make breakfasts every Sunday. At the end of the year, I gave the father [priest] $7,000. He was very happy. The school needed a new refrigerator and air conditioning, so they were able to get them.

Every weekend I got three or four different mothers from the school. I was there every weekend. I would go buy everything—the sisters would give me a blank check, and my husband would help a lot. After I bought the food, I gave the sister the receipts, and after the sale, we would figure the profits. We would make about $400 to $500 profit!

Parish and parochial school activities occupied a significant portion, but not all, of the women's community activities. Outside of the church arena, the core activists also shaped conditions in their communities by making use of state resources. In each case, the women stated that the work they did bettered the community in general.

Gaining State Resources through Collective Action

The work of bridging the gaps between the community's needs and the community's resources may require different actions. In order to bring needed resources into the community, eastside women have used several strategies. In the first case discussed, community mobilization was necessary. In the second case, a small group of neighbors persistently communicated needs to a city commission, and, after volunteering time to keep a recreational area open, successfully gained city resources to develop recreational services.

The Case of Driver's Training Instruction

In 1966, Erlinda Robles chaired the Evergreen Parents Steering Committee and worked to obtain an adult driver's training program through the recreation center (*Eastside Journal* 1964). Erlinda described the situation:

I would take my kids to the Evergreen Recreation Center, and a temporary director, a Russian man who had grown up in this neighborhood, asked the ladies who went there what kind of programs they would like. One lady from Talpa [church] said,

"Driving, I want to learn how to drive." But as hard as he tried, he couldn't get the classes for us. Then one day there was a representative from the Urban Affairs office and he told me, "Don't start at the bottom; start at the top." So we got about 150 women together and went to the Board of Education and made our request for a driver's training class.

The strategy of using mass numbers—150 people taking buses to the Board of Education—to stress a "request" speaks to the context of 1960s protest tactics. For most of the women in the group, this was a novel experience. The presentations to the board, letter writing, and phone calls finally led to success. She continued:

They finally said we could have a pilot program for driver's training. We got about 150 women and two men to sign up for the course, but they wouldn't give us behind-the-wheel training. We never had a formal group. We just went and met with a few other women and Henry Ronquillo. I remember my phone would be ringing constantly. Sometimes, I would just start crying. . . . Especially when the California Driving School started attacking us on the news and saying bad things against the program, like "a little knowledge is dangerous." If kids could get behind the wheel, why couldn't we? The California Driving School said they were going to put a bunch of women behind the wheel and let them free. We chartered two buses two times and got the women enrolled in the course to go before the Board of Education and ask for the program.

The women opposed the driving school's degrading portrayal of women as incompetent, dangerous, and less responsible than teens, and argued that their access to driver's training, at minimum, should be commensurate with that offered to youth.

Erlinda, who never liked speaking in front of large groups, always enjoyed being involved in community issues. But, as one of the key organizers, a community liaison with the Office of Urban Affairs pushed her to make a presentation before the Board of Education:

Henry Ronquillo would make me speak. I think when I get mad things come out of me. I spoke in front of the Board of Education and told them we wanted

this program for the last ten years and that we were
limited in our school and community volunteer
activities because we didn't know how to drive. We
could not afford to enroll in a private driving school;
at that time they charged between nine and twelve
dollars per hour.

Erlinda argued that the ability to drive would contribute
to the women's effectiveness as volunteers and also allow some
to seek work outside the home:

A lot of those ladies wanted to work, but the work
was too far by a bus. A lot of ladies got jobs after
they got their licenses. The women really needed to
drive, and the recreation director backed us up
because they needed more people to be able to drive
the kids to field trips. The mothers wanted to learn
for the kids, for jobs, and to help around the
community. Everything we said was true—a lot of
those women began driving other kids around too.
It was not a luxury; it was a necessity.

Here, the women who participated as mothers and unwaged
community workers gained community resources that would
give them options to enter the labor force. They argued from
the standpoint of women who were fulfilling the needs of their
children and of their community.

After an eleven-week battle, the parents' group composed
of women won a victory over a group of determined private
driving school owners. The driving schools blasted the program, "as big government again throttling private enterprise"
(Kaywood 1967, 4). In a unanimous decision, the Los Angeles
Board of Education authorized pilot programs at two adult
schools and added driver's training programs to the regular
adult classroom instruction. Later, Erlinda found out that
social services incorporated driver's training into a work incentive and training program for women on welfare. They actually brought the driver's education instructor who taught
the Evergreen pilot program out of retirement so he could develop the program.

The issue of driver's training may sound insignificant in
the context of 1990. But in 1970, the community's population was described as highly transit-dependent because of a
high percentage of young people (40 percent of the population were under twenty years of age), a significant percentage
of elderly (12 percent over sixty years of age), and low income

(median family income 40 percent below the citywide average). More than one-third of the families did not own autos, and 42 percent owned only one auto (Escobedo 1979).

Erlinda Robles and several other women completed the driver's training course and decided to celebrate their success by having a potluck and inviting the instructors and other community members. As a main course, they planned to make tamales for everyone. The priest hesitated upon the first request to use the church facilities. There were similarities to the way the women promoted the purchase of the station wagon for the nuns and the way they obtained access to church facilities for a non–church-related event. Erlinda explains how they used their extensive volunteer work for the church as leverage to use the church hall to celebrate their victory:

> The majority of the ladies who worked on getting driver's training classes were the ones who always did all the cooking for the church fundraisers at Talpa Church. Since the church had a large kitchen available, we asked the priest for permission to use it, but he said no at first. But we reminded him that we used to cook in the church about once a month, and if he didn't let us he wouldn't see us around anymore. So he changed his mind.

The collective work of women in the parish and their efforts in local political arenas merged. They combined the two spheres of activity when they demanded the use of the church to celebrate a success not directly church-based.

The Case of the Boyle Heights Recreation Center

Juana Gutiérrez lives across the street from a recreation center exactly one block square. The conditions of her immediate living space stand in direct contrast to the small neglected park across a narrow street from her home. She expressed her concern for the safety of her children and illustrated another way women mobilize to gain state resources. Juana describes the problem as it existed in the mid-1980s:

> We had a lot of problems with drug dealers in the park across the street. I didn't want my kids or my neighbors' kids involved in drugs. I made Neighborhood Watch meetings with the police and city commissioners. At the time Councilman Snyder was in office. He answered when we called—not like the

one we have now. We told him about the problems in the park. He could not *believe* [stressing his disbelief] it because he had never been to the park. I told him to go right down there and see the burned car that is parked in the middle of the park. When it happened, we called the police, and nothing happened.

Juana's efforts gained small concessions from the Parks and Recreation Department. Juana continued:

So, the park commissioner finally ordered lights for the park. Then, he came and talked to me. He said, "Mrs. Gutiérrez, I know because of the budget, we don't have anyone to turn on the lights at night or open the restrooms. Would you like to have the keys and do it?" I said, I will do it, not for pay, but as a volunteer. I will open the restrooms every morning and close them at night. Someone else would come and clean them. Sometimes my husband or my kids would turn on the lights at night.

When I mentioned that this must have been a tiresome job for her, she answered:

Yes, but for my community and my kids, I did it. You know some nights, I would say, I am not going to turn on the lights; I am tired. Then the phone would ring, and the neighbors would tell me, "Mrs. Gutiérrez, no va a poner las luces?" [Aren't you going to turn on the lights?] For five years I did it.

Instead of stressing the sacrifice, Juana's account stressed the necessity of her work, much as did Erlinda's story about the "Tamaleras de Talpa." Juana further explained how her diligence won stable staffing for the park.

When Assemblywoman Lucille Roybal-Allard informed Juana about some moneys available for hiring recreation directors in the local parks, she mobilized her neighbors:

When I heard the city had the money for other parks, I called to see if we could get some for our park. They told me they didn't have the money for Boyle Heights [a neighborhood in eastside Los Angeles]. I got the people together and went to talk to the Parks and Recreation Commissioners. For two years, about eight neighbors and I tried to get the position for a recreation director for the park. We called the office,

we sent letters, and we went to the office of parks
and recreation. Finally we got a position. Now the
kids get trips to the beach and other places.

Juana Gutiérrez took me on a walking tour of the park where
about sixty children and some adults played and relaxed well
before four o'clock in the afternoon. As we walked through the
park, I took for granted the green grass and newly planted
shrubs. Juana recalled the brown and barren untended hill-
sides of the previous years. Quite fittingly, the newly hired
young Latina gardener planted cuttings from Juana's rose-
bushes, and they now grow in the park. Juana commented
on how well the park is doing and saw her job as complete,
"Now we have a director and four or five helpers, and thank
goodness I don't have to do anything over there."

These two examples—the acquisition of driver's training
for community members and the staffing of the park—illustrate how the community activism of the women extended
beyond the simply defensive or reactive. The accounts illustrate the women's conscious proactive use of power in gar-
nering additional resources and services sorely needed in their
immediate neighborhoods. In the case of the driver's training
classes and the subsequent celebration at the church, the
women combined access to resources from secular and sacred
volunteer activities. Furthermore, they clarify how family units
may often form a network in blue-collar neighborhoods and
reach out for state resources.

Household Organization: "As Long As His Meals Are Ready. . . ."

Approximately half of the women interviewed worked for wages
only during brief periods of time. Among the married women
I interviewed who were over fifty years old, none currently
worked for wages. A few had worked intermittently when
school tuition increased beyond the capacity of their husbands'
earnings. Most women stated they preferred to care for their
children rather than work and have to send them to day care.
Because their husbands had stable employment and a salary
sufficient to support the family, they chose to stay home after
they married.

The women's husbands worked in a variety of predominantly unionized blue-collar jobs—baker, construction worker,
machinist, armed service, and plant maintenance. None of the
women stated that their husbands did not allow them to work.

Sociological studies often attribute the lower labor-force participation rates of Mexican American women to the cultural inclinations of jealous husbands (Sowell 1981; Briggs, Fogel and Schmidt 1977). The freedom of movement in the wider community of nonemployed Mexican American women certainly contradicts the notion that their husbands controlled them. The women, several of retirement age now, often referred to the decision not to work in relation to the types of jobs for which their education prepared them.

Angie Flores, a sixty-five-year-old mother of three sons, speaks of her experiences at Roosevelt High School in 1941:

> In my senior year [of high school], I had to go to Roosevelt, but they didn't have room in "Commercial" [clerical track]. They wanted me to take "Home Economics." I said, "Well, in that case, I wanted to quit school because I already know how to cook and sew!" Then, the war [World War II] broke out and we moved, and later in my senior year I lacked the money for graduation clothes and I quit high school.

> She worked for a short time in a spinach-packing house next door to her home, then quit work when she married. When I asked if her husband preferred she not work, she recalled his words, "Well, Angie, if you want to go on working, go ahead; but, I married you so I could support you. . . ." According to Angie, she quit work because her husband earned good wages as a construction worker.

The married women who did work for wages were a bit younger than the other women—just turning forty. For the younger women in the group, increasing inflation eliminated the option to remain home and raise children. According to these women, the current cost of living required two salaries. Other married women entered the labor force only at particular points in family life when the need was great—particularly when their children entered high school and tuition escalated beyond what one wage could cover. As soon as the child graduated, the women left work. One woman worked so that her son, attending college out of state, could afford the trips back home.

Women who took an active part in their communities accepted the management of the household as first priority. Once they completed household work, they attended to community work outside of the home. The husbands of the majority of active women worked at blue-collar jobs that often demanded rising before dawn. For example, Angie Flores's husband, Robert, worked laying cement. I asked Angie how he felt about her extensive volunteer work and how she balanced out her household responsibilities. She recalled that her mother, who lived with her at the time, shared her wisdom regarding the proper way to treat a husband:

> My mother used to live here with me, and she used to help take care of the kids. She would say, "Just have his [Angie's husband] food already set up so he can serve himself when he comes home at night." And, he wouldn't say anything as long as he didn't have to change diapers. . . . We [Angie and her mother] used to take the kids with us when we went shopping or to the movies in the evening.

Angie's husband did not dictate the conditions under which she could go out on evening entertainment excursions, and she felt they had worked out a mutual agreement about responsibilities. The agreement allowed her flexibility. She recognized and respected "changing diapers" as his absolute outer limit. He accepted a self-serve dinner waiting for him on top of the stove, rather than demanding she be home to serve him.

Rosa Villaseñor, now fifty-one years old, described similar household arrangements. She has two daughters in their early twenties who are attending college and living at home. She described her husband as very dedicated to their daughters; so, just in case something happened, he stayed home when she went to meetings:

> Like I said, my husband used to work two jobs—sixteen hours a day for about five years. Poor thing. Now he gets up at 4:00 A.M., and like most of these guys [in eastside Los Angeles] he doesn't have an easy job. When they come home, they take a shower and want to relax. The men you find at meetings are retired or they don't even work. He never objected to me doing anything. As long as I feed him and do his clothes. I had to take care of that if I wanted to do what I wanted to do!

Clearly, the dominant theme throughout the passages above illustrates how the women did community work while continuing to do the private household work of mothers and wives. The women recognized that maintaining household stability allowed them to do the work in the community. So, the exchange may be understood not simply as women's compliance but rather as a way to assert independent activity in the public sphere.

The organization of households tells much about the flexibility of women's time and their assertiveness in defining the boundaries of their work. The intensity of volunteer community work and activism ebbed and flowed in relation to the time they spent working for wages. Some community members explain, and in essence make trivial, women's volunteer work, by saying, "They do it because they have the time."[16] Having the time may be a necessary condition for doing volunteer work, but not all women and men who are not employed engage in unpaid work for community betterment.

Conclusion

When feminists coined the slogan "the personal is political," they expressed the relation between the private sphere of family and the public sphere of community. Conceptualized as separate spheres by some social scientists, the work women do to mediate between family and community institutions clearly reveals how the two are interconnected (Ackelsberg 1988; Thiele 1986). Although the women explain their community work in relation to family responsibilities, class and ethnicity further specify the work they do to create kinship networks (di Leonardo 1987; Harley 1990). If we ignore class, we miss the complexity and meaning of women's work under particular economic circumstances and in particular community contexts.

Similar to situations involving other women of color, the examples above suggest that everyday life and organized politics overlap in eastside Los Angeles. The women expressed a sense of belonging to the community and to their families; conversely, they perceive their families and their communities as belonging to them. Their activities and their life stories support a strong notion of integration and membership in the larger community. The neighborhood comprised the immediate physical and social space for the family and, as such, the women devised ways to influence its formation with limited resources.

In some instances, the women do not identify their community work as "political"; for them, the work holds a kind of middle ground and reveals the integrated character of the "social" and "political" spheres. The women's volunteer work in local parishes, on blocks, and in neighborhoods demonstrated a civic consciousness intertwined with, not solely defined by, family responsibilities. In practical everyday life, women who are mothers do carry out gender-specific responsibilities. But this is only part of the story, not the entire story.

The church, priests, and nuns were all significant resources in the community. The women negotiated with priests to have input into the expenditure of resources, the use of space, and the administrative procedures that affected their children's education. The women worked to include the participation of nuns and get them the resources to purchase what they needed, e.g., the station wagon. Women expressed a consciousness rooted in collective goals and work. Instead of individual advancement, they pressured to maintain the system of volunteer labor necessary to create collective resources.

Gender identity, ethnic identity, and class/community identity gave meaning to their community work. When they spent endless hours preparing the Mexican food preferred for parish fundraisers, they did so as women who were members of a Mexican community. Symbols of Mexican culture and origin color the community and social relations. Food and bilingual communication stand as obvious expressions of Mexican American culture; volunteer work for immigrant rights signifies an empathy for new Latino immigrants derived from a common cultural past. Although these relations were sometimes characterized by tension, women used language and social skills to establish communication between immigrants and long-established residents.

Through unpaid community work, women gained skills and experience fundraising, organizing neighborhood groups; negotiating with authority figures such as priests, husbands, and city officials; and managing households and family. The gendered nature of women's community work informed the strategies they used to create neighborhood networks that have significantly improved the quality of life in their communities. The women implicitly expressed their conception of civic membership as they bridged the spaces between their homes and the community.

Notes

1. Sacks 1989 argues for an understanding of "working class" that recognizes " . . . [membership] rooted in the relations to the means of production that are collective and grounded in community rather than individual and restricted to the workplace."

2. Also, see Evans 1989 for a historical account of how women in the United States redefined the boundaries between the private sphere of home and the public sphere of the larger community.

3. The data are drawn from a larger study of Mexican American women community activists (Pardo 1990). For a discussion of life history methods, see Bertaux and Kohli 1984.

4. The designations "eastside" Los Angeles and East Los Angeles are used to refer to the area east of the downtown Civic Center. Often used interchangeably and similarly in demographic profiles, eastside Los Angeles, immediately east of the Los Angeles river, is part of the City of Los Angeles and represented by the same political structure; the geographical area East Los Angeles proper is unincorporated. The neighborhoods immediately east of the river include Boyle Heights, Lincoln Heights, and El Sereno. The statistics used in this section are for Boyle Heights, Lincoln Heights, and El Sereno. All have historically shared public services and territory.

5. All quotations without sources are from interviews conducted in our study. See Rodríguez and Nuñez 1986, 138–56, for a study focused on a community in Houston, Texas.

6. The Spanish word for "wetbacks" is *mojados*; "TJ" refers to Tijuana, a city that borders California. *Ranchos* suggests the new immigrants' rural origins and connotes that they are country bumpkins. See Sahagun 1983, 1.

7. The Wyvernwood complex includes 130 two-story buildings housing 1,100 units with spacious rooms. The management discriminated against Latinos until the mid-1960s. See Acuña 1984.

8. Of the possible alternatives in Spanish for prefacing a woman's name, "Doña" denotes respect, often indicating moral authority and sometimes affection.

9. Sgt. Hurtado of Hollenbeck Police Station, L.A.P.D., stated that women outnumbered men in Neighborhood Watch groups about five to one. Along with three men and fifteen women who belong to Neighborhood Watch, I visited the L.A.P.D. Dispatch Center.

10. Termed an "amnesty law," the sponsors of IRCA designed it to "regain control of our borders," legalize perhaps millions of undocumented workers who came to the United States before the cut-off date of January 1, 1982, and impose harsh sanctions on employers who knowingly hire undocumented immigrants. The cut-off date is particularly punitive for the bulk of Central American refugees whose numbers began increasing in 1982. See Fuentes 1990.

11. The older women observed that increasing tuition fees result in fewer families being able to afford to send their children to parochial school. This has implications for community cohesiveness. The Los Angeles Archdiocese acknowledged that school tuition is beyond the reach of most Latino families and established a new education tuition fund for the 1990–1991 school year. See Dart 1990.

12. See Williams 1984, 113–26. Williams describes the labor-intensive work of making tamales—buying, cleaning, cooking, stuffing, wrapping, and steaming. She discusses how Mexican American migrant women workers in Texas and Illinois blur the boundaries between family and public affairs by preparing and distributing tamales in the interest of promoting kinship, cohesiveness, and channels of reciprocity among nonfamily members.

13. Drawing together secondary sources, Kalcik 1984 suggests that foodways operate as symbols in the performance of ethnic identity. She cites a scene in front of a church in Youngstown, Ohio, where a sign announces "*Pierogi*, This Friday"; Slovak women gather early Friday mornings to begin preparation.

14. Until the 1970s, nuns formed the teaching force for parochial schools. Because the nuns were paid literally room and board, the cost of parochial schooling was accessible to the poor. As fewer women became nuns, the teaching force changed over to predominantly lay persons, increasing the costs and the tuition.

15. See Grebler, Moore, and Guzman 1979, 451. Religious order priests, Claretian Fathers from Spain, have come to Los Angeles since the early 1900s. Many of the Spanish priests served at several East L.A. churches, including the one above. According to one interviewee, they were accustomed to a mid-day siesta and did not want to be disturbed by parishioners from 12:00 to 2:00 P.M.

16. See Dabrowski 1983 for a study of working-class white women and civic action that documents the contribution of the "civic activities and presence" of women and then attributes it to the "personal lifestyles of women which are conducive to community work."

Bibliography

Ackelsberg, Martha A. 1988. "Communities, Resistance, and Women's Activism: Some Implications for a Democratic Polity." In *Women and the Politics of Empowerment*, ed. Ann Bookman and Sandra Morgen. Philadelphia: Temple University Press.

Acuña, Rodolfo F. 1984. *A Community Under Siege: A Chronicle of Chicanos East of the Los Angeles River: 1945–1975*. Los Angeles: Chicano Studies Research Center Publications.

Aptheker, Bettina. 1989. *Tapestries of Life: Women's Work, Women's Consciousness, and the Meaning of Daily Experience.* Amherst: University of Massachusetts Press.

Bertaux, Daniel and Martin Kohli. 1984. "The Life Story Approach: A Continental View." *Annual Review of Sociology* 10: 215–37.

Briggs, Vernon, Walter Fogel, and Fred Schmidt. 1977. *The Chicano Worker.* Austin: University of Texas Press.

Dabrowski, Irene. 1983. "Working Class Women and Civic Action: A Case Study of an Innovative Community Role." *Policy Studies Journal* 11, no. 3 (March): 427–35.

Dart, John. 1990. "Outreach Plan for Catholic Latinos Has Mixed Success." *Los Angeles Times* (5 June): sec. A, p. 3.

di Leonardo, Micaela. 1987. "Female World of Cards and Holidays: Women, Families and the Work of Kinship." *Signs* 12, no. 3 (Spring): 440–53.

Eastside Journal. 1964. "Congressman Lauds CSO Service." 28 May.

Escobedo, Raúl. 1979. *Boyle Heights Community Plan.* Los Angeles: Department of City Planning.

Evans, Sara. 1989. *Born for Liberty.* New York: The Free Press.

Fuentes, Annette. 1990. "Immigration 'Reform': Heaviest Burden on Women." *Listen Real Loud.* Philadelphia: American Friends Service Committee.

García, Philip. 1985. "Immigration Issues in Urban Ecology: The Case of Los Angeles." In *Urban Ethnicity in the United States,* ed. Lionel Maldonado and Joan Moore. Beverly Hills, Calif.: Sage Publications.

Geiger, Susan. 1982. "Women's Life Histories: Method and Content." *Signs* 11, no. 2 (Winter): 334–51.

Grebler, Leo, Joan W. Moore, and Ralph C. Guzman. 1979. *The Mexican American People.* New York: The Free Press.

Harley, Sharon. 1990. "For the Good of Family and Race: Gender, Work and Domestic Roles in the Black Community, 1880–1930." *Signs* 15, no. 2 (1990): 336–49.

Horowitz, Ruth. 1987. "Community Tolerance of Gang Violence." *Social Problems* 34, no. 5 (December): 437–50.

Kalcik, Susan. 1984. "Ethnic Foodways in America: Symbol and the Performance of Identity." In *Ethnic and Regional Foodways in the United States,* ed. Linda Keller Brown and Kay Mussell. Knoxville: University of Tennessee Press.

Kaywood, Richard. 1967. "The Los Angeles Board Authorized Driver Training." *CALDEA Calendar* (January): 4.

McNamara, Patrick Hayes. 1957. "Mexican Americans in Los Angeles County: A Study in Acculturation." Master's Thesis, St. Louis University.

Moore, Joan. 1966. *Mexican Americans: Problems and Prospects.* Madison: Institute for Research on Poverty, University of Wisconsin.

———. 1985. "Isolation, Stigmatization in the Development of an Underclass: The Case of Chicano Gangs in East L.A." *Social Problems* 33, no. 1: 1–12.

Pardo, Mary. 1990. "Identity and Resistance: Mexican American Women and Grassroots Activism in Two Los Angeles Communities." Ph.D. dissertation, University of California, Los Angeles.

Rodríguez, Nestor, and Rogelio T. Nuñez. 1986. "An Exploration of Factors That Contribute to Differentiation between Chicanos and Indocumentados." In *Mexican Immigrants and Mexican Americans: An Evolving Relation,* ed. Harley L. Browning and R. O. de la Garza. Austin: Center for Mexican American Studies, University of Texas, Austin.

Sacks, Karen Brodkin. 1989. "Toward a Unified Theory of Class, Race, and Gender." *American Ethnologist* 16, no. 3 (August): 534–50.

Sahagun, Louis. 1983. "Boyle Heights: Problems, Pride and Promise." *Los Angeles Times* (31 July): sec. I, p. 1.

Sowell, Thomas. 1981. *Ethnic America: A History.* New York: Basic Books.

Stansell, Christine. 1990. "Women, Children and the Uses of the Streets: Class and Gender Conflict in New York City, 1850–1860." In *Unequal Sisters,* ed. Vicki L. Ruiz and Ellen DuBois. New York: Routledge.

Stein, George. 1989. "Surge of Violence Breaks Calm at Housing Project." *Los Angeles Times* (24 May): sec. B, p. 1.

Susser, Ida. 1988. "Working-Class Women, Social Protest, and Changing Ideologies." In *Women and the Politics of Empowerment,* ed. Ann Bookman and Sandra Morgen. Philadelphia: Temple University Press.

Thiele, Beverly. 1986. "Vanishing Acts in Social and Political Thought: Tricks of the Trade." In *Feminist Challenges, Social and Political Theory,* ed. Carole Pateman and Elizabeth Gross. Boston: Allen & Unwin.

Williams, Brett. 1984. "Why Migrant Women Feed Their Husbands Tamales." In *Ethnic and Regional Foodways in the United States,* ed. Linda Keller Brown and Kay Mussell. Knoxville: University of Tennessee Press.

Organizing Latina Garment Workers in Los Angeles

Maria Angelina Soldatenko

Recent literature on Chicanas and organized labor celebrates Chicanas' participation in unions and its links to family, community, and ethnicity. Ruiz's and Zavella's work demonstrates the creation of a work culture and system of networks among Mexicana and Chicana cannery workers. Both trace the participation and leadership roles of Mexicanas and Chicanas in United Cannery, Agricultural, Packing and Allied Workers of America and the way in which active participation in organized labor had an impact on the lives of these women (Ruiz 1987; Zavella 1987; Ruiz 1990). The picture I will paint of Latinas[1] in the Los Angeles garment industry is very different. Workers are still not formally organized, and women are excluded from leadership positions in the union.[2] In fact, the long- and short-term strategies of the International Lady's Garment Workers Union, in conjunction with the nature of the industry, have effectively disenfranchised Latinas from their right to organize.[3] This situation rests on the racist and sexist nature of organized labor in the Los Angeles garment industry. My aim in this essay is to demonstrate how race and gender have been used to keep Latinas from organizing.

Before describing any research on Latinas, I would like to posit a theoretical and political position. In the particular case of garment workers, Latina *costureras* must be placed at the center of our analysis. This means two things: First, we must consider their lived experiences and their conditions of work; and second, we must examine these within the construct of standpoint methodology.

Latina costureras do not exist in a vacuum. Political and social structural factors have an impact on the conditions of Latinas' working lives. In the particular case of the Los Angeles garment industry, a mutual relationship exists between the existence and development of sweatshops and the availability of undocumented Latina workers in Los Angeles (Soldatenko 1990). The garment industry in Los Angeles did not arise by chance. The historical move from the Northeast was triggered by a desire for cheaper nonunionized labor (Lamphere 1987; NACLA 1980). Latinas are locked into an industry that offers little possibility for advancement yet represents one of the few options in a gender/ethnic stratified labor market. We therefore need to understand the position of Latinas in the structure of the industry and their immigrant status if we are to understand why Latinas remain without union representation. This does not mean that our understanding of the costureras is subsumed by a purely economic study. Gender, race/ethnicity, class, and immigrant status are essential in any study of Los Angeles costureras.

Second, if we place women at the center of the analysis, we need to step away from traditional academic approaches. The work of Dorothy Smith provides an excellent point of departure. She vigorously argues that women must stand at the center of any analysis intended to understand them:

> We have not known, as poets, painters, and sculptors have known, how to begin from our own experience, how to make ourselves as women the subject of the sociological act of knowing. (Smith 1987, 69)

In the process of placing women at the center, we necessarily open to question epistemological issues in the social sciences. Women of color are excluded, not only from the social sciences, but from the conceptualizations of Euro-American feminists as well.[4] Traditional approaches must be reformulated in order to account for women who have been either excluded or reduced to stereotypical accounts. It is simply not good enough to use existing mainstream methodologies uncritically. When interpreting Latinas' lived experience, pertinent cultural knowledge must be brought to bear (Stanfield 1988). Oppositional ethnographies and life histories can assist in this task to give voice to these women by recording their perspectives on their experiences (hooks 1990; Mani 1990; Chabram 1990).[5]

Costureras and Theories of Work

To get an idea of the problems Latinas face, we can begin by
looking at a recent study of the history of ILGWU in Los Angeles by Laslett and Tyler. The book opens with a remarkable
observation:

> When people refer to the ladies' garment industry,
> they tend to assume that it is composed exclusively
> of female workers . . . the overwhelming majority of
> employees in the industry have always been women.
> . . . In the West, the majority have nearly always
> been Latinas. But the . . . industry has also
> employed men, mostly in skilled positions; and men
> have always dominated the officer cadre of the
> union. (Laslett and Tyler 1989, 3)

This statement demonstrates the typical exclusion of
Chicanas, Mexicans, and Latinas within the ILGWU. Women
of color do the work; white men lead.[6] We should not simply
reject this situation as inequitable; we need to understand how
this sexist and racist view permeates both Latinas' reality and
the analyses of Latinas. We therefore need to explain, on one
hand, how the ILGWU in Los Angeles has been and continues to be controlled by white males, while the vast majority
of workers are unorganized Latinas.[7] On the other hand, we
need to be aware that research that does not include standpoint methodology is flawed. The only way to find answers is
to begin to openly discuss the racist and sexist nature of organized labor from the point of view of Latinas themselves. I
will begin by examining some of the theories of work.

The participation of women of color in unions must be put
in the context of particular job settings and historical periods. By looking at particular case studies of working women
of color, it is possible to discern the main factors that contribute to their participation, or lack of it, in organized labor.
I would like to look at four issues that have appeared in the
recent literature concerning women and unions: gender segregation, work culture and resistance, the exclusionary practices of unions, and the role of the state in organized labor.

Historically, a fragmentation of jobs considered appropriate for women and men arose out of patriarchal practices
within particular economic and social contexts (Walby 1986;
Milkman 1987). This gender segregation at work has been
detrimental to women. As Tilly and Scott explain:

139

> From the preindustrial period to the present, jobs
> have been segregated by sex, and women's work has
> persistently been associated with low skill and low
> pay. Sex-segregated labor markets are not simply
> differentiated markets, they are also asymmetrical;
> women's work is consistently ranked lower than
> men's. (Tilly and Scott 1987, 2)

This separation must be addressed at the outset of any discussion about work. This process justifies and legitimizes the existence of men's and women's work and the inferiority of the latter. The debate on gender segregation has recently been extended to account for the gender/race segregation in the lowest occupations. Gender/ethnic-specific occupations have appeared and been assigned to women of color in the United States.[8] These occupations, such as jobs in the service industry, electronics, and garment manufacturing, are accompanied by terrible working conditions and extremely low wages. In the case of Latinas in the garment industry, their undocumented status further restricts their job options. The interlinking of gender, race, class, and immigrant status has led to the creation of an industry that operates like any other industry in underdeveloped societies.

Organized labor must therefore be studied in the context of gender/ethnic segregation at work. The level of segregation by gender and ethnicity affects the character of the labor organizing that can take place and its ultimate success or failure. Some scholars argue that it is possible to create a work culture on the shop floor. Networks are developed among women in the same ethnic group or across ethnic lines. These networks created at work extend from work to lifecycle and family events celebrated at the workplace. Solidarity arises among workers, resulting in some cases in effective union participation and resistance against management (Lamphere 1987; Sacks 1988; Ruiz 1990; Zavella 1987; Westwood 1984). Ruiz, for instance, argues that in some cases the ghettoization of an ethnic group and crowded conditions at work, as in the case of Mexican cannery workers, might result in effective unionization (Ruiz 1990, 281).

For Latinas in Los Angeles's sweatshops, the development of a work culture did not occur. This does not disprove the existence of work cultures among women workers; rather it illuminates the pervasive effect that a particular set of working conditions, and a fragmented and extended community, has on the possibility that Latina costureras could effectively resist management and deteriorating working conditions. Even though Latinas sit next to each other, they are completely absorbed in their sewing machines. The noise level does not allow for conversation and exchange at work. Furthermore, these women are constantly forced to compete for the good bundles that are distributed according to the supervisor's criteria—sometimes unfairly—to particular groups of women.

Though Latinas come into contact during work breaks, the conditions of work are so competitive that they must always be on guard. Moreover, new workers who will eventually take the place of the senior garment workers are constantly entering the shop. The working conditions are complicated by the high turnover rate; women do not stay long enough at the shop to establish networks. New immigrant workers constantly replace those already on the line. Another factor that retards the development of networks is the geographical character of Los Angeles. Latina garment workers do not live close to each other in a differentiated community. They are spread across multiple communities throughout the city and beyond its limits. Their family and coworker networks are not connected by geographic immediacy. As a result, my research did not corroborate the findings of those who reported community ties among women workers (Lamphere 1987; Sacks 1988; Zavella 1987; Westwood 1984).

Many scholars have analyzed the sexist practices of union officials and rank-and-file males in U.S. labor (Ruiz 1990; Zavella 1988; Lamphere and Grenier 1988; Bookman and Morgen 1988; Sacks 1988). It has been pointedly argued that men have kept women out of unions because women were seen as competitors in the labor market. Together with a patriarchal ideology in which women were assigned roles as mothers and wives, men kept women without options by marginalizing them in the labor market (Kessler-Harris 1975; Walby 1988; Bradley 1989).

In the case of working-class Chicanas and Latinas there exists little question as to their long history in the labor market. Latinas have been relegated to the lowest-paying and most onerous of occupations in the labor market, placing them in "ethnic niches" (Ruiz 1990; Phizacklea 1988). In Los Angeles, the garment industry represents one of these niches that has been sustained and exists because of the available pool of immigrant Latina and Asian working women.[9]

The state plays an important role as well in the marginalization of women in both employment and union organizing. The efforts of the unions to confine women to certain "unskilled" jobs is compounded by the passage of certain types of labor legislation. For example, some protective labor legislation excluded women from performing certain jobs considered dangerous and "immoral."[10] As Strom notes, women did not receive the kind of assistance that men did through labor legislation in the 1930s. Married women were constantly under attack, were condemned for working outside the home, and were not allowed to fully participate in government and union policies (Strom 1983).

In the case of the Los Angeles garment industry, we can observe the role of the state through the failure of the labor department and labor legislation to effectively protect immigrant Latina working women. There are few inspectors in the garment industry, and their numbers appear to be decreasing. Abuses on the part of garment contractors have rarely been stopped. The National Labor Relations Board's process of complaints is long and complicated; it might take from thirty months to three years for a complaint to be resolved (Douglas 1986, 207). A recent attempt at implementation of new state legislation, the Hayden initiative, to make manufacturers jointly liable with contractors and subcontractors for violations against workers was vetoed by Governor Deukmeijian in August 1990. Thus the state, through the lack of protection and labor violation regulation, leaves Latinas vulnerable to all forms of abuse.

The lack of a protective state policy for worker rights is further evident in the implementation of immigration laws and labor restrictions that effectively segregate immigrant women into underground shops in the garment industry (Laslett and Tyler 1989; Phizacklea 1988). In the sweatshops it is the employers who suggest that workers purchase false work permits. Delia, a Mexican garment worker, describes such an incident:

> El dueño me daba para . . . [The owner offered me some money to buy fake papers. My husband did not let me . . . the owner offered me the minimum wage with fake papers. He got fake papers for this other guy at the shop . . . he used to say that even if the papers were not good, he would take them.]

Many Latinas remain silent about these abuses. They are afraid to lose their meager salaries. There are, however, some Latinas who are ready to risk deportation by complaining. Adela, a Mexican garment worker, reported her employer. She knows that she is going to face deportation, but she explains why she had to do it:

> No le hace que me deporten . . . [It doesn't matter if they deport me, I will just go away. This is a vicious circle, there should be a law . . . they should deport the drug addicts, to me (sigh) . . . I cannot see my people humiliating themselves for money . . . I leave and there will be someone else to take my place.]

Even though Chicanas and Mexicanas have a long history in union organizations, they are kept outside of union leadership. They were always circumscribed by the manipulations of non-Latino male-dominated unions who in the end did not integrate them into the different unions. Union leaders continue to be shortsighted as to the possibilities and the subsequent prospects for organizing if Chicanas, Mexicanas, and Latinas are included in real leadership positions (Ruiz 1990; Zavella 1987; Durón 1984). The ILGWU in Los Angeles, for example, unlike the ILGWU in San Francisco, which has an Asian woman as manager of the Pacific North West District Council, hires Latinas but never to positions of importance.

The ILGWU has not been able to accommodate Latinas in leadership positions even though the majority of garment workers are Latinas. The union typically hires Latinas to positions of minor importance when their expertise is needed to deal directly with Latina garment workers. In general, however, Latinas are excluded from positions of power, leadership, and decision making, even though it is clear that their opinions and leadership could be valuable to any attempts at unionization.

The structure of the garment industry, management, the state, and organized labor have worked in harmonious ways to the detriment of immigrant Latina workers in the garment industry of Los Angeles. The garment industry in Los Angeles illuminates the processes by which immigrant women, who historically have this occupation in this industry, are left completely unprotected by any form of regulation from the state via the board of labor relations or by labor organizations such as the ILGWU. This situation by which garment workers are attempting to survive is taking place at the same time that the state is enforcing a new immigration law (Immigration Reform and Control Act, IRCA). This immigration law is supposed to sanction employers who hire undocumented workers. In practice it has exacerbated a situation in which undocumented workers have to work in illegal contractor shops where there is no regulation or enforcement of basic labor laws, such as minimum wage, hours of work, and industrial homework, not to mention unsanitary and dangerous working conditions.

Latina Garment Workers in Los Angeles

While it is a very legitimate issue to discuss lack of representation of Latinas in leadership positions in unions, I want to argue that our point of departure must be the masses of Latinas. I propose that in order to study Latina garment workers in Los Angeles and their lack of participation in unions we must start from the lived experiences of Latinas themselves. It is no longer enough to focus on the unions, the ILGWU, and its officials and organizers. We already know that unions are heavily male and non-Latino and that racist perceptions are common among the leadership of the AFL-CIO.[11] The ILGWU in no way reflects the population of Latina garment workers who form the majority of that labor sector in Los Angeles. If we want to understand the problems of unionization we must explore the life histories of Latinas who are nonunionized, concentrated in contractor's shops, and doing industrial homework. The future of the garment workers in Los Angeles depends on that majority of Latinas who continue to be exploited and are nonunion. The life history approach is important in looking at Latinas and their participation in the industry. We need to know where Latinas are located in the structure of the garment industry. How do Latinas look at unions? What do Latinas need in terms of organizing, from their own perspective?

Methods

From 1987 to 1990 I did participant observation at the ILGWU and sewing schools where Latinas are trained and placed in shops at the end of their training. Working in a contractor's shop in order to accurately assess the working conditions, I learned to operate industrial sewing machines and worked piece rates, in an effort to learn what it means to be a garment worker in Los Angeles. Later, I interviewed key informants and collected the life histories of some Latina garment workers of various ages working at shops or doing industrial homework.

Through participating with Latina garment workers in Los Angeles, it is clear that one of the main problems that Latinas face in the apparel industry is the lack of unionization. This lack of unionization has usually been explained by union officials and scholars as a result of Latinas' (1) naiveté and lack of past union experience in their country of origin;[12] (2) their lack of English skills; (3) their lack of schooling and ignorance about U.S. social institutions; and (4) the *machismo* of Latino husbands.[13] I intend to debunk these myths reproduced by both scholars and union officials.

Many scholars argue that immigrant European garment workers back East at the turn of the century were able to organize because they had a history of struggle behind them (Asher 1984). According to Schlein, regarding the case of the garment industry in Los Angeles:

> The original Los Angeles garment workers and union leaders were transplanted New Yorkers with European roots. They came replete with the tradition of socialist ideas and a strong regard for unions. As the labor force changed in favor of Latin American workers the union lost much of its force. Its efforts to communicate and organize among people who could not relate to unions became frustrated, leading to the present situation. (Schlein 1980, 116)

Given the worker struggles of late-nineteenth-century Europe, some scholars point to the rapid unionization in certain industries on the East Coast. They carried over, if you wish, a culture and history of unionization. In contrast, their argument continues, Latinas in the twentieth century lack this culture and history. Latinas are again depicted as less sophisticated, more ignorant, and politically inferior to their European counterparts.

To begin with, Latinas who come to the United States and participate in the apparel industry are a heterogeneous population. It is difficult to establish their class origins, levels of education, and labor experience in their countries of origin. In fact, we encounter a collage of experiences: Latinas come from urban and rural areas; some garment workers have worked in various types of industrial settings, including the garment industry, while others were rural laborers.[14] For all, the apparel industry offered the only entry into the U.S. labor market.

Many of the Latinas had a sixth- to eighth-grade education or higher but due to lack of English skills chose to enter the garment industry. Some Latinas I talked to were secretaries, teachers, or nurses in their countries of origin. If they wanted to continue their own professions in this country, they would have had to take exams and learn English. It would be too costly and time-consuming, and their economic situation did not allow them to opt for this choice.

More important, these women are not ignorant of unions and labor organizing. They know that the United States has labor laws and are aware of the existence of the ILGWU. The Spanish-language media, furthermore, informs them about daily labor events—strikes, boycotts, state or federal investigations, and the like. Many of these women clearly understand or have experienced some type of labor organizing, especially if they came from urban areas. Ignorance about Latin American countries' labor histories greatly hampers scholars, union officials, and anyone interested in organizing Latinas. Latinas do not come to the United States as blank slates; they already have experienced or witnessed the repressive forces used by governments against legitimate unionization efforts on the part of workers. It is common in Mexico or El Salvador to make use of the police or the military to suppress any attempt by independent unions to organize.[15] Furthermore, Los Angeles has a labor history in which Mexican garment workers since the 1930s have actively participated (Laslett and Tyler 1989; Pesotta 1945; Vásquez 1980; Monroy 1980; Durón 1984).

It was Chicanas who worked closely with Rose Pesotta and the ILGWU. Rose Pessota was a Jewish immigrant worker from Ukraine who became a union organizer and vice-president of the ILGWU from 1934 to 1944. Because Pesotta had a vision for the ILGWU, she advocated the inclusion of women in different ethnic groups as union organizers. Her strategy worked with Mexican-origin women in Los Angeles during the 1930s and 1940s. Pessota drew influence from her ability to work with Mexican-origin women. She saw them as equal workers with the potential for organizing—unlike her male counterparts who saw Mexican women as unorganizable.[16] Even though

Pesotta was able to communicate with Chicanas, her interactions revealed a paternalistic bent (Monroy 1980). Nevertheless, we must recognize that she was more effective than anyone else at that time.

Therefore, the question we need to ask is why these Latinas have not organized. No simple answer exists. One aspect of the problem lies in the organizational structure of the garment industry and the place that Latinas occupy within this structure.[17] For an illustration we have the case of a Salvadoran garment worker who has been in the industry for nine years. This is what she told me when I asked if she knew about a garment workers' union:

> Sí, yo ya sabía que había un sindicato . . . [Yes, I already knew about the union, and I wanted to become a member. But then I found out that the ILGWU only accepts membership from stable shops or large manufacturers who can respond to union demands.]

She was working for a small contractor shop where a large number of Latinas are concentrated. She continued:

> Y pensar . . . [And to think that people like us that really need the union cannot be part of it! . . . I have worked in less than human conditions. I have been exposed to thievery, they (the owners) have stolen from me, they have not paid me for work that I have done . . . . I would talk about all these things to people in the union. But the union people would tell me that those were shops that could close overnight and open somewhere else.]

Thus the decision of the ILGWU not to get involved with workers in small contracting shops affects a large number of Latinas who have no hope for fair representation. At the same time, a large number of unscrupulous contractors take advantage of this situation. The ILGWU has a valid claim when its leadership points out that as soon as they try to organize small shops the owners threaten to inform immigration officials,[18] or they move to a different location and leave the workers out of work again. The structure of the garment industry lends itself to this type of intimidation and manipulation of immigrant workers. The big manufacturers subcontract their work; it is hard to trace them—though not impossible. A couple of Latinas who were not paid for their work traced a label from a contractor's shop in downtown Los Angeles all the way to a manufacturing firm in Santa Monica. They asked the manager to give them any lead on the unscrupulous contractor who had made them work for a week without any remuneration. The manager understood the situation but never called them on the phone as she promised to do when that contractor came back to the factory.

Latinas are doing industrial homework throughout Los Angeles County even though a ban exists on industrial homework in California. Walking through the Latino communities in and around downtown Los Angeles one hears the roar of industrial machines running at any time during the day or night and sees garbage dumpsters close to apartment houses filled with fabric remnants from the overlock sewing machines.[19] During the last week of March in 1988, hearings with the Labor Relations Board took place in Los Angeles, and many people from the garment industry, unions, and community organizations testified, as did Latina homeworkers. The deplorable work conditions for homeworkers and their children were denounced; however, as one Latina homeworker asked me after two days of hearings:

> Ahora ya les dijimos a todos . . . [Now we have told everyone how bad it is doing homework, and now what? What are the unions and community groups going to do about it? What about us, the women who are still working at it?]

If it is difficult to organize in contractors' shops, it is even more difficult to organize homeworkers. These women are isolated, working day and night, because the factory is their home. These Latinas understand that homework is illegal, but one homeworker explained why she preferred staying home:

> Tengo que cuidar . . . [I have to look after my grandson and my younger daughter who is going to school. My older daughter is working, and I have to babysit for her. Before I used to pay for gas and lunch in order to go to the factory. I had to pay for a babysitter as well. Now I can be with my family.]

When I asked her how much was she getting paid, she assured me that it was the minimum wage. However, when I began to ask for the hours that she had worked and how much money she got the week before, she was no longer sure. She showed me a finished cocktail gown with a lot of work and fancy pleats, for which she was paid only $3.75 apiece. It took her about two hours to do the whole garment.

At another level the immigrant status of some Latinas inhibits union organization. For Latinas, their ethnicity, gender, class, and often their immigrant status are interrelated. A garment worker explained it to me this way.

> Organizarse para la gente . . . [To get organized for some people will be a double-edged sword; some people have no documents, and it is precisely these types of shops (referring to small contractor's shops) that accommodate people who do not have papers; some people prefer to earn one dollar an hour to deportation.]

From my own experience as a participant observer I can attest to the anonymity and easy entrance into contractors' shops, the lack of regard for new immigration laws, and the way in which they operate to accommodate immigrant workers. I was admitted with no questions asked; they did not even know my name. My sewing machine had a number, and I was referred to as "number four." The converted warehouse had a heavy metal screen door that remained locked at all times, partly to prevent INS officials from just walking in. There was a garage exit at the other end of the building.

I asked Olga, a Salvadoran garment worker, if Latinas could be organized without the help of a union. She responded:

> Sí se podría hacer . . . [It could be done, but people who have no documents are very vulnerable. Even people with documents do not get organized. I do know that they are not interested in getting organized. Why do we not get organized? . . . I would like to test that idea. I think that we could come up with some norms of work that we could present to the employers. But we have to study this carefully. This should be studied. . . . There are possibilities, but this would not benefit the organizers, only the people that are being organized.]

She came up with ideas for how to go about organizing, always aware of the discrepancy between those with documents and those who did not have them. The documented workers are very sensitive regarding the position of their undocumented peers and avoid exposing them to the possibility of deportation or economic hardship. Olga was infuriated by all her experiences as a garment worker in the United States. She summarized it this way:

> En mi país . . . [Back home they said that over here we were going to sweep dollars with the broom . . . that is a big lie! Over here we are going to sweep, and we will not see any dollars . . . . Since I came to this country I have worked and I have not seen any money. . . . It is totally unfair.]

To exclude Latinas from important positions in union leadership has repercussions for the future of predominately Latina unions and working Latinas. The following example illustrates the lack of gender/ethnic awareness on the part of the union's cadre. In 1990, the ILGWU opened a new center for legal aid. It is located in the heart of the garment district. Free legal aid is available to garment workers who want to complain about employers. I asked one of the ILGWU leaders if Latinas had been consulted on the usefulness of the center in addressing their complaints. He explained that the question of the center was decided among the leadership (mainly male). The ILGWU intention is to encourage Latinas to complain to the NLRB about employers who commit labor violations. This center might function to deter unscrupulous contractors and to attract Latinas to the ILGWU. It remains to be seen if this will be the net result. One major problem remains—undocumented Latinas who avail themselves of the center's services risk deportation.

When I asked Latinas what their immediate needs were and how the ILGWU could best serve them and effectively attract the women as members, they cited child care issues. The lack of child care is one of the major problems for Latinas and an issue that produces a great deal of anxiety and family instability. As Pilar, a Mexican trimmer, explained:

> Mi problema más grande . . . [My biggest problem is child care for my little girl. One goes to work, and the child stays in this environment (referring to the inner city area). . . . We want to move out of this area. Yesterday at six in the afternoon there was a shooting. . . . I am going to send my daughter to Mexico with her grandparents.]

And according to Dolores, a Mexican trimmer and mother of five children ranging in age from eighteen to two years old.

> Mi hija, la grande . . . [My oldest daughter has to
> stay and take care of her two little sisters . . . she
> goes to school at night to learn English . . . the other
> day one of the little ones went out into the street,
> and we found her at the police station.]

In ignoring those issues of greatest concern to Latinas,
their largest constituency, the union diminishes its effectiveness as a political force. The union effort to aid Latinas with
free legal advice and support must be recognized as a legitimate strategy by the potential membership. Yet by not taking
into consideration the needs of Latinas, the process of organizing is retarded.

Conclusion

In order to analyze the lack of unionization among Latina
garment workers in Los Angeles, we have to understand the
complexity of issues that Latinas face in the industry. Inad-
vertently, the union has worked in harmony with the state
through labor legislation and immigration laws. Not organizing the sector of the industry in which the majority of Latinas
are concentrated negatively affects Latinas.

We must note that the garment industry has became an
"ethnic niche" for immigrant Latinas in Los Angeles. In this
niche, they suffer the terrible labor conditions and miserable
wages of the piece-rate system. The segregation at work along
gender/ethnic lines occurs simultaneously with the gender/
racial exclusionary practices of organized labor and the sanctions of the state that exacerbate the exploitation of Latina
garment workers.

We need to understand the lived experiences of Latinas
in the apparel industry in Los Angeles if we want to understand the issues of gender, race, and ethnicity in trade unions.
The histories of the women who have been in this industry
since the 1920s have not been sufficiently documented or
studied. It is already assumed that this population is ignorant and culturally unsuited to unionization. We need to ask
Latinas what problems they face as women of color outside of
and in the union—and what is it that Latinas want from community organizations and unions. In many ways the working
conditions for these immigrant women have deteriorated; proportionately, their wages have decreased in the last forty years.
There is a qualitative difference between the conditions of work

in the 1980s and the 1960s. Unionization efforts have died down as compared to earlier years, a phenomenon closely related to the present structure of the garment industry and the Union's decision not to organize shops where Latinas are concentrated. The ILGWU could organize as it did under the leadership of Pesotta in the 1930s when the union advertised on Spanish-language radio stations. The majority of garment workers then were Mexican women who were willing to strike and demand fair wages and hours of work. Perhaps in the 1990s Latinas are not a priority on the agenda of union organizers and leaders in Los Angeles.

Notes

1. Historically in the garment industry in Los Angeles, the majority of sewing machine operators were Chicanas and Mexicanas. At the present time, younger Chicanas have moved to other occupations, and many older Chicanas have retired or are in the process of retiring from this industry. Immigrant Mexicanas remain the majority of garment workers in the different types of shops—though there is an increasing number of women from other parts of Latin America. Here "Latinas" refers to the group of women that I studied in the Los Angeles garment industry. It does not mean, however, that they form a homogeneous group.

2. In 1988, the ILGWU claimed membership of only 1 percent of the total number of garment workers, estimated by the ILGWU at around 100,000 workers (Ferraro 1988).

3. The ILGWU can trace its history back to 1910–1911 (Laslett and Tyler 1989, 15).

4. Several feminists have demonstrated how research by Euro-American feminists has attempted to subsume the experience of women of color into their own theories and agendas (Spelman 1988; hooks 1984; Collins 1990).

5. I do not want to argue that ethnography is the method that will allow us truly to give marginalized populations their voices. This is not the case. Ethnography, whatever its variant, began as and continues to be the tool of colonization; it restricts voice. As a tool for domination, it is never neutral. I simply want to argue that when we approach ethnography critically, understanding its deficiencies, we can use it to initiate our study.

6. The hidden assumption is that immigrant and minority women are traditional and familistic and therefore incapable of organizing. This position has been effectively critiqued by Zavella (1988), Durón (1984), Bookman and Morgan (1988), and Ruiz (1990).

7. Scholars have documented the ways in which the ILGWU in Los Angeles has excluded Mexicanas and Latinas from leadership positions (Laslett and Tyler 1989; Monroy 1980). At best the leadership in the ILGWU have paternalistically tried to "guide" Latina workers (Monroy 1980).

8. This also occurs in Great Britain (Phizacklea 1990).

9. Asian women represent a smaller significant sector of the garment workers in Los Angeles. At the beginning they were only Chinese concentrated in Chinatown, but they have extended geographically to other areas. There are other groups as well, such as Koreans, Vietnamese, Thai, and Cambodians.

10. In the 1800s some critics believed that women who spent long hours at the pedal sewing machine were sexually aroused (Chapkis and Enloe 1983, 69).

11. According to some observers, people of color are unwelcome and misunderstood by organized labor in Los Angeles. In the words of Miguel Machuca, an ex-ILGWU organizer, "I remember attending meetings at the AFL-CIO . . . when the tone of the meetings was very antagonistic towards Mexicans, or wetbacks, a term I heard very often. I heard organizers saying, 'what are we going to do about the damn wetbacks? . . . why don't we call immigration on them?'" (Machuca 1988, 8–11).

12. According to Laslett and Tyler 1989, "Latino workers tended at first to be swayed by the paternalistic blandishments of the contractors." Latinos also looked upon white organizers with suspicion. "ILGWU organizers, most of whom were still white, were sometimes wrongly seen by the newcomers as 'agents of authority,' who may also seek to have them deported" (Laslett and Tyler 1989). Also note Schlein 1980, who argues that only European workers have a trade unionist tradition.

13. "The machismo associated with Latino culture could also make it difficult to organize the married women in the trade" (Laslett and Tyler 1989).

14. Lourdes Arguelles argues that Mexicanas who migrate to the U.S. Southwest are not the landless and/or the poorest of their society (Arguelles 1990). There is little information on women from Central and South America (Peñalosa 1986).

15. The labor history of women in Mexico is extensive (Ruiz-Funes 1990). For a short account of Mexican garment workers in Mexico see Arbalaez 1990.

16. According to the ILGWU regional representative in Los Angeles, in the early 1980s married Latinas could not get organized because of the machismo among Latino husbands (Laslett and Tyler 1989, 108). These culturalist explanations demonstrate the racism inherent in perceptions of the ILGWU's leadership.

17. The garment industry in Los Angeles is structured to function at several levels. We first have the manufacturers where designing, cutting, sewing and finishing are done in the same place. The "jobbers" do designing and cutting and contract out the sewing of garments. The contractors, who may or may not be licensed, do the sewing themselves; sometimes they subcontract as well. At the bottom are the homeworkers who can work for all of them in their own homes.

18. The Immigration and Naturalization Service has been involved in union organizing drives by the ILGWU. In the strike of Lilli Diamond Fashions in 1977, the INS was privotal in the demoralization and deportation of activist Latina workers (Vásquez 1980).

19. The Bush administration pressed to have that ban lifted throughout the nation, but it was not lifted on garment production.

Works Cited

Arbalaez, A. Marisol. 1990. "Impacto social del sismo, Mexico 1985: Las costureras." In *Between Borders: Essay on Mexicana/Chicana History*, ed. Adelaida R. Del Castillo. Encino, Calif.: Floricanto Press.

Arguelles, Lourdes. 1990. "Undocumented Female Labor in the United States Southwest: An Essay on Migration, Consciousness, Oppression, and Struggle." In *Between Borders: Essay on Mexicana/Chicana History*, ed. Adelaida R. Del Castillo. Encino, Calif.: Floricanto Press.

Asher, Nina. 1994. "Dorothy Jacob's Bellanca: Women Clothing Workers and the Run Away Shops." In *A Needle, a Bobbin, a Strike: Women Needle Workers in America*, ed. Joan M. Jensen and Sue Davidson. Philadelphia: Temple University.

Bookman, Ann, and Sandra Morgen. 1988. "'Carry It On': Continuing the Discussion and the Struggle." In *Women and the Politics of Empowerment*, ed. Ann Bookman and Sandra Morgen. Philadelphia: Temple University Press.

Bradley, Harriet. 1989. *Men's Work, Women's Work: A Sociological History of the Sexual Division of Labor in Employment*. Minneapolis: University of Minnesota Press.

Chabram, Angie. 1990. "Chicana/o Studies as Oppositional Ethnography." *Cultural Studies* 4, no. 3.

Chapkis, Wendy, and Cynthia Enloe, eds. 1983. *Of Common Cloth: Women in the Global Textile Industry.* Amsterdam: Transnational Institute.

Collins, Patricia Hill. 1990. *Black Feminist Thought: Knowledge Consciousness, and the Politics of Empowerment.* Boston: Unwin/ Hyman.

Douglas, Sara U. 1986. *Labor's New Voice: Unions and the Mass Media.* Norwood, N.J.: Ablex Publishing Corporation.

Durón, Clementina. 1984. "Mexican Women and Labor Conflict in Los Angeles: The ILGWU Dressmakers' Strike of 1933." *Aztlán* 15, no. 1.

Ferraro, Cathleen. 1988. "Fragmentation, Competition Inhibit L.A.'s Union Growth." *California Apparel News* (February): 12–18.

hooks, bell. 1984. *Feminist Theory: From Margin to Center.* Boston: South End Press.

———. 1990. *Yearning: Race, Gender and Cultural Politics.* Boston: South End Press.

Kesser-Harris, Alice. 1975. "Where Are the Organized Women Workers?" *Feminist Studies* (fall).

Lamphere, Louise. 1987. *From Working Daughters to Working Mothers: Immigrant Women in a New England Industrial Community.* Ithaca, N.Y.: Cornell University Press.

Lamphere, Louise, and Guillermo J. Grenier. 1988. "Women's Unions, and 'Participative Management': Organizing in the Sun Belt." In *Women and the Politics of Empowerment,* ed. Ann Bookman and Sandra Morgen. Philadelphia: Temple University Press.

Laslett, John, and Mary Tyler. 1989. *The ILGWU in Los Angeles 1907– 1988.* Inglewood, Calif.: Ten Star Press.

Machuca, Miguel. 1988. "Organizing Asian and Latino Workers." In *Organizing Asian Pacific Workers in Southern California,* ed. June McMahon. Los Angeles: Institute of Industrial Relations.

Mani, Lata. 1990. "Multiple Mediations: Feminist Scholarship in the Age of Multi-National Reception." *Feminist Review* 35.

Milkman, Ruth. 1987. *Gender at Work: The Dynamics of Job Segregation by Sex during World War II.* Urbana: University of Illinois Press.

Monroy, Douglas. 1980. "La Costura en Los Angeles, 1933–1939: The ILGWU and the Politics of Domination." In *Mexican Women in the United States: Struggles Past and Present,* ed. Magdalena Mora and Adelaida R. Del Castillo. Los Angeles: Chicano Studies Research Center.

NACLA Report of the Americas. 1980. "Capital's Flight: The Apparel Industry Moves South." In *Mexican Women in the United States: Struggles Past and Present,* ed. Magdalena Mora and Adelaida R. Del Castillo. Los Angeles: Chicano Studies Research Center.

Pesotta, Rose. 1945. *Bread Upon the Waters.* New York: Dodd, Mead and Company.

Phizacklea, Annie. 1988. "Entrepreneurship, Ethnicity, and Gender." In *Enterprising Women: Ethnicity, Economy, and Gender Relations*, ed. Sally Westwood and Parminder Bhachu. London: Routledge Press.

———. 1990. *Unpacking the Fashion Industry: Gender, Racism and Class in Production.* London: Routledge Press.

Ruiz, Vicki L. 1987. *Cannery Women, Cannery Lives.* Albuquerque: University of New Mexico.

———. 1990. "A Promise Fulfilled: Mexican Cannery Workers in Southern California." In *Between Borders: Essays on Mexicana/ Chicana History*, ed. Adelaida R. Del Castillo. Encino, Calif.: Floricanto Press.

Ruiz-Funes, Concepción and Enriqueta Tuñón. 1990. "Panorama de las luchas de la mujer mexicana en el siglo XX." In *Between Borders: Essays on Mexicana/Chicana History*, ed. Adelaida R. Del Castillo. Encino, Calif.: Floricanto Press.

Sacks, Karen Brodkin. 1988. *Caring by the Hour: Women, Work, and Organizing the Duke Medical Center.* Urbana: University of Illinois Press.

Schlein, Lisa. 1980. "Los Angeles Garment Industry Sews a Cloak of Shame." In *Mexican Women in the United States: Struggles Past and Present*, ed. Magdalena Mora and Adelaida R. Del Castillo. Los Angeles: Chicano Studies Research Center.

Smith, Dorothy E. 1987. *The Everyday World as Problematic: A Feminist Sociology.* Boston: Northeastern University Press.

Soldatenko, María. 1990. "Made in the U.S.A.: Latina Garment Workers in the Sweatshops of Los Angeles." Paper presented at Stanford Law School at Palo Alto, Calif., in October.

Spelman, Elizabeth V. 1988. *Essential Women: Problems of Exclusion in Feminist Thought.* Boston: Beacon Press.

Stanfield II, John. 1988. "Not Quite in the Club." *The American Sociologist* (winter).

Strom, Sharon Hartman. 1983. "Challenging 'Women's Place': Feminism, the Left, and Industrial Unionism in the 1930s." *Feminist Studies* (summer).

Tilly, Louise A., and Joan W. Scott. 1987. *Women, Work, and Family.* New York: Methuen Press.

Vásquez, Mario F. 1980. "The Election Day Immigration Raid at Lilli Diamond Originals and the Response of the ILGWU." In *Mexican Women in the United States: Struggles Past and Present*, ed. Magdalena Mora and Adelaida R. Del Castillo. Los Angeles: Chicano Studies Research Center.

Walby, Sylvia. 1986. *Patriarchy at Work: Patriarchal and Capitalist Relations in Employment.* Cambridge, Mass.: Polity Press.

———, Sylvia. 1988. "Segregation in Employment in Social and Economic Theory." *In Gender Segregation at Work*, ed. Sylvia Walby. Philadelphia: Open University Press.

Westwood, Sally. 1984. *All Day, Every Day: Factory and Family in the Making of Women's Lives.* Urbana: University of Illinois Press.

Zavella, Patricia. 1987. *Women's Work and Chicano Families: Cannery Workers of the Santa Clara Valley.* Ithaca, N.Y.: Cornell University Press.

———. 1988. "The Politics of Race and Gender: Organizing Chicana Cannery Workers in Northern California." In *Women and the Politics of Empowerment,* ed. Ann Bookman and Sandra Morgen. Philadelphia: Temple University Press.

Part Two:
Negotiating the Family

"Work Gave Me a Lot of *Confianza*": Chicanas' Work Commitment and Work Identity

Beatriz M. Pesquera

Sociological investigation has tended to bifurcate the analysis of workers along gender lines. Typically, the "job model" focusing on the specific work context is used in studies that analyze male work attitudes and behaviors. A "gender model," on the other hand, has unduly influenced studies of women's employment. Conceptually this model appears skewed toward assuming that women's family experiences (e.g., gender socialization, the division of household labor) unduly influence their employment attitudes and behaviors, with work-based dynamics considered as only tangentially contributing to our understanding of women workers (Feldberg and Nakano Glenn 1979). Highlighting women's gender socialization and familial duties distorts our analysis of the significance of the work context in shaping women's level of work commitment and work identity.

To get at these issues, I have interviewed a select group of professional, clerical, and blue-collar married Chicana workers. In this essay I argue that an integrative conceptual approach drawing on both "job" and modified "gender" models illuminates the complex interactive effect between women's experiences in the domestic realm and outside employment, as well as their level of work commitment and work identity.

The division of household labor on the basis of gender must be incorporated in any analysis of female workers as long as women continue to be primarily or solely responsible for the reproduction (both biologically and socially) of the family.

Women's incorporation into wage labor has not significantly reduced their unpaid labor in the home (Miller and Garrison 1984; Shelton 1990). Because women allocate a considerable amount of both physical and emotional labor to their familial responsibilities, their role within the domestic domain shapes their identity. To assume otherwise would be misleading and distorts the intersection of domesticity and paid labor.

Equally misleading is the assumption that only the domestic sphere shapes women's identities. The "job model" that locates workers within a specific set of social relations in the labor market must also be incorporated in the study of women workers. Employed women, like men, also define and identify themselves within the context of their work (Feree 1976; Pistrang 1984; Segura 1992). However, because most employed married women simultaneously perform two jobs—one at home and the other at work—their familial responsibilities and domestic-based identities may color their employment experiences.

In this paper, I explore familial and employment factors that influence levels of work commitment and work identity among a small group of professional, clerical, and blue-collar married Chicana workers. For my analysis, I rely on Chappell's (1980) analytical distinction between work commitment and work identity. According to Chappell, commitment to work refers to behavioral factors that include activity within the work role and a determination to continue within that role (Chappell 1980, 85). While work commitment refers to role-specific behavior, identification with work is more general and subjective. Work identity pertains to the subjective meaning of paid labor in peoples' lives. It refers to the importance of the work role for a person's sense of self (Chappell 1980, 86). It is possible for individuals to hold a high level of work commitment because of economic need and not highly identify with their jobs. Chappell provides a framework to explore the motivation, behavior, and relevance of work in people's lives.

Methodology and Sample Characteristics

I obtained my data through twenty-four in-depth interviews with Mexican-origin women between the ages of twenty-five and forty, married to Mexican-origin men. Two of the women were born in Mexico and migrated to the United States with their parents as children; the others are United States–born

Chicanas. Two-thirds of their spouses are also United States–born. The remainder migrated to the United States at varying ages—from childhood to adolescence. I generated data through a convenience sample in the greater San Francisco Bay area and Sacramento. The sample includes twenty-four women evenly divided among professional, clerical, and blue-collar occupations. The limitations of the sample preclude wholesale generalizations.

I selected women who had been in the labor force for at least five years because I wanted a sample whose members had substantial work histories. All professional workers have graduated from college, and five earned graduate degrees. They all work in the public sector, six as administrators and two as teachers. Clerical workers are also employed primarily in the public sector. These women completed high school, and all but one have from one to two years of community college or business school training. Blue-collar laborers earned high school diplomas, and the majority also attended community college, but more sporadically than the clerical workers. One blue-collar worker drives a delivery truck; the rest labor in factories. All women had at least one child living at home at the time of the interview. The majority had preschool and elementary school children.

Women in this sample grew up in farm labor camps or working-class or lower-middle-class neighborhoods. Those from migrant-worker families eventually settled in urban areas. Thus, these women have lived the majority of their lives in urban settings. At the time of the study they resided in northern California, in predominantly lower- and middle-class neighborhoods. About a fourth of the professional women lived in affluent areas.

Early Introduction to Work

Chicanas from farmworker backgrounds began to toil in the fields at an early age. As members of families working as an economic unit, they picked fruits and vegetables on a piece-rate scale, with the father as head of the family receiving the collective family earnings.[1]

Families that previously labored in the fields eventually combined agricultural work with cannery employment. Often families continued to work together in the canneries. After following the migrant stream, Lupe's family settled in

Sacramento where they combined field with food processing work. Lupe recalls the shift from a collective family wage her family received as agricultural workers to individual wages when they began to work in the canneries. As the family's economic situation improved, offsprings' earnings were distributed between the family unit and their own personal consumption. Lupe comments on this change:

> When I was in junior high school we started working on the tomato machine, and we would each get our own checks. At first I started to give it all to my mom until she told me to start putting money in the bank for myself. So I would give half the check to my mom and save the rest.

Most urban Chicanas entered the labor force in their early teens, usually in the service and clerical sectors, with a smaller number as seasonal cannery workers. Their earnings supplemented the family income either as direct contributions to the family wage or as supplements for their own personal use for clothing or extra spending money.

Some women experienced conflicts regarding the allocation of their earnings. Celia, a professional worker, expresses her feelings:

> From the time I turned fourteen or fifteen I have been working at various jobs in restaurants and stores. It was a hassle knowing that I was working and I couldn't spend any of the money. But I also felt satisfaction that I was helping out at home.

For some Chicanas employment provided an avenue for establishing minimal personal and financial independence. Rosaura, a professional worker, recalls this strategy:

> I started working when I was fourteen. I lied about my age, and I was busing dishes in a cafeteria after school and on the weekends. Two things made me want to get a job: I needed the money, and I wanted to get out of the house. My dad was so strict that the only way to get out was to get a job.

By the time the majority of these women graduated from high school, they had considerable work experience. They also established work patterns in their childhood and teen years that would influence their level of work commitment and work identity as adult women. Furthermore, they were socialized within a collective family economic strategy, whereby a strong work ethic provided a means to economic and social betterment. Their early training shaped their conceptions regarding the meaning of work in their lives. The majority expected that as adult women they would combine marriage, childbearing, and employment. For Chicanas, employment has familial as well as personal dimensions. Their outside employment as married women provides an economic advantage that permits their families to sustain a lower-middle- to middle-class lifestyle. Thus, they contextualized their employment within the context of familial responsibility. Equally important, however, is the sense of personal autonomy they gain from their economic role. In the words of Norma, a clerical worker: "If I wasn't working, he would have me eating out of his hands." Thus, employment can be construed as an avenue for familial and personal satisfaction and as an important source of identity.

I must caution, however, that not all of the women in this sample expected to combine marriage and wage work. They grew up in families organized along a traditional division of gender roles and were socialized accordingly. Some expected to marry, have children, and reproduce the traditional middle-class division of labor. Others expressed the idea that the "man goes to work, and the woman stays home to raise the children," a 1950s "Cleaver family" model, inconsistent with their own upbringing, as many of their own mothers had held jobs. Thus, although many Chicanas in this sample expected to combine employment and family, some initially entered the labor force solely for economic reasons.

Full-Time Employment

Full-time employment among this sample varied according to the age of marriage, childbearing, and the level of education. All but two professional workers delayed marriage, and all but one delayed childbearing until after completing educational goals and establishing careers. This group appeared to be the most homogeneous in terms of career trajectories and began full-time employment later than most of the other women in this sample.

In contrast, half of the clerical workers began full-time employment directly out of high school or after completing between one to three semesters of community college or business school.

Married in their early twenties, they began having children within the first two years of marriage. Nonetheless, they remained in the workforce except for maternity leaves. The remaining half of the clerical sample married upon completion of high school, began families, and did not enter the labor force immediately.

As a group, women in the blue-collar sector displayed several unique characteristics. Half of the blue-collar workers became pregnant early in the marriage, remained full-time homemakers until their children began school, at which point they entered the labor force full-time. Three women obtained jobs immediately after high school, quit for a number of years for childbearing and childrearing, and then reentered the labor force three to four years later. Only one Chicana in a blue-collar job had consistently remained in the labor force, except for brief maternity leaves, since graduation from high school.

Chicana professionals experienced the least difficulty finding jobs. They secured employment in agencies that serve the Chicano community or through affirmative action programs. These women benefited from the gains garnered through Chicano/Latino community and university student activism during the late 1960s and early 1970s. This activism represents a part of a broader Chicano/Latino civil rights movements that challenged the lack of access to social services, educational institutions, and the political process. As a result of political pressure exerted at various levels of society, human service and educational programs were instituted to meet community and student needs. Some became institutionalized within existing structures and agencies, such as educational opportunity programs. Others became part of the blossoming community-based movement. Examples within the greater Bay area include: Centro Legal, a legal aid center; La Familia, a mental health agency; El Centro Infantil de la Raza, a preschool; La Escuelita, a primary school; and Adelante, a job training program. These programs offered bilingual and bicultural services.

Chicano/a students and professionals worked with grassroots community people in a collective effort to institutionalize services and affirmative action programs to meet community needs. All of the professional women in this sample and a small percentage of the clerical and blue-collar workers participated in these efforts. The career benefits derived by the Chicana professionals in this study resulted from the political activism in which they had participated. At the time the interviews took place, they all worked in either community-based programs, educational institutions, or county and state programs. Those who held administrative positions at the county and state level held affirmative action appointments. Graciela discusses her appointment:

> I have the highest position of any Chicano within this agency. I am also the only female department head. My job is not permanent yet; I am an appointee. My position is very political. I was appointed because I am a Mexican, a woman, and because of my experience and orientation to community-based organizations.

Prior to her present position, Graciela had worked in a community-based organization. She started there as a graduate student intern and eventually rose to become executive director.

Although Chicana professionals did not experience difficulties in obtaining jobs, most of them lacked clearly defined career goals. Interestingly, several women used identical phrases to explain their professional success such as: "I fell into the job," "it was an accident," or it was "luck and chance."

In contrast to the professional workers, clerical workers experienced varying degrees of difficulty in obtaining jobs they considered desirable. The majority reported anxiety and frustration in reaching their job goals. Entry into jobs of their choice proved difficult even though they expressed high levels of job commitment and had previous work histories. Moreover, three-fourths of the clerical workers had business training or community college education. Some clerical workers eventually obtained jobs of their choice through affirmative action programs in the public sector. Although the majority of the clerical workers do not have an activist background, some benefited from political pressure to hire minorities and women.

Gloria, who works for a telephone company, believes that she was initially hired because of a pending lawsuit against the telephone company regarding its employment practices. Furthermore, she discusses how her promotion to her current job resulted from affirmative action:

> About five years ago, the federal government told them they didn't have enough minorities in

particular jobs. There weren't enough women and minorities in the higher titles. I was asked if I wanted to transfer to a higher-level job. And I told them that I had a request for a transfer for years.

Blue-collar workers had little difficulty in securing employment in their initial job searches. They secured employment as production workers. One woman initially began full-time employment as a clerical worker but found the job too confining. When a position came up as a delivery-truck driver, she applied and got the job. Some of the production workers experienced temporary or permanent layoffs. With downturns in the economy, which resulted in production cutbacks or plant closures, their subsequent job searches became more difficult as fewer jobs became available.

In addition, some blue-collar workers moved into male-dominated jobs due to affirmative action. They experienced considerable hostility from male workers who perceived them as a threat to their male privilege. Luz, a sorter, recalls her entry into a "man's" job:

One time they put me to train for a job, and the men didn't like it. They felt that I was taking their job away. They let me know that they didn't like it. The men wouldn't show me the shortcuts to make the job easier.

María works full-time at a furniture factory and part-time as a maid in a hotel on the weekends and also attends a welding training program at a local community college. She has received considerable harassment from her fellow white male students and course instructor. Their pejorative comments are directed at her race/ethnicity and gender:

I have gotten a lot of hassles by men because I want to be a welder. As a matter of fact, I have gotten hassles from my own instructor. It's because I'm a woman mainly; the men say I have no business being there. At the same time, they discriminate against me because of my race. They tell me I should get papers or go back to Mexico. I'm not from Mexico, I'm from Texas. I'm an American citizen.

Numerous other women reported experiences with harassment and discrimination on the basis of race/ethnicity and/or gender. Maria's case represents the most extreme. None of the women filed official complaints. Instead they either tried to ignore the comments or discuss the problem with their coworkers or supervisors. María, like the rest of the women in this sample, demonstrated a deep commitment to full-time employment. She views her jobs at the furniture factory and at the hotel as temporary until she can complete her welding program. At that point she hopes to seek employment in that field.

Commitment to Work

A person's employment behavior evidences her or his level of work commitment. Work commitment refers to the willingness to attain employment and sustain a work role. Although Chicanas differed with respect to the timing of full-time employment, the degree of difficulty in obtaining jobs, and the types of jobs, they all shared a strong commitment to work. This held true for women who had anticipated combining family and jobs and those who initially sought full-time employment after marriage solely for economic reasons. Regardless of their reasons for entering the labor force, women indicated they expected to work until retirement age and asserted that they would not quit work even if it was no longer economically necessary.

Celia, a professional worker who has the option of staying home during the summer months, described her preference for full-time employment:

> I will stay home for a few weeks. I enjoy being home
> with the kids, but to stay home and become a mother
> and a housewife full time, I wasn't meant for that.
> When I am home for a week or two with the kids I
> really get frustrated . . . and I really want out.

Similarly, Norma, a clerical worker who has worked since childhood, stated: "I think the only time I didn't work was for about three months. It drove me up the wall." Angie, a blue-collar worker, began full-time employment after high school. She became a full-time homemaker after her first child was born, reentered the job market a year later, and then returned home again after the birth of her second child. Due to economic considerations, she went back to work after her second child was only six months old. She expressed her commitment to work as follows:

> I enjoy being out of the house. It's like my own part of life. I think mentally it's better. After working for nine years, I can't see myself staying home. I'm home two days a week, and that's enough time to get the house and the laundry done.

Moreover, both sets of women, those who had expected to reproduce a middle-class division of labor (breadwinner husband and homemaker wife) and those who had anticipated combining employment and family, eventually converged in their perception that the traditional nuclear family structure was either unattainable and/or undesirable. As Laura, a clerical worker, explained: "The days when you expected your husband to take care of you, those days are gone, they are over. The way I figure, I plan to work whether it's part-time or full-time. That is something I have pretty much accepted."

The strength of the work commitment shared by these women can be traced to their childhood and adolescent work experiences, a strong work ethic developed within their families of origin, their contemporary socioeconomic circumstances, and, most important, an ideological commitment to a dual-earner household. For the Chicano families in this sample, women's earnings are essential to maintain a more comfortable lifestyle than would be possible with only their husbands' earnings.

Work Identity

Work commitment denotes role behavior; work identity refers to the subjective meaning of work in people's lives. This subjective meaning can be gauged by analyzing the centrality of the work role to a person's self-identity. While work commitment appeared strong and fairly consistent, the strength of work identity fluctuated among this sample of Chicana workers. They all acknowledged the importance of their work role to their sense of self; however, its impact on their self-identity varied. For some women, their identification with work significantly affects the sense of self. Their identities seem intricately fused with their work roles. Others do not consider their work role as pivotal to their identity.

Several components contextualize the meaning of work to their self-identity. These components combine economic and noneconomic sources of reward and empowerment. Of primary significance in the development of a work identity is their role as economic providers. In the words of María, a blue-collar worker: "I'm happy to receive a check. . . . It's my labor . . . I can spend it any way I like. I don't have to ask permission." Earning their own wages cultivates pride, self-esteem, and a degree of economic independence. Yolanda, a professional worker, expresses these sentiments:

> Women gain independence from money; they have the option to leave. Power relations change not only due to economic considerations but also because women gain a sense of self-worth. I have gained respect at my work site and also in my community. This gives me something to identify with outside of the home.

Chicanas perceived work as important not only for family economic gain but for personal benefits as well. Flor, a clerical worker, stated: "I wouldn't ever leave my job because I'm taking care of myself." Equally significant, women's economic role offers intangible sources of identification and reward. As Laura, a clerical worker, acknowledges: "I feel good knowing I have done a good job." Angie, a blue-collar worker, expresses her feeling regarding her sense of self in relation to work: "It makes me happy. I think if I didn't work I would be grouchy. It's like my own identity, doing something for me." Victoria, a blue-collar worker, concurs: "Work gave me a lot of confianza. It gave me confidence."

Women express the intrinsic nature of work identity through monetary and personal motivations for wage labor. Their words speak to the manner in which employment enhances their options and empowers them. They blur the tangible (economic) with the subjective (empowerment) to reflect an enhanced sense of themselves, of their self-identity. Employment confers a degree of independence that includes economic rewards for their families and themselves and personal satisfaction and confidence in their abilities beyond the domestic sphere.

Among the overwhelming majority of the couples, women's employment appeared accepted as necessary for family economic survival and upward mobility. For blue-collar Chicanas, whose husbands were also predominately production workers, their combined income seemed essential for economic survival. Clerical workers' spouses hold blue-collar craft jobs, with a small number in production-related employment.

Chicana professionals are predominantly married to Chicano professionals or men involved in graduate training. Among the majority of these couples women's employment offers the opportunity to move up to a middle-class lifestyle.

Chicanas do not consider their economic contribution as "helping" their husbands but rather as a component of their familial obligation. All women viewed their employment as a family duty but acknowledged receiving personal benefits associated with contributing to their families' economic well-being. To these women, work becomes a responsibility, and a right. Work provides a means to attain a degree of economic independence and personal identification apart from the family. For them, adult identity incorporates both roles of worker and wife/mother, as Consuelo, a clerical worker, stated: "I don't feel a complete person when I'm not working."

For these Chicanas, their senses of identity becomes influenced by their work role. Nonetheless, there existed qualitative distinctions between professional, clerical, and blue-collar workers on the centrality of this role to their overall self-identity. Such factors as job status and the reward system for various occupations must be considered because they affect the level of work identity. Women in high-status employment situations that offer autonomy, greater intrinsic rewards, higher educational training, and more subjective evaluation appear likely to be more identified with their work roles than those in low-status jobs with limited opportunities and rewards. Not surprisingly, then, professional women have the highest level of work identification among the women in this sample.

An added dimension for Chicana professionals relates to their unique social location. Their degree of work identification appears accentuated by their sense of historic mission. They constitute part of the first wave of Chicanas to enter the professional ranks. As pioneers breaking class, race/ethnic, and gender barriers, they embody a collective representation of the aspirations of the Chicano community and a deep sense of commitment and responsibility to that community. This sense of mission heightens their level of work identity. It also, however, entails enormous responsibility and increases their self-expectation and stress. Gloria, a high-ranking state administrator, discusses this tension:

> Well, the first thing is that you are working in a nontraditional environment. You are a pioneer.

> People expect a lot out of you since you are the one
> and only. There is a lot riding on you from your
> family, from other Chicanas and Chicanos, other
> minorities. Whether it is real or not, you feel it. It's
> the fact that you are a woman. If you are a minority,
> it even complicates it further.

For Chicana professionals, work identity fuses political and
personal dimensions. These factors enhance their level of work
identity while placing tremendous pressure on their lives.

Another means to gauge the level of work identity involves
analyzing how Chicana workers reconcile the "competing urgencies" of work and family.[2] Reconciling the competing urgencies means that women have to balance job and family
responsibilities with identity investment. While all women in
this sample expressed a degree of difficulty in reconciling these
claims, professional workers expressed the highest level of
anxiety and conflict. In order to understand this, we need to
separate the factors associated with the job performance from
those associated with the level of work identification. This includes the amount of both physical and emotional investment
in the work role. That is, on the manner in which workers dis-
tribute their subjective involvement among adult roles (Bielby
and Bielby 1984).

In general, women are comfortable with their dual roles
as workers and wives/mothers, although they find it difficult
to manage the "competing urgencies" of work and family. Professional workers expressed a high level of concern regarding
their dual roles. They seemed unsure of their ability to adequately perform both sets of expectations. In addition,
Chicana professionals expressed anxiety over "role overlap" or
their tendency to bring work home with them. As Sonia reveals: "Keeping priorities is important. Things can get
muddled. Sometimes things are at odds between what is important at work and what is important for the family. What is
more important is difficult to decide."

At an ideological level, women appear caught in a contradiction between traditional social and cultural expectations,
which reinforce women's familial roles, and their needs and
identification as working women. Linda articulates how this
pull between family and self affects her life: "There is a tendency to believe that if the women were home with the children things would be a lot better at home, that the woman is
not able to devote all of her attention to her family. I don't

believe that for myself." Linda, like other Chicana professionals, rejects traditional social norms regarding women's work and family welfare. Although she says that she doesn't agree with these normative expectations, she nonetheless expresses some ambivalence regarding the impact of work on her children: "I know sometimes I do feel guilty. I can think very selfishly. There is nothing wrong with that. But when it has a direct affect on the kids, then I start feeling uncomfortable."

Sonia's and Linda's comments highlight professional workers' feelings of anxiety, guilt, and ambivalence. They appear caught in a contradiction shared by many women, what Berg (1986) refers to as "the guilt that drives mothers crazy." This contradiction appears strikingly evident among professional workers.

Although clerical and blue-collar workers tended to identify with their work roles to a lesser degree than professional workers, they must also contend with similar contradictions between sociocultural expectations and their own needs.

In an angry voice, Christina, a delivery truck driver, conveys shared sentiments regarding the social pressure exerted on women to conform to a traditional domestic role: "My mother says that I should be home with the kids, that I have no business working. But when I had the babies and was home, it wasn't enough. Besides, my job is important to me."

Laura, a clerical worker, expresses a sense of loyalty to her family role beyond the pride and satisfaction she derives from her job:

> A lot of us identify with our jobs. I try not to, but I do. I'm proud. But that isn't the biggest drive in my life. The way I look at it right now, my primary concern is my family. Whatever I do for a living, that is a separate issue. The day I'm gone and buried they are not going to remember me for the achievements that I did, the fantastic job that I did, or whatever, they are going to remember me for being a good mother.

Christina's and Laura's voices echo those of professional workers. Like them, Christina rejects the notion that she should stay home. For her, like the other women in this sample, the domestic role is not sufficiently satisfying. Laura identifies with and gains pride from her job; however, her domestic role appears to win over her work role in social prestige.

The magnitude of work identity investment fluctuates according to the prestige and reward structure of occupations. Chicana professionals' higher level of work identity reflects their higher-status location in the labor market hierarchy. Their professional status enhances their identification with work. Furthermore, some hold highly visible, political positions. Their sense of mission and responsibility to the Chicana/o community strengthens their level of work identity.

While women in this sample reject normative expectations that women's first priority must be the family, they acknowledge the possibility that their employment may have a negative impact on family well-being. They also express frustration with the guilt-producing attitudes of family members regarding the presumed negative impact of their employment on their family, particularly on their children.

Laura, a clerical worker, acknowledges her identification with work but suppresses it and emphasizes her identity investment in the domestic sphere. Although she identifies with her work, her identity shift to the domestic sphere reflects her perception that her social status as a clerical worker is unlikely to confer high levels of prestige. By emphasizing her domestic role as a wife and mother, she can draw upon traditional means to gain social status as a "good mother."

Laura's stance reflects her location in the labor market, which influences her level of work identity. She, like other clerical and blue-collar workers, is cognizant of the fact that although she does identify with her job and is proud of her role as a worker, her job does not confer a high degree of social status. This factor, in conjunction with the social pressure to conform to traditional female norms, tends to curtail the development of a higher level of work identity among clerical and blue-collar workers.

Professional workers must also contend with similar pressure regarding women's roles. They tended to view their employment as having the potential for placing greater stress on their families, particularly their children, than that of clerical or blue-collar workers. Holding higher-status jobs, they more highly identified with their work than did the other women in this sample.

Conclusion

Work commitment, the willingness to engage and sustain a work role, appears strikingly evident among the Chicanas in this sample. This commitment is conditioned by family socialization, work histories, economic need, and monetary and emotional rewards.

This study both confirms and challenges the gender model that asserts that women's employment attitudes and behavior are unduly influenced by their experiences in the domestic sphere. The high level of work commitment among this sample can be related to their socialization in their working-class families of origin. Their families' economic need fostered a strong work ethic and attachment to work as a family economic strategy for survival and betterment. The economic strategy of their working-class families of origin resembles the "family wage economy" whereby all economically viable members contribute to the household's needs.[3] This factor kindled an initial identification with work, which influenced their commitment to work as adult women. Family socialization positively shapes their work attitudes and behavior. This runs counter to the notion that female socialization within the family has a negative impact on their work attitudes and behavior.

Yet they were also socialized within a traditional division of labor. Although many of their mothers worked for wages, mothers and daughters assumed responsibility for the child-rearing and household work. Raised in patriarchal households, they were subservient to male authority. However, because many of their mothers worked and they also began working at an early age, either to contribute to the family economy, to be able to buy personal items their families could not afford, or (for some) to obtain a semblance of economic autonomy, most developed an early attachment to work. Their socialization instills two sets of messages: Women could work for wages and simultaneously maintain their traditional role within the household division of labor.

Not surprisingly then, when they married, their domestic responsibilities did not affect overall work commitment. An important reason for their high level of job commitment remains economic need. Among clerical and blue-collar workers, their earnings prove essential for their families' economic survival or betterment. While the majority of Chicana professionals are married to males with similar professional backgrounds and could survive on one income, their combined income enables the maintenance of a middle-class lifestyle.

Chicanas' work commitment is also conditioned by subjective criteria such as the rewards gained from a sense of accomplishment in doing a good job, pride in their ability to provide economically for their families, and a degree of relative economic independence. While work commitment appears similar among this sample of Chicana workers, work identity seems more variable. One can apply both job and gender models in analyzing differences in the level of work identity.

Job-related issues such as the amount of control over the labor process, mobility opportunities, and economic and status rewards differ substantially among occupations. Although differences do exist between blue-collar jobs and clerical work, Chicanas in these occupations expressed similar levels of work identity. Clerical labor in postindustrial society has increasingly taken on characteristics of production work (Davis 1979; Glen and Feldberg 1977). While Chicanas in the clerical sector have slightly more control over their labor process and greater opportunities for job mobility, their earning power is not significantly higher than those of their blue-collar counterparts.

The similarities in job-related factors among clerical and blue-collar Chicana workers in this sample set them apart from Chicana professionals. These differences bolster the higher level of work identity expressed by Chicana professionals. Furthermore, for them the social and political dimension of their jobs intensifies their level of work identity.

The level of work identity, the importance of work to a person's sense of self, seems more significantly influenced by gender factors than work commitment. Sociocultural norms indicating that women should give priority to their domestic role and derive their main source of identity from the domestic sphere have a greater influence on women's work identity. That is, ideological factors mediate the manner in which women in this sample evaluate the degree of self-identity drawn from their employment and family roles to a much greater extent than for work commitment. This dynamic is played out in how they attempt to reconcile the competing urgencies of work and family. All women expressed some ambivalence regarding the distribution of subjective investment between work and family. They experience conflict between the norms of "family first" and their identity as workers.

Clerical and blue-collar workers appear more likely to play down or submerge the work identity. Zavella (1987) reported similar findings among Chicana cannery workers. Professional workers acknowledge the centrality of work identity and ideologically reject, in a somewhat ambivalent fashion, cultural expectations. They appear caught in a "consciousness gap" between competing claims on their self-identity. They are not as likely as clerical or blue-collar workers to disregard the extent to which they invested themselves in the work role and derive a sense of identity from work. This often produces a higher level of anxiety and guilt among Chicana professionals, specifically with regard to motherhood.

The data do not indicate that professional workers' children suffer more from having working mothers than children of clerical or blue-collar working women. I contend, rather, that sociocultural expectations regarding women's appropriate role in society affect the manner in which Chicana workers reconcile competing claims. The gender-specific cultural mandate to mother bears upon the manner in which Chicana workers attempt to reconcile ideologically the extent to which work identity contributes to the sense of self.

Both job and gender factors influence Chicanas' work identity. Job-related concerns, including control over the labor process and status rewards, affect the extent of self-investment in the work role and bear upon work identity. Professional jobs seem more likely than clerical and blue-collar jobs to confer greater opportunity for the development of higher levels of work identity. These job-related factors account for some of the variance in work identity among this sample of Chicana workers.

Gender factors, specifically the ideological tug-of-war between work and family, also have an impact on their level of work identity as illustrated by how women negotiate the competing urgencies of work and family and their sense of identity. Gender plays a significant role in the ideological sphere—in the manner in which women couch identity within work.

Notes

1. For the historical pattern, see Ruiz 1987, 14–20.
2. This phrase was coined by Arlie Hochschild in personal discussion with Lilian Rubin and quoted in Rubin 1983.
3. According to Tilly and Scott (1978), the family wage economy is characterized by wage labor of numerous members of the family. Wives and daughters enter and exit the labor force according to the overall economic needs of the family. Daughters were usually family wage-earners, and wives/mothers' labor allocation fluctuates between production and reproduction. I suggest that many of the families of origin of these women resemble to some degree the family wage economy as characterized by Tilly and Scott. That is, daughters' earnings were either direct or in-kind contributions to the overall family economy.

Works Cited

Berg, Barbara. 1986. *The Crisis of the Working Mother.* New York: Summit Books.

Bielby, Denise Del Vento, and William T. Bielby. 1984. "Work Commitment, Sex-Role Attitudes, and Women's Employment." *American Journal of Sociology* 49: 234–47.

Chappell, Neeve L. 1980. "Paid Labor: Confirming a Conceptual Distinction Between Commitment and Identification." *Sociology of Work and Occupations* 7, no. 1: 81–116.

Davis, Margery. 1979. " 'Women's Place is at the Typewriter': The Feminization of the Clerical Labour Force." In *Capitalist Patriarch and the Case for Socialist Feminism*, ed. Zillah R. Eisenstein. New York: Monthy Review Press.

Feldberg, Roslyn L., and Evelyn Nakano Glenn. 1979. "Male and Female: Job Versus Gender Models in the Sociology of Work." *Social Problems* 26: 524–38.

Feree, Myra. 1976. "Working Class Jobs: Housework and Paid Work as Sources of Satisfaction." *Social Problems* 23: 431–41.

Glenn, Evelyn N., and Roslyn Feldberg. 1977. "Degraded and Deskilled: The Proletarianization of Clerical Work." *Social Problems* 25: 53–64.

Miller, Joanne, and Howard H. Garrison. 1984. "Sex Roles and the Division of Household Labor at Home and at the Workplace." In *Family Studies Yearbook*, vol 2, ed. David H. Olson and Brent C. Miller. Beverly Hills, Calif.: Sage Press.

Pistrang, Nancy. 1984. "Women's Work Involvement and Experience of New Motherhood." *Journal of Marriage and the Family* 45: 433–47.

Rubin, Lilian. 1983. *Intimate Strangers: Men and Women Together.* New York: Harper and Row.

Ruiz, Vicki. 1987. *Cannery Women, Cannery Lives: Mexican Women, Unionization, and the California Food Processing Industry, 1930–1950.* Albuquerque: University of New Mexico Press.

Segura, Denise. 1991. "Chicanas in White Collar Jobs: 'You Have to Prove Yourself More.'" *Sociological Perspectives* 35, no. 1: 163–82.

Shelton, Beth Anne. 1990. "The Distribution of Household Tasks: Does Wife's Employment Status Make a Difference?" *Journal of Family Issues* 11: 115–35.

Tilly, Louise A., and Joan W. Scott. 1978. *Women, Work, and Family.* New York: Holt, Rinehart and Winston.

Zavella, Patricia. 1987. *Women, Work and Chicano Families: Cannery Workers of the Santa Clara Valley.* Ithaca, N.Y.: Cornell University Press.

Ambivalence or Continuity?: Motherhood and Employment among Chicanas and Mexican Immigrant Women Workers

Denise A. Segura

The social construction of motherhood exerts a powerful influence on individual behaviors, social institutions, labor market structures, and social policy. The ideology of motherhood posits a woman's biological ability to bear and suckle children as her "natural" and therefore "most fulfilling" social destiny rather than as a culturally informed role whose meanings can vary and are subject to change. In our society the social construction of motherhood assigns responsibility to women to raise their own children while staying at home during the child's early or "formative" years and asserts that activities that take married mothers out of the home (i.e., paid employment) are less important or "secondary" to their domestic duties (Wearing 1984; Berg 1986; Folbre 1984).[1] This set of assumptions is embedded in labor market structures (i.e., sex segregation of economic sectors and occupations) that reinforce women's reproductive role and their economically subordinate position vis-á-vis men, as well as help legitimize existing gender and class relationships (Smith 1987; Hartmann 1976).

Despite the ideological impetus to mother at home, over half of all women with children work for wages (Grossman 1982; Hayghe 1984; U.S. Bureau of the Census 1991).[2] The growing discrepancy between ideology and behavior has prompted some researchers to suggest that traditional gender role expectations

181

are changing to accommodate greater acceptance of women working outside the home.[3] The profuse literature on the "ambivalence" and "guilt" employed mothers often feel when they work outside the home, however, reminds us that changes in expectations are neither absolute nor uncontested.

Some researchers argue that the ambivalence felt by some employed mothers stems from their discomfort in deviating from the socially constructed image of an "idealized mother" who stays home to care for her family (Hochschild 1989; Gerson 1985; Berg 1986). This image of motherhood, popularized in the media, schoolbooks, and public policy, implies that the family and the economy constitute two separate spheres, private and public. According to Zaretsky (1976), the development of industrial capitalism gave rise to a privatized family sphere outside of economic production and removed women from commodity production and exchange, thereby reinforcing their social subordination to men.[4] Motherhood, notes Johnson (1988, 26), is typically characterized as a liability because it is associated with wifehood and confinement to the nuclear family. Sacks (1979), however, points out that in a majority of societies, women's childbearing and childrearing has not impeded their effective involvement in the economic, political, and cultural activities integral to their societies. In light of variation in women's economic and cultural roles, DuBois and Ruiz (1990) argue that the private/public dichotomy largely rests on the experiences of white, leisured women and lacks immediate relevance to less privileged women (e.g., immigrant women, women of color).[5] This suggests that the relationship between motherhood and employment varies by class, race, and/or culture.

Does the ideology of motherhood and the ambivalence of employed mothers depicted within American sociology and feminist scholarship appertain to women of Mexican descent in the United States? Is motherhood mutually exclusive from employment among women from varying social locations? This paper explores both questions from qualitative data gathered from thirty women of Mexican descent in the United States— both native-born Chicanas (including two Mexican-born women raised since preschool years in the United States) and resident immigrant Mexicanas.[6] I illustrate that conceptualizations of the relationship between motherhood and employment differ between Chicanas and Mexicanas. Contrary to the expectations of acculturation models, I find that Mexicanas' views of motherhood are more conducive to a consistent labor market presence than those articulated by Chicanas. I argue that this distinction—typically bypassed in the sociological literature on motherhood, women and work, or Chicano studies—is rooted in their dissimilar social locations, that is, the "social spaces" they engage within the social structure created by the intersection of class, race, gender, and culture (Zavella 1991, 75).

I propose that Mexicanas, raised in a world where economic and household work often merged, do not dichotomize social life into public/private spheres but appear to view employment as one workable domain of motherhood. Hence, the more recent the time of emigration, the less ambivalence Mexicanas express regarding employment. Chicanas, on the other hand, raised in a society that celebrates the expressive functions of the family and obscures its productive economic functions, express higher adherence to the ideology of stay-at-home motherhood and correspondingly more ambivalence to full-time employment.

The differences I discuss between Mexicanas and Chicanas challenge current research on Mexican-origin women, which treats them as a single analytic category, as well as challenging contemporary views of motherhood, thereby contributing to the formulation of frameworks on diversity among women. My examination of the intersection of motherhood and employment among immigrant Mexican women also reinforces emerging research that focuses on women's own economic motivations to immigrate to the United States as opposed to immigration at the behest of husbands and/or fathers (the traditional view) (Solórzano-Torres 1987; Baca and Bryan 1985; Guendelman and Pérez-Itriago 1987).

My analysis begins with a brief review of relevant research on the relationship between motherhood and employment. Then, I explore this relationship in greater detail using in-depth interview data. I conclude by discussing the need to recast current conceptualizations of the dilemma of choosing between motherhood and employment in a way that reflects women's different social locations.

Theoretical Concerns

The theoretical concerns that inform my research integrate feminist analyses of the hegemonic power of patriarchy in the organization of work and the social construction of motherhood with a critique both of rational choice models and the overemphasis on modernity and acculturation within research on Chicana and Mexicana employment. In much of the literature on women and work, familial roles, in particular motherhood, tend to be portrayed as important constraints on both women's entry into the labor market and mobility. Differences among women related to immigrant status, however, challenge this view.

Within rational choice models, motherhood represents a prominent social force behind women's job decisions. Becker (1975, 1981, 1985) and Polachek (1975, 1979, 1981), for example, argue that women's "preference" to mother is maximized in jobs that exact fewer penalties for interrupted employment such as part-time, seasonal, or clerical work.[7] According to this view, women's pursuit of their rational self-interest reinforces their occupational segregation within low-paying jobs (e.g., clerical work) and underrepresentation in higher-paying, male-dominated jobs that typically require significant employer investments (e.g., specialized training). Employers may be reluctant to invest in or train women workers who, they perceive, may leave a job at any time for familial reasons.[8] This perspective views motherhood as a major impediment to employment and mobility. But it fails to consider how the organization of production developed in ways that make motherhood an impediment. Many feminist scholars view this particular development as consistent with the hegemonic power of patriarchy.

Distinct from rational choice models, feminist scholarship directs attention away from individual preferences to consider how patriarchy (male domination/female subordination) shapes the organization of production resulting in the economic, political, and social subordination of women to men (Kuhn 1978; Hartmann 1976, 1981; Barrett 1980). While many economists fail to consider the power of ideological constructs such as "family" and "motherhood" in shaping behavior among women, employers, and the organization of production itself, many feminist scholars focus on these power dynamics.

Within feminist analyses, motherhood as an ideology obscures and legitimizes women's social subordination because it conceals particular interests within the rubric of a universal prerogative (reproduction). The social construction of motherhood serves the interest of capital by providing essential childbearing, child care, and housework at a minimal cost to the state and sustains women as a potential reservoir of labor power, or a "reserve army of labor" (Beneria and Roldan 1987; Beneria and Sen 1986; Smith 1987). The strength of the ideology of motherhood is such that women continue to try to reconcile the "competing urgencies"[9] of motherhood and employment despite the lack of supportive structures at work or within the family.

Because women are viewed by employers as mothers (or future mothers), they encounter discrimination in job entry and advancement (Kanter 1977).[10] Because women are viewed as mothers, they also work a "second shift" at home (Hochschild 1989). The conflict between market work and family work has caused considerable ambivalence within women. Berg, for example, notes that one of the dominant themes in analyzing women and work is the guilt of employed mothers based on "espousing something different" from their own mothers (1986, 42).

The notion of "conflict" or "guilt" Berg describes rests on several suppositions. The first assumption is that motherhood is a unilaterally oppressive state; the second is that employed mothers feel guilt; and the third is that today's employed mothers do not have working mothers (which partially explains their guilt feelings). Inasmuch as large numbers of working-class, immigrant, and racial/ethnic women have long traditions of working in the formal and informal economic sectors, such assumptions are suspect.

Research on women of Mexican descent and employment indicates that their labor force participation is lower than that of other women when young children are present (Hayghe 1984; U.S. Bureau of the Census 1987, 1991).[11] Moreover, Chicanas and Mexicanas are occupationally segregated in the lowest-paying of female-dominated jobs (Dill, Weber Cannon, and Vanneman 1987; Malveaux and Wallace 1987; Ruiz 1988). Explanations for their unique employment situation range from analyses of labor market structure and employer discrimination (Barrera 1979; Almaguer 1975; Segura 1984) to deficient individual characteristics (e.g., education, job skills) (Tienda and Guhleman 1985) and cultural differences (Kranau, Green, and Valencia-Weber 1982; Mirandé and Enríquez 1979).

Analyses of Chicana/Mexicana employment that utilize a cultural framework typically explain their lower labor force participation—particularly when young children are present—by higher fertility, lower levels of education, and higher levels of unemployment as part of an ethnic or cultural tradition (Kranau, Green, and Valencia-Weber 1982; Mirandé 1985). That is, that the Chicano/Mexican culture emphasizes a strong allegiance to an idealized form of motherhood and a patriarchal ideology that frowns upon working wives and mothers and does not encourage girls to pursue higher education or employment options. These attitudes are supposed to vary by generation, with immigrant women (from Mexico) holding the most conservative attitudes (Ortiz and Cooney 1984).

There are two major flaws in the research on Chicana/ Mexicana employment. First, inconsistency in distinguishing between native-born and resident immigrant women characterizes much of this literature. Second, overreliance on linear acculturation models persists. Both procedures imply either that Chicanas and Mexicanas are very similar, or that they lie on a sort of cultural continuum with Mexican immigrants at one end holding more conservative behaviors and attitudes grounded in traditional (often rural) Mexican culture, and U.S.–born Chicanos holding an amalgamation of cultural traditions from Mexico and the United States (Keefe and Padilla 1987; Mendoza 1984). In terms of motherhood and employment, therefore, Mexicanas should have more traditional ideas about motherhood than U.S.–born Chicanas. Because the traditional ideology of motherhood typically refers to women staying home to mother children rather than going outside the home to work, Mexicanas theoretically should not be as willing to work as Chicanas or American women in general—unless there is severe economic need. This formulation, while logical, reflects an underlying emphasis on modernity—or the view that "traditional Mexican culture lags behind American culture in developing behaviors and attitudes conducive to full participation in modern society" (Baca Zinn 1979, 1980, 1982). Inasmuch as American views of motherhood exalt labor market exit to care for children, embracing this ideal may be more conducive to maintaining patriarchal privilege (female economic subordination to men) than facilitating economic progress generally. In this sense, conceptualizations of motherhood that affirm its economic character may be more accommodating to women's market participation in the United States.

The following section discusses the distinct views of motherhood articulated by Chicanas and Mexicanas and their impact on employment. In contrast to the notion that exposure to American values enhances women's incentive to work, proportionately more Chicanas than Mexicanas express ambivalence to paid employment when they have children at home. I analyze these differences among a selected sample of clerical, service, and operative workers.

Method and Sample

This paper is based on in-depth interviews with thirty Mexican-origin women—thirteen Chicanas and seventeen Mexicanas—who had participated in the 1978–1979 or 1980–1981 cohorts of an adult education/employment training program in the greater San Francisco Bay area.[12] All thirty respondents had been involved in a conjugal relationship (either legal marriage or informal cohabitation with a male partner) at some point in their lives before I interviewed them in 1985 and had at least one child under eighteen years of age. At the time of their interviews, six Chicanas and fourteen Mexicanas were married; seven Chicanas and three Mexicanas were single parents.

On the average, married Chicanas have 1.2 children at home; Mexicanas report 3.5 children. Both Chicana and Mexicana single mothers averaged 1.6 children. The children of the Chicanas tend to be preschool age or in elementary school. The children of the Mexicanas exhibit a greater age range (from infant to late adolescence) reflecting their earlier marriages and slightly older average age.

With respect to other relevant characteristics, all but two Mexicanas and five Chicanas had either a high school diploma or its equivalent (GED). The average age was 27.4 years for the Chicanas and 33 years for the Mexicanas.[13] Upon leaving the employment training program, all the women secured employment. At the time of their interviews, about half of the Chicanas (n = 7) and three-fourths of the Mexicanas (n = 12) were employed. Only 2 out of the 7 (28 percent) employed Chicanas worked full-time (35 or more hours per week), whereas 9 out of the 12 employed Mexicanas (75 percent) worked full-time. Most of the Chicanas found clerical or service jobs (e.g., teacher assistants); most of the Mexicanas labored in operative jobs or in the service sector (e.g., hotel maids), with a small minority employed as clerical workers.

I gathered in-depth life and work histories from the women to ascertain (1) factors motivating them to enter, exit, and continue employment in their specific occupations; (2) whether familial roles or ideology influenced their employment consistency; and (3) the degree to which other barriers limited their job attachment and mobility. My examination of the relationship between motherhood and employment forms part of a larger study of labor market stratification and occupational mobility among Chicana and Mexican immigrant women (Segura 1986).

Motherhood And Employment

Nearly all of the respondents, both Chicana and Mexicana, employed and nonemployed, speak of motherhood as their most important social role. They differ sharply, however, with respect to the place employment holds in this configuration. Figure 1 illustrates some of these behavioral and attitudinal differences.

Figure 1

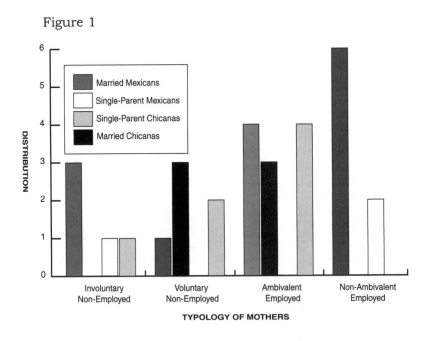

Figure 1 shows that women fall into four major groups. The first group consists of five involuntary nonemployed mothers who are not employed but care full-time for their children. All of these women want to be employed at least part-time.

Either they cannot secure the job they want and/or they feel pressured to be at home mothering full-time.

The second group consists of six voluntary nonemployed mothers who are not employed but remain out of the labor force by choice. They feel committed to staying at home to care for preschool and/or elementary school-age children.

The third category, ambivalent employed mothers, includes eleven employed women. They have either preschool- or elementary school-age children. Women in this group believe that employment interferes with motherhood and feel guilty when they work outside the home. Despite these feelings, they are employed at least part-time.

The fourth group, nonambivalent employed mothers, includes eight employed women. What distinguishes these women from the previous group is their view that employment and motherhood seem compatible social dynamics irrespective of the age of their children ($n = 8$). All eight women are Mexicanas. Some of these women believe employment could be problematic, however, if a family member could not care for their children or be at home for the children when they arrived from school.

Chicanas tend to fall into the second and third categories, whereas Mexicanas predominate in the first and fourth groups. Three reasons emerged as critical in explaining this difference: (1) the economic situations of their families; (2) labor market structure (four-fifths of the nonemployed Mexicanas were involuntarily unemployed); and (3) women's conceptualizations of motherhood, in particular, their expressed need to mother. Age of the women and number of children did not fall into any discernable pattern, therefore I did not engage them in depth within my analysis.

First, I consider the situation of the voluntary nonemployed mothers' group composed of three married Chicanas, two single-parent Chicanas, and one married Mexicana. All but one of these women exited the labor market involuntarily (e.g., layoffs, disability) but all remain nonemployed by choice. Among these five women, the need to mother appears strong, overriding all other concerns. They view motherhood as mutually exclusive from employment. Lydia, a married Chicana with a small toddler, articulates this perspective:

> Right now, since we've had the baby, I feel, well he [her husband] feels the same way, that I want to

spend this time with her and watch her grow up. See, because when I was small my grandmother raised me so I felt this *loss* [her emphasis] when my grandmother died. And I've never gotten that real love, that mother love from my mother. We have a friendship, but we don't have that "motherly love." I want my daughter to know that I'm here; especially at her age, it's very important for them to know that when they cry that mama's there. Even if it's not a painful cry, it's still important for them to know that mommy's there. She's my number one—she's all my attention . . . so working-wise, it's up to . . . [her husband] right now.

Susana, a Chicana single parent with a five-year-old child, said:

I'm the type of person that has always wanted to have a family. I think it was more like I didn't have a mother and a father and the kids all together in the same household all happy. I didn't have that. And that's what I want more than anything! I want to be different from my mother, who has worked hard and is successful in her job. I don't want to be successful in that way.

Lydia, Susana, and the other voluntarily nonemployed Chicanas adamantly assert that motherhood requires staying home with their children. Susana said, "A good mother is there for her children all the time when they are little and when they come home from school." All the Chicanas in this category believe that motherhood means staying home with children, even if it means going on welfare (AFDC). This finding is similar to other accounts of working-class women (Wearing 1984).

The sense shared among this group of women that motherhood and employment are irreconcilable when preschool-age children are present is related to their social locations. A small minority of the Chicanas had been raised by nonemployed mothers ($n = 3$). They feel they should stay at home with their children as long as it's economically feasible. Most of the Chicanas, however, resembled Lydia and Susana, who had been raised by employed mothers. Although these women recognized that their mothers had worked out of economic need, they believed they had not received sufficient love and care from their mothers. Throughout their interviews, this group of Chicanas expressed hostility and resentment against their employed mothers for leaving them with other caretakers. They either stay at home with their children or feel guilty when they are employed. Their hostility and guilt defies psychoanalytic theories that speculate that the cycle of gender construction that can lock women into "exclusive mothering" roles can be broken if the primary caretaker (the mother) undertakes more diverse roles (e.g., Chodorow 1979). Rather, Chicanas appear to value current conceptionalizations of motherhood that prioritize the expressive work of the mother as distinct from her economic activities.

This group of Chicanas seems to be pursuing the social construction of motherhood idealized within their ethnic community, their churches, and society at large (Ramírez and Castañeda 1974; Peck and Díaz-Guerrero 1967; Escobar and Randolph 1982). Among Chicanos and Mexicanos the image of *la madre* as self-sacrificing and holy is a powerful standard against which women often compare themselves (Mirandé and Enríquez 1979; Melville 1980; Anzaldúa 1987; Fox 1983). The Chicana informants also seem to accept the notion that women's primary duty is to provide for the emotional welfare of the children and that economic activities that take them outside the home are secondary. Women's desire to enact the socially constructed motherhood ideal was further strengthened by their conviction that many of their current problems (e.g., low levels of education, feelings of inadequacy, single parenthood) are related to growing up in families that did not conform to the stay-at-home mother, father-as-provider configuration. Their evaluation of the close relationship between motherhood and economic or emotional well-being of offspring parallels popular emphasis on the primacy of individual efforts and the family environment for emotional vigor and achievement (Parsons and Bales 1955; Bradley and Caldwell 1984; Caspi and Elder 1988; Parcel and Menaghan 1990).

Informants in this group demonstrate a complex dimension to mothering and gender construction in the Chicano/Mexicano communities. These women reject their employed mothers' organization of family life. As children, most had been cared for by other family members and now feel closer to their grandmothers or other female relatives than to their own biological mothers. This causes them considerable pain—pain they want to spare their own children. Many, like Susana, do not want to be "successful" in the tradition of their own employed mothers. Insofar as success means leaving their children with other caretakers, it contradicts their conceptualization of motherhood. Rather, they frame success in more affective terms: having children who are happy and doing well in school. This does not suggest that Chicanas disagree with the notion that having a good job or a lucrative career could and should be deferred until their children are older (i.e., the upper grades of elementary school) and doing well academically and emotionally.

Only one married Mexicana, Belén, articulated views similar to the Chicanas. Belén left the labor market in 1979 to give birth and care for her newborn child. It is important to note that she has a gainfully employed husband who does not believe mothers should work outside the home. Belén, who has two children and was expecting a third when I interviewed her, said:

> I wanted to work or go back to school after having my first son, but my husband didn't want me to. He said, "No one can take care of your child the way you can." He did not want me to work. And I did not feel right having someone else care for my son. So, I decided to wait until my children were older.

Belén's words underscore an important dynamic that impacted on both Mexicana and Chicana conceptualizations of motherhood: spousal employment and private patriarchy. Specifically, husbands working in full-time, year-round jobs with earnings greater than those of their wives tended to pressure women to mother full-time. Women who succumb to this pressure become economically dependent on their husbands and reaffirm male authority in the organization of the family. These particular women tend to consider motherhood and employment in similar ways. This suggests that the form taken by the social construction of motherhood involves women's economic relationship to men as well as length of time in the United States

Four Mexicanas and one Chicana were involuntarily nonemployed. They had been either laid off from their jobs or had taken disability leave. Three women (two Mexicanas/one Chicana) were seeking employment; the other two were in the last stages of pregnancy but intended to look for jobs as soon as possible after their children's birth. All five women reported feeling good about being home with their children but wanted to rejoin the labor force as soon as possible. Ideologically these women view motherhood and employment as reconcilable social dynamics. As Isabel, an unemployed production worker, married, with eight children, said, "I believe that women always work more. We who are mothers work to maintain the family by working outside but also inside the house caring for the children."

Isabel voiced a sentiment held by all of the informants—that women work hard at motherhood. Since emigrating to the United States over a decade ago, Isabel had been employed nearly continuously with only short leaves for childbearing. Isabel, and nearly all of the Mexicanas, described growing up in environments where women, men, and children were important economic actors. In this regard they are similar to the nonambivalent employed mothers, all of whom are also Mexicanas. They tended not to dichotomize social life in the same way as the voluntary nonemployed Chicanas and ambivalent employed informants.

Although all of the Chicanas believe that staying home best fulfills their "mother" roles, slightly fewer than half actually stay out of the labor market to care for their young children. The rest of the Chicanas are employed and struggling to reconcile motherhood with employment. I refer to these women as "ambivalent employed mothers." They express guilt about working and assert they would not work if they did not have to for economic reasons. As Figure 1 shows, seven of these women are Chicanas; four are Mexicanas.

In order to alleviate their guilt and help meet their family's economic goals, most of the Chicanas work in part-time jobs. This option permits them to be home when their children arrive from school. Despite this, they feel guilty and unhappy about working. As Jenny, a married Chicana with two children, ages two and four, who is employed part-time, said:

> Sure, I feel guilty. I *should* [her emphasis] be with them [her children] while they're little. He [her husband] really feels that I should be with my kids all the time. And it's true.

Despite their guilt, most of the women in this group remain employed because their jobs offer them the means to provide for family economic betterment—a goal that transcends staying home with their children. Women's utilization of economic rationales for working sometimes serves as a smokescreen for individualistic desires to "do something outside the home" and establish a degree of autonomy by having their "own money."

The ambivalently employed Mexicanas tend to work part time ($n = 3$). Their ambivalence stems from their desire to work full time—a desire thwarted by gainfully employed husbands who hold their wives accountable to the notion of full-time motherhood.[14] One Mexicana in this group works full-time because her husband is irregularly employed. She feels guilty working full-time because she has not been able to find a good child-care situation for her child.

All ambivalent employed mothers report worrying about their children while at work. While this does not necessarily impair their job performance, it adds another psychological or emotional burden onto their shoulders. This burden affects their ability to work full-time—overtime is especially problematic—or seek the means (especially schooling) to advance in their jobs. Women seem particularly troubled when they have to work on weekends, which robs them of precious family time. As Elena, a Chicana single parent with two children, ages nine and three, who works part-time as a hotel maid, said:

> Yes, I work on weekends. And my kids, you know how kids are—they don't like it. And it's hard. But I hope to find a job soon where the schedule is fixed and I won't have to work on weekends, because that time should be for my kids.

There is a clear sense among the women I interviewed that a boundary between "time for the family" and "market time" should exist. During the times this boundary folds, women experience both internal conflict (within the woman herself) and external conflict (among family members). They regard jobs that overlap on family time with disfavor and accept them reluctantly. When economic reasons compel women to work during what they view as family time, they usually try to find a different job that allows them to better meet their mother roles as quickly as possible.

Interestingly, the Chicanas appear less flexible in reconciling the boundaries of family time and market time than the Mexicanas. That is, Chicanas overwhelmingly "choose" part-time employment to limit the amount of spillover time from employment on motherhood and family activities. Mexicanas, on the other hand, overwhelmingly work full time ($n = 9$) and attempt to do both familial caretaking and market work as completely as possible.

This leads us to consider the fourth category, which I refer to as nonambivalent employed mothers. This category consists of Mexicana immigrants, both married and single parent (six and two women, respectively). Mexicanas in this group do not describe motherhood as a need requiring a separate sphere for optimal realization. Rather, they refer to motherhood as one function of womanhood compatible with employment, insofar as employment allows them to provide for their family's economic subsistence or betterment. As Pilar, a married Mexicana with four children employed full-time as a line supervisor in a factory, said: "I work to help my children. That's what a mother should do." This group of Mexicanas does not express guilt over the leaving the children in the care of others so much as regret over the limited amount of time they could spend with them. As Norma, a Mexicana full-time clerical worker who is married with two children, ages three and five, said:

> I don't feel guilty for leaving my children, because if I didn't work they might not have the things they have now. . . . Perhaps if I had to stay at home I would feel guilty and frustrated. I'm not the type that can stay home twenty-four hours a day. I don't think that would help my children any, because I would feel pressured at being cooped up [*encerrada*] at home. And that way I wouldn't have the same desire to play with my daughters. But now, with the time we have together, we do things that we want to, like run in the park, because there's so little time.

All of the Mexicanas in this group articulate views similar to those of Norma. Their greater comfort with the demands of market and family work emanates from their social positions. All of the Mexicanas come from poor or working-class families where motherhood embraced both economic and affective features. Their activities were not viewed as equal to those of men, however, and ideologically women saw themselves as helping the family rather than providing for it.

Few Mexicanas reported that their mothers were wage-laborers ($n = 3$) but rather described a range of economic activities they remembered women doing "for the family."[15] Mexicanas from rural villages ($n = 7$) recounted how their mothers had worked on the land and made assorted products or food to sell in local marketplaces. Mexicanas from urban areas (n = 5) also discussed how their mothers had been economically active. Whether rural or urban, Mexicanas averred that their mothers had taught them to "help" the family as soon as possible. As Norma said:

> My mother said, "It's one thing for a woman to lie around the house, but it's a different thing to get the work done. As the saying goes, work is never done; the work does you in [uno nunca acaba con el trabajo, el trabajo acaba con uno.].

Lourdes and two other Mexicanas cleaned houses with their mothers after school. Other mothers sold clothes to neighbors, cooked and sold food, or did assorted services for pay (e.g., giving penicillin shots to neighbors). The Mexicanas do not view these activities as "separate" or less important than the emotional nurturing of children and family. Rather, they appreciate both the economic and the expressive as important facets of motherhood.

Although the Mexicanas had been raised in worlds where women were important economic actors, this did not signify gender equality. On the contrary, male privilege, or patriarchy, characterizes the organization of the family, the economy, and the polity in both rural and urban Mexican society (Fernández-Kelly 1983; Guendelman and Pérez-Itriago 1987; Baca and Bryan 1985). In the present study, Mexicanas indicated that men wield greater authority in the family, the community, and the state than women. Mexicanas also tended to uphold male privilege in the family by viewing both domestic work and women's employment as "less important" than the work done by men. As Adela, a married Mexicana with four children, said: "Men are much stronger and do much more difficult work than women." Mexicanas also tended to defer to husbands as the "head" of the family—a position they told me was both "natural" and "sacred."[16]

Continuity and Ambivalence

The differences presented here between the Chicanas and Mexicanas regarding motherhood and employment stem from their distinct social locations. Raised in rural or working-class families in Mexico, the Mexicanas described childhoods where they and their mothers actively contributed to the economic subsistence of their families by planting crops, harvesting, selling homemade goods, and cleaning houses. Their situations resonate with what some researchers term a "family economy," where all family members work at productive tasks differentiated mainly by age and sex (Rothstein 1983; Cowan 1987; Tilly and Scott 1978). In this type of structure, there is less distinction between economic life and domestic life. Motherhood in this context is both economic and expressive, embracing both employment and childrearing.

The family economy the Mexicanas experienced differs from the family organization that characterizes most of the Chicanas' childhoods. The Chicanas come from a world that idealizes a male wage earner as the main economic provider, and in which women are primarily consumers and only secondarily economic actors (Bernard 1974, 1981; Hood 1986). Women in this context are mothers first, wage earners second. Families that challenge this structure are often discredited or perceived as dysfunctional and the source of many social problems (Walker and Best 1991; Doherty and Needle 1991; Clark and Ramsey 1990). The ambivalence Chicanas recurrently voice stems from their belief in what Kanter (1977) calls "the myth of separate worlds." They seek to realize the popular notion or stereotype that family is a separate structure—a haven in a heartless world. Their attachment to this ideal is underscored by a harsh critique of their own employed mothers and themselves when they work full-time. Motherhood framed within this context appears irreconcilable with employment.

There are other facets to the differences between Chicanas and Mexicanas. The Mexicanas, as immigrant women, came to the United States with a vision of improving the life chances of their families and themselves. This finding intersects with research on "selective immigration." That is, that Mexican immigrants tend to possess higher levels of education than the national average in Mexico and a wide range of behavioral characteristics (e.g., high achievement orientation) conducive to success in the United States (Chávez and Buriel 1986; Buriel 1984; Chávez 1985).

The Mexicanas emigrated hoping to work—hence their strong attachment to employment even in physically demanding, often demeaning jobs. Mexican and Chicano husbands support their wives' desires to work so long as this employment does not challenge the patriarchal structure of the family. In other words, so long as the Mexicanas (1) articulate high attachment to motherhood and family caretaker roles, (2) frame their employment in terms of family economic goals, and (3) do not ask men to do equal amounts of housework or child care, they encounter little resistance from husbands or other male family members.

When Mexican and Chicano husbands secure good jobs, however, they begin pressuring wives to quit working or work only part time. In this way, Mexican and Chicano men actively pursue continuity of their superordinate position within the family. This suggests that the way motherhood is conceptualized in both the Mexican and Chicano communities, particularly with respect to employment, is wedded to male privilege or patriarchy. Ironically then, Mexicanas' sense of employment's continuity with motherhood enhances their job attachment but does not challenge a patriarchal family structure or ethos.

Similarly, Chicanas' preference for an idealized form of motherhood does not challenge male privilege in their community. Chicanas' desire to stay at home to mother exercised a particularly strong influence on the employment behavior of single-parent Chicanas and women with husbands employed in relatively good jobs. This preference reflects both an adherence to an idealized middle-class lifestyle that glorifies women's domestic roles as well as the maintenance of a patriarchal family order. Chicanas feel they should stay at home to try to provide their children with the mothering they believe children should have—mothering that many of them had not experienced. Chicanas also feel compelled by husbands and the larger community to maintain the status of men as "good providers." Men earning wages adequate to provide for their families' needs usually urged their wives to leave the labor market. While the concept of the good provider continues to be highly valued in our society, it also serves as a rationale that upholds male privilege ideologically and materially and reinforces the myth of separate spheres that emanates from the organization of the family and the economy.

Conclusion

The present study revealed important differences between Chicanas and Mexicanas concerning the relationship between motherhood and employment. The vitality of these differences underscores the need for frameworks that analyze diversity among women. It is essential to explore motherhood and discuss the problems and issues surrounding it, one of the primary lenses through which gender is interpreted, in ways that reflect sensitivity to women's different social locations. Among the study informants, differences in social origins, family economics, employment, and experience with manifestations of patriarchy influenced women's conceptualizations of motherhood and employment.

Mexicanas tended to hold a broad conceptualization of motherhood that demonstrated greater compatibility with employment than that of the Chicanas. Mexicanas' employment was not hampered by their cultural orientation to mother—this was an asset—but by the lack of supportive social structures, in particular good employment opportunities. Both married and single-parent Mexicanas worked in physically demanding jobs until they were laid off, became disabled, or were forced out of the labor market by gainfully employed husbands. For these women, a patriarchal division of labor that cast motherhood into women's sphere could (and did) extend to embrace full-time employment. This dual dimension of motherhood was, for the most part, accepted by the Mexicanas, whose major motivation was the socioeconomic betterment of their families.

Chicanas, on the other hand, described high levels of ambivalence concerning the interplay between motherhood and employment. This difference reflects Chicanas' desire to realize the prevailing social construction of motherhood that exalts child rearing over paid employment. Chicanas were more likely to feel compelled to exit from the labor market to care for young children even though they did not always enact their preference. Instead, they tended to seek part-time employment as their economic circumstances allowed. It is important to note that Chicanas usually were better able to access nonprofessional part-time service and clerical work than the Mexicanas. This suggests that the intersection of labor market structure with idealized notions of motherhood worked better for Chicanas than Mexicanas.

The finding that women from more traditional backgrounds (such as rural Mexico) are more likely to approach full-time employment with less ambivalence than more "American" women (such as the Chicanas) rebuts linear acculturation models that assume a negative relationship between ideologies (such as motherhood) constructed within traditional Mexican society and employment. It also complements findings on the negative relationship between greater length of time in the United States and high aspirations among Mexicanas (Buriel, Calzada, and Vásquez 1982; Buriel 1984; Nielsen and Fernández 1981).[17] This suggests that employment problems (e.g., underemployment, unemployment) are less related to traditional cultural configurations than labor market structure and employment policies.

The differences between the Chicanas and Mexicanas depicted here emphasize the need to distinguish between Mexican subgroups and argue against the common practice of merging all Hispanic-origin women into one group for analytic purposes. The challenge of analyzing differences among women is formidable but compelling, as we recognize the need to understand the processes whereby ideologies and behaviors are constructed and contested within the unique social spaces individuals engage within our society.

Notes

This article is a revised version of a paper presented at the XII World Congress of Sociology held in Madrid, Spain, 9–13 July 1990. I would like to thank Maxine Baca Zinn, Arlie Hochschild, Beatriz Pesquera, and Vicki L. Ruiz for their constructive feedback and criticism of earlier drafts of this paper. Any remaining errors or inconsistencies are my own responsibility. This research was supported, in part, by a 1986–1987 University of California President's Postdoctoral Fellowship.

1. The view that mothers should not work outside the home typically pertains to married women. Current state welfare policies (e.g., Aid to Families with Dependent Children [AFDC], workfare) indicate that single, unmarried mothers belong in the labor force, not at home caring for their children full time (Gerstel and Gross 1987; Zinn and Sarri 1984; Folbre 1984; Naples 1991).

2. In June 1990, over half (53.1 percent) of women between the ages of 18 and 44 who had a child in the last year were in the labor force. This proportion varied by race: 54.9 percent of white women, 46.9 percent of black women, and 44.4 percent of Latinas were in the labor force (U.S. Bureau of the Census 1991, 5).

3. Simon and Landis report that the 1986 Gallup Poll indicates that support for married women to work outside the home is considerably greater than 1938 levels: 76 percent of women and 78 percent of men approve (1989, 270). Comparable 1938 levels are 25 percent

and 19 percent of women and men respectively. The 1985 Roper Poll finds the American public adhering to the view that a husband's career supersedes that of his wife: 72 percent of women and 62 percent of men agree that a wife should quit her job and relocate if her husband is offered a good job in another city (1989, 272). Simon and Landis conclude: "The Women's Movement has not radicalized the American woman: She is still prepared to put marriage and children ahead of her career and to allow her husband's status to determine the family's position in society" (1989, 269).

4. The concept of "separate spheres" is approached in a variety of ways and often critiqued (e.g., Glazer 1984; Barrett 1980). Zaretsky contends that distinct family and market spheres arose with the development of industrial capitalism: "Men and women came to see the family as separate from the economy, and personal life as a separate sphere of life divorced from the larger economy" (1976, 78). This stance is substantially different from that of early radical feminist approaches, including Firestone 1970 who argued that the separation antedates history. Other scholars assert that the relations of production and reproduction are intertwined and virtually inseparable (e.g., Hartmann 1976, 1981; Barrett 1980).

5. Hood 1986 argues that the "ideal" situation of stay-at-home motherhood relying on male provider has historically been an unrealistic standard for families outside the middle and upper classes. She points out that early surveys of urban workers indicate that between 40 percent and 50 percent of all families supplemented their income with the earnings of wives and children.

6. It should be noted that native-born status is not an essential requirement for the ethnic label "Chicana/o." There are numerous identifiers used by people of Mexican descent including: Chicana, Chicano, Mexican, Mexican-American, Mexicana, Mexicano, Latina, Latino, and Hispanic. Often people of Mexican descent use two or three of the above labels, depending on the social situation (e.g., "Mexican-American" in the family or "Chicana/o" at school) (Garcia 1981; Keefe and Padilla 1987). My designation of study informants as either "Chicana" and "Mexicana" represents an analytic separation that facilitates demonstrating the heterogeneity among this group.

7. Becker's classic treatise, *Human Capital*, uses the following example borrowed from Stigler, "The Economics of Information," *Journal of Political Economy* (June 1961): "Women spend less time in the labor force than men and, therefore, have less incentive to invest in market skills; tourists spend little time in any one area and have less incentive than residents of the area to invest in knowledge of specific consumption activities" (1975, 74).

8. Some institutional economists argue that "statistical discrimination" is one critical labor market dynamic that often impedes women and minorities (Arrow 1976; Phelps 1980). This perspective suggests

that prospective employers often lack detailed information about individual applicants and therefore utilize statistical averages and normative views of the relevant group(s) to which the applicant belongs in their hiring decisions (e.g., college-educated men tend to be successful and committed employees; all women are potential mothers; or women tend to exit the labor force for childbearing).

Bielby and Baron 1987 pose an important critique to the underlying rationale of statistical discrimination. They argue that utilizing perceptions of group differences between the sexes is "neither as rational nor as efficient as the economists believe" (1987, 216). That is, utilizing stereotypical notions of "men's work" and "women's work" is often costly to employers and therefore irrational. This suggests that sex segregation is imbedded in organizational policies that reflect and reinforce "belief systems that are also rather inert" (1987, 221–22).

9. This phrase was coined by Arlie R. Hochschild and quoted in Lillian B. Rubin 1983.

10. Bielby and Baron note: "Employers expect certain behaviors from women (e.g., high turnover) and therefore assign them to routine tasks and dead-end jobs. Women respond by exhibiting the very behavior employers expect, thereby reinforcing the stereotype" (1987, 221).

11. In June 1986 (the year closest to the year I interviewed the respondents where I found relevant data), 49.8 percent of all women with newborn children were in the labor force. Women demonstrated differences in this behavior: 49.7 percent of white women, 51.1 percent of black women, and 40.6 percent of Latinas with newborn children were in the labor force (U.S. Bureau of the Census 1987, 5).

12. For additional information on the methods and sample selection, I refer the reader to Segura 1986.

13. The ages of the Chicanas range from twenty-three to forty-two years. The Mexicanas reported ages from twenty-four to forty-five. The age profile indicates that most of the women were in peak childbearing years.

14. For a full discussion of the interplay between economic goals and economic status of the respondents and their employment decisions, see Segura 1989.

15. Two of the Mexicanas reported that their mothers had died while they were toddlers and, therefore, were unable to discuss their economic roles.

16. Research indicates religious involvement plays an important role in gender beliefs (Baker, Epstein, and Forth 1981; Peek and Brown 1980). Of particular interest for the present study is that involvement in fundamentalist Christian churches is positively related to adherence to traditional gender role ideology (Wilcox and Cook 1989; Wilcox 1987). Half of the Mexicanas (and all but two

Chicanas) adhered to the Roman Catholic religion; half belonged to various fundamentalist Christian churches (e.g., Assembly of God). Two Chicanas belonged to other Protestant denominations. I noticed that the women who belonged to the Assembly of God tended to both work full-time in the labor market and voice the strongest convictions of male authority in the family. During their interviews many of the women brought out the Bible and showed me the biblical passages that authorized husbands to rule the family. Catholic women also voiced traditional beliefs regarding family structure but did not invoke God.

17. In their analysis of differences in educational goals among Mexican Americans, Buriel and his associates found that, "Third-generation Mexican Americans felt less capable of fulfilling their educational objectives" (1982, 50). Similar findings were reported by Nielsen and Fernández: "We find that students whose families have been in the U.S. longer have *lower* [their emphasis] aspirations than recent immigrants" (1981, 76). In their analysis of Hispanic employment, Bean and his associates (1985) reported an unexpected finding—that English-proficient Mexican women exhibit a greater "constraining influence of fertility on their employment vis-à-vis Spanish-speaking women." They speculate that more acculturated Mexican women may have "a greater desire for children of higher quality," and therefore "be more likely to devote time to the informal socialization and education of young children." They wonder "why this should hold true for English-speaking but not Spanish-speaking women" (1985, 241).

Works Cited

Almaguer, Tomás. 1975. "Class, Race and Chicano Oppression." *Socialist Revolution* 5.

Anzaldúa, Gloria. 1987. *Borderlands, La Frontera: The New Mestiza.* San Francisco: Spinsters/Aunt Lute Book Co.

Arrow, Kenneth. 1976. "Economic Dimensions of Occupational Segregation: Comment I.*" Signs: Journal of Women in Culture and Society* 1: 233–37.

Baca, Reynaldo, and Dexter Bryan. 1985. "Mexican Women, Migration and Sex Roles." *Migration Today* 13: 14–18.

Baca Zinn, Maxine. 1979. "Chicano Family Research: Conceptual Distortions and Alternative Directions." *Journal of Ethnic Studies* 7: 59–71.

———. 1980. "Employment and Education of Mexican-American Women: The Interplay of Modernity and Ethnicity in Eight

Families." *Harvard Educational Review* 50, no. 1 (February): 47–62.

———. 1982. "Mexican-American Women in the Social Sciences." *Signs: Journal of Women in Culture and Society* 8: 259–72.

Baker, Ross K., Laurily K. Epstein, and Rodney O. Forth. 1981. "Matters of Life and Death: Social, Political and Religious Correlates of Attitudes on Abortion." *American Politics Quarterly* 9: 89–102.

Barrera, Mario. 1979. *Race and Class in the Southwest: A Theory of Racial Inequality.* North Bend, Ind.: University of Notre Dame Press.

Barrett, Michele. 1980. *Women's Oppression Today, Problems in Marxist Feminist Analysis.* London: Verso Press.

Bean, Frank D., C. Gray Swicegood, and Allan G. King. 1985. "Role Incompatibility and the Relationship between Fertility and Labor Supply Among Hispanic Women." In *Hispanics in the U.S. Economy*, ed. G. J. Borjas and M. Tienda. New York: Academic Press.

Becker, Gary S. 1975. *Human Capital*, 2d ed. Chicago: University of Chicago Press.

———. 1981. *A Treatise on the Family.* Cambridge, Mass.: Harvard University Press.

———. 1985. "Human Capital, Effort, and the Sexual Division of Labor." *Journal of Labor Economics* 3, no. 1 (1985 Supplement): S33–S58.

Beneria, Lourdes, and Martha Roldan. 1987. *The Crossroads of Class and Gender: Industrial Homework, Subcontracting, and Household Dynamics in Mexico City.* Chicago: University of Chicago Press.

Beneria, Lourdes, and Gita Sen. 1986. "Accumulation, Reproduction, and Women's Role in Economic Development: Boserup Revisited." In *Women's Work: Development and the Division of Labor by Gender*, ed. E. Leacock and H. I. Safa. South Hadley, Mass.: Bergin and Garvey Publishers.

Berg, Barbara J. 1986. *The Crisis of the Working Mother: Resolving the Conflict between Family and Work.* New York: Summit Books.

Bernard, Jessie. 1974. *The Future of Motherhood.* New York: Penguin Books.

———. 1981. "The Rise and Fall of the Good Provider Role." *American Psychologist* 36: 1–12.

Bielby, William T., and James N. Baron. 1987. "Undoing Discrimination: Job Integration and Comparable Worth." In *Ingredients for Women's Employment Policy*, ed. C. Bose and G. Spitze. New York: State University of New York Press.

Bradley, Robert H., and Bettye M. Caldwell. 1984. "The Relation of Infants' Home Environments to Achievement Test Performance in First Grade: A Follow-up Study." *Child Development* 55: 803–809.

Buriel, Raymond. 1984. "Integration with Traditional Mexican-American Culture and Sociocultural Adjustment." In *Chicano Psychology*, ed. J. Martinez, Jr., and R. H. Mendoza. New York: Academic Press.

Buriel, Raymond, Silverio Calzada, and Richard Vásquez. 1982. "The Relationship of Traditional Mexican American Culture to Adjustment and Delinquency among Three Generations of Mexican American Adolescents." *Hispanic Journal of Behavioral Sciences* 4: 41–55.

Caspi, Avshalom, and Glen H. Elder. 1988. "Emergent Family Patterns: The Intergenerational Construction of Problem Behavior and Relationships." In *Understanding Family Dynamics*, ed. R. Hinde and J. Stevenson-Hinde. New York: Oxford University Press.

Chávez, John M., and Raymond Buriel. 1986. "Reinforcing Children's Effort: A Comparison of Immigrant, Native-Born Mexican American and Euro-American Mothers." *Hispanic Journal of Behavioral Sciences*, 8: 127–42.

Chávez, Leo R. 1985. "Households, Migration and Labor Market Participation: The Adaptation of Mexicans to Life in the United States." *Urban Anthropology* 14: 301–346.

Chodorow, Nancy. 1979. *The Reproduction of Mothering*. Berkeley: University of California Press.

Clark, E. Eugene, and William Ramsey. 1990. "The Importance of Family and Network of Other Relationships in Children's Success in School." *International Journal of Sociology of the Family* 20: 237–54.

Cowan, Ruth Schwartz. 1987. "Women's Work, Housework, and History: The Historical Roots of Inequality in Work-Force Participation." In *Families and Work*, ed. N. Gerstel and H. E. Gross. Philadelphia: Temple University Press.

Dill, Bonnie Thornton, Lynn Weber Cannon, and Reeve Vanneman. 1987. "Pay Equity: An Issue of Race, Ethnicity and Sex." Washington, DC: National Commission on Pay Equity (February).

Doherty, William J., and Richard H. Needle. 1991. "Psychological Adjustment and Substance Use Among Adolescents Before and After a Parental Divorce." *Child Development* 62: 328–37.

DuBois, Ellen Carol, and Vicki L. Ruiz. 1990. "Introduction." In *Unequal Sisters: A Multicultural Reader in U.S. Women's History*, ed. E. C. DuBois and V. L. Ruiz. New York: Routledge.

Escobar, Javier I., and E. T. Randolph. 1982. "The Hispanic and Social Networks." In *Mental Health and Hispanic Americans: Clinical Perspectives*, ed. R. M. Becerra, M. Karno, and J. I. Escobar. New York: Grune and Stratton.

Fernández-Kelly, M. Patricia. 1983. "Mexican Border Industrialization, Female Labor-Force Participation, and Migration." In *Women,*

Men, and the International Division of Labor, ed. J. Nash and M. P. Fernández-Kelly. Albany: State University of New York Press.

Firestone, Shulamith. 1970. *The Dialectic of Sex.* New York: Bantam Books.

Folbre, Nancy. 1984. "The Pauperization of Motherhood: Patriarchy and Public Policy in the United States." *Review of Radical Political Economics* 16, no. 4.

Fox, Linda C. 1983. "Obedience and Rebellion: Re-Vision of Chicana Myths of Motherhood." *Women's Studies Quarterly* (winter): 20–22.

García, John A. 1981. "Yo Soy Mexicano . . . : Self-identity and Socio-demographic Correlates." *Social Science Quarterly* 62, no. 1 (March): 88–98.

Gerson, Kathleen. 1985. *Hard Choices.* Berkeley: University of California Press.

Gerstel, Naomi, and Harriet Engel Gross. 1987. "Introduction." In *Families and Work,* ed. N. Gerstel and H. E. Gross. Philadelphia: Temple University Press.

Glazer, Nona. 1984. "Servants to Capital: Unpaid Domestic Labor and Paid Work." *Review of Radical Economics* 16: 61–87.

Grossman, Allyson Sherman. 1982. "More than Half of All Children Have Working Mothers." *Special Labor Force Reports—Summaries, Monthly Labor Review* (February): 41–43.

Guendelman, Sylvia, and Auristela Pérez-Itriago. 1987. "Double Lives: The Changing Role of Women in Seasonal Migration." *Women's Studies* 13: 249–71.

Hartmann, Heidi. 1976. "Capitalism Patriarchy and Job Segregation by Sex." In *Women and the Work Place,* ed. Martha Blaxall and Barbara Reagan. Chicago: University of Chicago Press.

———. 1981. "The Family as the Locus of Gender, Class and Political Struggle: The Example of Housework." *Signs: Journal of Women in Culture and Society* 6: 366–94.

Hayghe, Howard. 1984. "Working Mothers Reach Record Number in 1984." *Monthly Labor Review* 107, no. 12 (December): 31–34.

Hochschild, Arlie, with Anne Machung. 1989. *The Second Shift: Working Parents and the Revolution at Home.* New York: Viking Penguin Books.

Hood, Jane C. 1986. "The Provider Role: Its Meaning and Measurement." *Journal of Marriage and the Family* 48 (May): 349–59.

Johnson, Miriam M. 1988. *Strong Mothers, Weak Wives.* Berkeley: University of California Press.

Kanter, Rosabeth Moss. 1977. *Men and Women of the Corporation.* New York: Basic Books.

Keefe, Susan E., and Amado M. Padilla. 1987. *Chicano Ethnicity.* Albuquerque: University of New Mexico Press.

Kranau, Edgar J., Vicki Green, and Gloria Valencia-Weber. 1982. "Acculturation and the Hispanic Woman: Attitudes toward Women, Sex-Role Attribution, Sex-Role Behavior, and Demographics." *Hispanic Journal of Behavioral Sciences* 4: 21–40.

Kuhn, Annette. 1978. "Structure of Patriarch and Capital in the Family." In *Feminism and Materialism: Women and Modes of Production*, ed. Annette Kuhn and AnnMarie Wolpe. London: Routledge & Kegan Paul.

Malveaux, Julianne, and Phyllis Wallace. 1987. "Minority Women in the Workplace." In *Women and Work: Industrial Relations Research Association Volume*, ed. K. S. Koziara, M. Moskow, and L. Dewey Tanner. Washington, DC: Bureau of National Affairs.

Melville, Margarita B. 1980. "Introduction" and "Matrescence." In *Twice a Minority: Mexican American Women*, ed. M. B. Melville. St. Louis, Mo.: C. V. Mosby Co.

Mendoza, Richard H. 1984. "Acculturation and Sociocultural Variability." In *Chicano Psychology*, ed. J. L. Mártinez, Jr., and H. Mendoza. New York: Academic Press.

Mirandé, Alfredo. 1985. *The Chicano Experience: An Alternative Perspective*. North Bend, Ind.: University of Notre Dame Press.

Mirandé, Alfredo, and Evangelina Enríquez. 1979. *La Chicana: The Mexican American Woman*. Chicago: The University of Chicago Press.

Naples, Nancy A. 1991. "A Socialist Feminist Analysis of the Family Support Act of 1988." *AFFILIA* 6: 23–38.

Nielsen, François, and Roberto M. Fernández. 1981. *Hispanic Students in American High Schools: Background Characteristics and Achievement*. Washington, DC: National Center for Education Statistics.

Ortiz, Vilma, and Rosemary Santana Cooney. 1984. "Sex-Role Attitudes and Labor Force Participation among Young Hispanic Females and Non-Hispanic White Females." *Social Science Quarterly* 65, no. 2 (June): 392–400.

Parcel, Toby L., and Elizabeth G. Menaghan. 1990. "Maternal Working Conditions and Child Verbal Facility: Studying the Intergenerational Transmission of Inequality from Mothers to Young Children." *Social Psychology Quarterly* 53: 132–47.

Parsons, Talcott, and Robert Bales. 1955. *Family, Socialization, and Interaction Processes*. New York: Free Press.

Peck, Robert F., and Rogelio Díaz-Guerrero. 1967. "Two Core-Culture Patterns and the Diffusion of Values across Their Borders." *International Journal of Psychology* 2: 272–82.

Peek, Charles W., and Sharon Brown. 1980. "Sex Prejudice among White Protestants: Like or Unlike Ethnic Prejudice?" *Social Forces* 59: 169–85.

Phelps, Edmund. 1980. "The Statistical Theory of Racism and Sexism." In *The Economics of Women and Work*, ed. A. H. Amsden. New York: St. Martin's Press.

Polachek, Solomon W. 1975. "Discontinuous Labor Force Participation and Its Effect on Women's Market Earnings." In *Sex, Discrimination, and the Division of Labor*, ed. C. Lloyd. New York: Columbia University Press.

———. 1979. "Occupational Segregation among Women: Theory, Evidence, and Prognosis." In *Women in the Labor Market*, ed. C. B. Lloyd, E. S. Andrews, and C. L. Gilroy. New York: Columbia University Press.

———. 1981. "Occupational Self-Selection: A Human Capital Approach to Sex Differences in Occupational Structure." *Review of Economics and Statistics* 63: 60–69.

Ramírez III, Manuel, and Alfredo Castañeda. 1974. *Cultural Democracy, Bicognitive Development, and Education*. New York: Academic Press.

Rothstein, Frances. 1983. "Women and Men in the Family Economy: An Analysis of the Relations Between the Sexes in Three Peasant Communities." *Anthropological Quarterly* 56:10–23.

Rubin, Lillian B. 1983. *Intimate Strangers: Men and Women Together*. New York: Harper & Row.

Ruiz, Vicki L. 1988. " 'And Miles to Go . . .': Mexican Women and Work, 1930–1985." In *Western Women: Their Land, Their Lives*, ed. L. Schlissel, V. L. Ruiz, and J. Monk. Albuquerque: University of New Mexico Press.

Sacks, Karen. 1979. *Sisters and Wives: The Past and Future of Sexual Equality*. Westport, Conn.: Greenwood Press.

Segura, Denise A. 1984. "Labor Market Stratification: The Chicana Experience." *Berkeley Journal of Sociology* 29: 57–91.

———. 1986. "Chicanas and Mexican Immigrant Women in the Labor Market: A Study of Occupational Mobility and Stratification." Ph.D. dissertation, University of California, Berkeley.

———. 1989. "The Interplay of Familism and Patriarchy on Employment among Chicana and Mexican Immigrant Women." In *The Renato Rosaldo Lecture Series Monograph 5*. Tucson: University of Arizona, Center for Mexican American Studies.

Simon, Rita J., and Jean M. Landis. 1989. "Women's and Men's Attitudes about a Woman's Place and Role." *Public Opinion Quarterly* 53: 265–76.

Smith, Dorothy E. 1987. "Women's Inequality and the Family." In *Families and Work*, ed. N. Gerstel and H. E. Gross. Philadelphia: Temple University Press.

Solórzano-Torres, Rosalia. 1987. "Female Mexican Immigrants in San Diego County." In *Women on the U.S.–Mexico Border: Responses to Change*, ed. V. L. Ruiz and S. Tiano. Boston: Allen and Unwin.

Tienda, Martha, and P. Guhleman. 1985. "The Occupational Position of Employed Hispanic Women." In *Hispanics in the U.S. Economy*, ed. G. J. Borjas and M. Tienda. New York: Academic Press.

Tilly, Louise A., and Joan W. Scott. 1978. *Women, Work, and Family*. New York: Holt, Rinehart and Winston.

U.S. Bureau of the Census. 1987. "Fertility of American Women: June 1986." *Current Population Report*, Series p-20, No. 421. Washington, DC.: United States Government Printing Office.

————. 1991. "Fertility of American Women: June 1990." *Current Population Report*, Series p-20, No. 454. Washington, DC.: United States Government Printing Office.

Walker, Lorraine O., and Mary Ann Best. 1991. "Well-Being of Mothers with Infant Children: A Preliminary Comparison of Employed Women and Homemakers." *Women and Health* 17: 71–88.

Wearing, Betsy. 1984. *The Ideology of Motherhood: A Study of Sydney Suburban Mothers*. Sydney, Australia: Allen and Unwin.

Wilcox, Clyde. 1987. "Religious Attitudes and Anti-Feminism: An Analysis of the Ohio Moral Majority." *Women and Politics* 48: 1041–51.

Wilcox, Clyde, and Elizabeth Adell Cook. 1989. "Evangelical Women and Feminism: Some Additional Evidence." *Women and Politics* 9: 27–49.

Zaretsky, Eli. 1976. *Capitalism, the Family and Personal Life*. New York: Harper Colophon Books.

Zavella, Patricia. 1991. "Reflections on Diversity among Chicanas." *Frontiers* 2: 73–85.

Zinn, Deborah K., and Rosemary C. Sarri. 1984. "Turning Back the Clock on Public Welfare." *Signs: Journal of Women in Culture and Society* 10: 355–70.

Levels of Acculturation, Marital Satisfaction, and Depression among Chicana Workers: A Psychological Perspective

Yvette G. Flores-Ortiz

Social scientists have highlighted both the sociological and cultural context of Chicana work patterns (De la Torre and Pesquera 1993; Pesquera 1984; Zavella 1984) and have noted the important contribution of cultural values, social networks, and marital support to the overall well-being of Chicana workers. The psychological correlates of work for these women, however, seem less clear.

Only in the last decade have feminist scholars systematically studied the context of work. Typically, these essays provide an analysis of the impact of women's work on their relationships (e.g., Nieva and Gutek 1982), but these studies have all but ignored Chicanas.

This essay attempts to elucidate the existing knowledge regarding the psychological impact of wage work among Chicanas and to report the findings of an empirical study of sex roles, marital satisfaction, and mental health among Mexican and Chicana workers.

The Psychology of Women and Work

Psychological health is usually determined by the absence of psychiatric symptomatology (e.g., symptoms of depression, anxiety, psychosomatic concerns) and the presence of socially determined criteria, in particular, conformity to traditional expectations of behavior. Thus, the psychological well-being of women is determined on the basis of their ability to perform socially expected and mandated roles. In traditional psychiatric literature, an emotionally healthy woman is one who conforms to stereotypic depictions of femininity (Broverman et al. 1972) and who prioritizes family roles above individual needs. In the last two decades, a woman's sense of well-being often has been judged on the basis of her ability to balance career, family, and individual obligations.

Thus, the extent to which a woman is viewed as psychologically healthy often depends upon her ability to manage the stress experienced in fulfilling multiple role obligations. In general, the psychological literature considers a woman "psychologically fit" if the individual has high regard for herself and accepts herself in terms of her job, her marital status, and her role as mother. Health data would suggest that women pay a high price for this balancing act, given their increasing rates of heart disease, hypertension, stroke, and substance abuse, all perceived correlates of stress.

In general, the psychology of women and work has been studied from the perspective that wage work forms an added dimension to women's fundamental roles in the family. Research has therefore focused on the stress experienced by women in their multiple roles. The majority of psychological studies on women and work have operationalized emotional or psychological well-being on the basis of stress indicators (Cartwright 1978; Ducker 1983, 1987) and have relied on professional Euro-American samples. Little is known about the level of stress experienced by blue-collar and lower-level white-collar workers, who invariably face less desirable working conditions and less financial security.

Few studies have been conducted among Chicana professionals. However, Valtierra's (1989) investigation of Latina physicians found high levels of stress, particularly related to role fragmentation or role strain (the experience of having two or more conflicting claims on time and energy). For these women, however, social support, particularly the support offered by family, served to alleviate the stress inherent in the medical profession and the stress of role fragmentation. Interestingly, the women in Valtierra's study adhered to traditional cultural values of *familismo* but had postponed certain roles in order to achieve their educational aspirations. Of the fifty-two Latina physicians in the study, twenty-nine were married, three divorced, and eighteen never married. Thirty-four women had no children; of the eighteen women with children, thirteen had children under five years of age. Valtierra does not specify whether marital or parenting status was related to role fragmentation. However, the data do indicate that support from family did alleviate the stress of role fragmentation.

Anthropologist Patricia Zavella (1984) also found social support as a key variable for Chicana cannery workers. Work friends were sources of advice and emotional support, particularly for marital and role conflicts (e.g., how much husbands should help in the home). Zavella's sample reported work friends as the central persons with whom they could talk, especially concerning issues of role strain.

While psychological studies of women and work hypothesize a relationship between role strain and emotional distress, few studies have analyzed this relationship empirically or with non-Anglo samples. Moreover, scholars generally agree that for Chicanas the major sources of stress will result from difficulties balancing familistic values, economic necessities, or individual desires to work or pursue a career (Gibsen 1983; Valtierra 1989).

A few sociological studies (e.g., Ybarra 1977) have suggested that Chicanas increasingly participate in egalitarian marital arrangements. The extent to which this finding can be generalized across diverse economic groups of Chicanos remains open to question. Furthermore, the impact of egalitarianism on work satisfaction has not been assessed. Moreover, the extent to which sex-role practices, marital satisfaction, and work status have an impact on Chicana mental health has not been studied to any extent. Although family pressures, traditional sex role expectations, and lack of economic opportunity often are cited as correlates of depression among Chicanas (Gibson 1983; Roberts and Roberts 1982), the degree to which these factors affect working women remains an empirical question.

Scholars have often cited the level of acculturation as influencing role strain and marital satisfaction among Chicanas. While there has been much debate in the literature regarding the conceptual and cultural accuracy of prevailing acculturation models (see Keefe and Padilla, 1987), researchers continue to suggest that level of acculturation will determine the type of family and marital arrangements Chicanas will form. Furthermore, level of acculturation often is used as a predictor of both degree and quality of marital satisfaction, work satisfaction, and mental health (Castro 1977; Griffith 1983; Roberts and Roberts 1982; Szapocznick et al. 1980). These studies typically conclude that more acculturated Chicanas and Latinas, that is, those less familistic and less attached to traditional sex-role expectations, experience greater job satisfaction and less anxiety. Often, however, these women report greater marital difficulty, particularly if their spouses are less acculturated.

This study proposes to examine the relationships among level of acculturation, marital satisfaction, and psychological distress in a sample of Chicana and Mexican workers and thereby examine two interrelated hypotheses: (1) that increased acculturation would correlate with a preference for more egalitarian household and marital arrangements; and (2) that higher acculturation would also correlate with increased symptoms of depression, somatization, and anxiety (indicators of stress). The study also proposes to examine whether wage earners experienced greater stress than women who did not work outside the home. Finally, the study aims to elucidate the relationship of work, marital satisfaction, and levels of stress experienced by the informants.

The study reported here is part of a larger multivariate investigation of forty Chicano and Mexican families conducted in northern California (Flores-Ortiz 1982). The sample consisted of twenty-eight two-parent households and twelve single-parent families. The larger study examines the impact of acculturation on the structure and functioning of Mexican and Chicano families with a focus on the relationship of marital satisfaction, employment, and psychiatric symptomatology among the couples in the study. The study explored the families' coping and adaptation after migration and the influence of culture change on the balance of power between spouses and on childrearing methods.

Methodology

Forty families were selected and interviewed. Whenever possible, I administered to both spouses a number of research instruments including: (1) Values Acculturation Scale (Flores-Ortiz, Coyne, and Mesa 1978); (2) Hopkins Symptom Checklist (Derogatis et al. 1974); (3) Social Environment Questionnaire and Social Supports Questionnaire (Cohen and Lazarus 1977 a,b); and (4) Who Does What and Who Decides

What scales (Cowan et al. 1978). All instruments were translated and backtranslated and presented in bilingual format. In addition to the questionnaires, each respondent was interviewed using a semistructured guide to elaborate on specific themes (e.g., views on sex roles, attitudes about work, and levels of stress).

Sample Characteristics. The sample consisted of thirty-seven women ranging in age from eighteen to fifty-eight years, with a mean age of 36.4. Twenty (54.1 percent) of the women were married, six (16.2 percent) were living with a male partner, five (13.5 percent) were divorced, three (8.1 percent) were widowed, and three (8.1 percent) separated from their spouses at the time of the study.

Twenty-six of the women were born in Mexico but had lived in the United States for at least ten years. Ten were United States–born, primarily second generation. The sample consisted primarily of blue-collar (31.4 percent) informants. Nineteen (53.8 percent) of the women engaged in full-time work, two were students (5.6 percent), and fifteen worked in seasonal agricultural labor (e.g., cannery and packing work). Interestingly, most of the women described themselves primarily as homemakers.

Results. The hypotheses of the study were tested by examining the interrelationship of family characteristics and level of acculturation (predictive variables) with level of marital satisfaction and stress (outcome variables). Interview data serve to elucidate and highlight the quantitative data obtained.

Predictive Variables

Level of Acculturation. Acculturation was measured on the basis of generation, religion, socioeconomic status (SES), cultural participation, and ethnic loyalty (Keefe and Padilla 1989). On the basis of religion, generation, and SES, the women in this sample appeared low in acculturation. Seventy-five percent ($n = 28$) were Catholic, two Jewish, two described themselves as agnostics, and the remaining five were Protestant. Twenty-seven respondents (73 percent) were immigrants, four (10 percent) were second generation, five (13.5 percent) third generation, and one respondent was a sixth-generation Californian.

As Table 1 indicates, this sample was predominantly blue collar and low in income. Despite the relatively high educational attainment of the women (43.3 percent had finished high school and 24.3 percent had some college education), only four could be described as holding lower-level white-collar jobs (e.g., secretary, clerk in a law office, sales representative). One of the professional women was a social worker, the other a junior college instructor.

Table 1

Socioeconomic Indicators

Occupation	n	%	Income	n	%	Education	n	%
Blue Collar	11	31.4	$0–5,000	14	53.8	Elementary	10	27.0
White Collar	4	11.4	$5–10,000	11	42.3	Secondary	16	42.3
Professional	2	5.7	$10–15,000	1	3.8	College	7	18.9
Domestic	1	2.9				Post-Graduate	2	5.4
Homemaker	13	27.1				Vocational	1	2.7
Unemployed	3	8.6				None	1	2.7

A Spanish-dominant sample, most of the respondents spoke Spanish as children (75.7 percent, $n = 28$) and continued to speak it in their present homes (48.6 percent, $n = 18$), socially with friends (59. 5 percent, $n = 22$), with employers (34.6 percent, $n = 9$), and in their family relationships (72.7 percent, $n = 24$ with their children; $n = 21$, 75 percent with their spouse). Twelve of the women considered themselves bilingual but preferred to speak Spanish. Twenty-four of the women chose to be interviewed in Spanish. Such preference for Spanish appears consonant with a lower level of acculturation.

The women in the sample had high rates of Mexican cultural participation, as demonstrated by their practice of cultural rituals such as baptism ($n = 33$, 89.2 percent), *quinceañeras* ($n = 20$, 54.1 percent), and *compadrazgo* ($n = 32$, 94.1 percent). Furthermore, the sample was primarily Mexican in cultural orientation; 49.6 percent ($n = 18$) self-identified as Mexican. Only five respondents self-identified as Chicanas (13.9 percent), while only two respondents preferred the label "Mexican American" (5.6 percent).

To address the limitations of acculturation research that excludes a measurement of cultural values, the women's ethnic loyalty (or value system) was measured by the Flores-Ortiz et al. (1978) Acculturation Scale. The scale measures sex-role views, familism, educational attitudes, and identification with

Chicano cultural and political values. As Table 2 shows, the women adhered to a traditional view of familism and philosophy of life; that is, views that reflect Mexican cultural ideals. Moreover, views on sex roles were characteristic of a transition toward preference for more egalitarian arrangements. In particular, the women highly endorsed items that placed a great value on education; 93.7 percent of the women agreed that "education is the key to success," and 89 percent agreed that "a college education is necessary for finding a good-paying job." In effect, among the immigrant women, a major impetus for the family's migration to the United States had been a desire to afford their children a better education.

Relationship among Acculturation Variables. An analysis of the relationship among the various acculturation factors found a significant negative relationship between socioeconomic indicators and ethnic loyalty, so that women who earned more money, had more education, and could be described as white collar or professional reflected less traditional values, particularly with regard to gender roles.

María, a thirty-two-year-old divorced college instructor with three children (two daughters and a son), helps illustrate this finding:

Table 2

Ethnic Loyalty (Value Dimension of Acculturation)

Item	% Agreement (Traditional)	Scale
Religion is essential in life	83.8	World View
There is something wrong with a person who lacks religious feelings	64.9	
Abortion is a sin	64.9	
Death is the begining of eternal life	75.7	
Life is a long chain of sacrifice	65.7	
Children are the essence of the family	94.6	Familism
A family must be kept together whatever the cost	81.1	
For poor people too many children are a burden	83.8	
Children should provide for their parents when the parents get old	89.2	
Older children should help in the raising of their younger siblings	86.1	

Item	% Agreement (Traditional)	Scale
It is good to have children because they are cute and lots of fun	64.9	Child rearing
A good child will be obedient and helpful to his or her parents	97.2	
To be a godparent means to have responsibility for the child's entire life	81.1	
A man's character is shown by his authority in the home	70.3	Sex Role
A woman's highest achievement is motherhood	73.0	
Education is the key to success	97.3	Educational Achievement
It is good for parents to pressure their children to get as much education as possible	86.5	
A college degree is necessary for finding a good-paying job	89.2	
Anglo teachers do not understand the problems of Chicano students	64.9	
It is not lack of skills and abilities that keeps many Chicanos from getting a job, it's discrimination against them	70.3	
Chicanos and Latinos should be taught their language and culture at school as well as at home	94.6	
Anglos should try to become more educated and learn about Chicanos and Latinos	81.1	
A Chicano is a person with a certain political ideology	74.3	

Yo no creo que la mujer debe depender de un hombre o servirle como esclava. En la pareja debe haber igualdad. Es muy difícil ser buena chicana, buena madre, y buena esposa. Yo me conformo con ser buena proveedora para mis hijos, darles un buen ejemplo de moral, y enseñarlos a no depender de un hombre para subsistir.

[I don't think a woman should depend on a man or serve him like a slave. There should be equality between the spouses. It's very difficult to be a Chicana, a good mother, and good wife. I settle for being a good provider for my children, being a good moral role model, and teaching them to not depend on a man for a living.]

Elena, a forty-year-old married secretary, added:

> Mi esposo sabe que para mantener el hogar se requieren dos personas. Yo trabajo fuera de casa todo el día, sigo siendo ama de casa, pero él me ayuda. A veces cocina, a veces lava la ropa. Lo importante es que él respete mis derechos humanos y no me trate como burra. Yo eso se lo implanté desde la noche de bodas.

> [My husband knows that to maintain our home, two people are necessary. I work outside the house all day and continue to be a housewife, but he helps me. Sometimes he cooks and sometimes does the laundry. What's important is that he respects my rights and doesn't treat me like a burro. I made that clear since our wedding night.]

However, Julia, a thirty-seven-year-old cannery worker, disagreed:

> El hombre se casa para tener quien lo atienda, lo cuide y lo mime. Si quisiera lavarse su propia ropa, cocinarse y plancharse, se quedaría soltero. Aunque yo trabajo duro mi responsabilidad principal sigue siendo el hogar. Pues para eso me casé.

> [A man marries to have someone to take care of him and to spoil him. If he wanted to wash his own clothes, cook for himelf, and iron, he'd remain a bachelor. Although I work hard, my main responsibility remains the house. That's why I got married.]

Thus, for these women, white-collar and professional work apears to have influenced their gender role views away from a traditional perception, as described by Julia, and toward a preference for a partnership. Similarly, religious beliefs among the informants were negatively correlated with awareness of and participation in Mexican cultural rituals (baptism, quinceañeras), so that less-religious women were higher in Mexican cultural awareness. While there was no statistically significant difference in the religious identification of Mexican versus Chicana women, Chicanas did appear to participate more in "Mexican" cultural rituals that have a religious basis (Feast of Our Lady of Guadalupe, compadrazgo) than did Mexican self-identified women. With regard to religious practices in general, however, Mexican women appeared to be more involved with church activities. This suggests that for Mexican women religious beliefs may in fact supercede cultural values. It also may be that for Chicanas a sense of connection to Mexican culture is manifested through religiously based cultural rituals and not through religiosity per se. Moreover, there was a positive correlation between religion and ethnic loyalty, indicating that for these women religion and cultural values were deeply intertwined, so that Catholics were less acculturated than non-Catholics.

Generational Differences. A comparison of first- and second-generation women found that immigrant women attained higher education levels and income than second-generation women, suggesting a drop in social status between first and second generation, because the women did not differ in terms of socioeconomic *background*; immigrant women who worked simply earned more than second-generation women who worked, irrespective of job category. Similarly, first-generation women scored higher in cultural awareness than United States–born respondents, paralleling the drop in cultural knowledge found by Keefe and Padilla among second-generation Chicanos.

Family Characteristics. The women's family characteristics are determined by their familism (as measured by the Acculturation Scale), family structure, and familial integration. The latter factor is based on the degree of interdependence with kin, contact, and mutual aid (as measured by the Social Supports Questionnaire). While the sample scored high in familism, a trend toward less traditional values appeared evident. For example, 37 percent of the women disagreed with the statement that "a woman should live with her parents until she gets married," and 40.5 percent disagreed that "one should not question the word of an adult." Married women reported that if they could relive their lives, they would postpone marriage until they had obtained more schooling and a better job "and had lived a little more." Moreover, 94.6 percent of the women agreed that "children are the essence of the family," and 83.8 percent agreed that "children give women an identity within the family." Thus, while views on adult relationships may have changed for this sample, the meaning and value of children remained very traditional.

Half of the women in the sample grew up in nuclear households, the rest in extended families. Moreover, regardless of structure, the households were large, averaging seven children.

The extended families often included at least one grandparent and several unmarried aunts. Most of the women, however, currently lived in nuclear households. Most of the immigrant women had migrated with their spouses from Mexico, leaving their own families behind. As a result, most of these women described having few family-of-origin resources. As a result, many of the women scored low in familial integration. That is, their responses indicated that they did not rely on their own families for assistance and had little contact with them. This was due to the geographic separation and not to estrangement. This finding highlights the problems inherent in using instruments not standardized on immigrant populations to measure kinship patterns, because the data would suggest that the women do not have family resources when in fact the resources exist but are diminished by the migration.

Mutual aid patterns, another variable of familial integration, indicated that most of the women exchanged aid with their mothers and siblings. Similarly, the women reported having little contact with members of the extended kin, with the exception of compadres. Most of the frequent contact was with children not living at home (63.9 percent reported seeing them daily). Despite the absence of extended family and low levels of familial integration, the women contacted close relatives daily by phone. None of the women felt isolated or lonely. Women who had daughters reported relying on them for comfort, emotional support, and often friendship. They engaged in moderate sharing of activities with close family, in particular going out to dinner and attending parties or baptisms. None of the married women reported going out alone with their husbands. Many felt that such practices are not central to their culture nor predictive of a good marriage. In fact, many of the women found that question to be particularly strange. Unmarried women, however, described an ideal of a more balanced couple relationship wherein parental and marital roles would be more independent. Unmarried women indicated they would prefer to marry a man who would be their equal and who would value them as individuals, not only as wives or mothers. None of the married Chicanas or Mexicanas indicated those as values in their marriages.

In summary, the women in this sample appeared moderately integrated with kin, particularly with close nuclear relatives and compadres. While there seemed to be no difference in the level of familism among the women, as measured by the scales, in the course of the interview unmarried women did describe significantly different ideals for marriage than did the married women.

Jane, a twenty-eight-year-old single college student who identified as Chicana, stated:

> I want a different type of marriage than my mother had. She sacrificed for us kids, waited on Dad as though he was disabled, and never complained. But she was always suffering from nerves. I want a man who will respect and support me emotionally; I can take care of me financially. My mother says respect from a man is shown by not cheating. I say respect is belief in the woman's sense of worth. I want a partner, not a father, not a boss, not a master.

The women in the sample who came from close-knit families valued family contact and family activities and relied on family members for financial, social, and emotional assistance. They espoused values of familism and actively tried to instill these values in their children. However, *generational differences* began to emerge when first- and second-generation informants were compared on these variables. Specifically, immigrant women relied to a greater extent on family for all types of aid, while second- generation women were more likely to utilize social and friendship networks for support. This finding parallels Zavella's (1984) data with cannery workers. While both groups of women scored high in familism, second-generation women relied less on their families for support, even though they valued such mutual aid in theory. In summary, the women in the sample differed in terms of demographic variables, with immigrant women having attained higher socioeconomic status than second-generation Chicanas. Overall the sample of women appeared low in acculturation, highly familistic, and moderately integrated with kin. There were no differences between the full-time workers and the part-time workers in terms of predictive variables. However, single women described more egalitarian marital ideals than did married women. Despite high adherence to a traditional view of family relationships, the women evidenced a shift toward a preference for more egalitarian sex roles.

Outcome Variables

This study examined the relationship of acculturation and family characteristics to the degree of intergenerational conflicts, sex-role division, marital satisfaction, and psychiatric symptomatology among Mexicans and Chicanas.

Intergenerational Conflicts. The women reported experiencing a moderate degree of conflict with their children, particularly in the areas of friends of children (n = 20, 54.1 percent), use of money by the children (n = 19, 51.4 percent), and discipline (n = 23, 65.7 percent). Similarly, the women indicated having had recent difficulties with the children's conduct (n = 17, 53.1 percent) and 66.7 percent of the sample found their children difficult to get along with. This finding was stronger for women with adolescent children. A number of respondents expressed worry over their children's work and marital situations and over their children's preference for speaking English. However, the majority of the women expressed satisfaction with their children (n = 32, 88.8 percent) despite the stated difficulties. None of the women expressed dissatisfaction with the maternal role.

Sex-Role Division. An examination of women's actual roles (as measured by the Cowans' scale) indicated a clear division of chores along gender lines. For example, women appeared primarily responsible for planning and preparing meals, house cleaning, laundry, and writing letters and making calls to friends and family, while the men took care of cars and home repairs, took out the garbage, paid the bills, and were primarily responsible for providing income for the family. However, they were not dissatisfied with the arrangement, as evident in the congruence between ideal and actual task performance, because the women received help with these chores from their daughters. Thus, despite values reflecting a desire for more egalitarian sex roles, the women appeared content with the division of roles within the home. The study did not assess, regrettably, how content the daughters felt with their responsibilities in the home. A number of respondents, however, volunteered that it was not chore division per se that dissatisfied them; rather than assistance with household tasks, the women desired greater respect from their spouses.

In terms of decision-making, a pattern of shared responsibility emerged. Over 50 percent of the women indicated that they shared decisions with their spouses on a number of areas (see Table 4). Most notably, however, women reported that men had more influence in decisions concerning initiation and frequency of lovemaking, religious practices in the home, and the teaching of cultural traditions to the children. Of particular interest is the reported *lack of differences* in the decision of how much time each partner should work outside the home. This finding would suggest that such decisions are jointly made, even though in the interviews the women often confided that they had gone to work without their husband's knowledge and had only informed them after several paychecks had been collected and saved.

Despite the objective evidence that both partners shared in the decision making, only 29.9 percent of the women felt that both spouses had equal influence in decision making. This finding suggests that even though actual decisions often are shared, women felt the man had more influence. Many women stated that this perceived lack of influence contributed to feelings of not being respected in their marriages. Elena, a forty-seven-year-old married Mexican woman, stated:

> I know my husband loves me; he buys me things; he honors our vows. Pero a veces siento que no valoriza lo que opino [but sometimes I feel he does not value my opinion]. If he asked me what I thought about the car or his job, I would feel more appreciated, más respetada, you know.

Marital Satisfaction. While 85.7 percent of the women (*n* = 24) reported having had marital difficulties at some time, only a few areas of high conflict and problem frequency appeared. Interestingly, only 20 percent of the men reported difficulties with their spouses. The greatest areas of conflict concerned work, money, and children. Eighteen of the respondents (64.3 percent) reported conflicts with their husbands because they viewed the wife as too overinvolved with her work. Thus, even though the women reported equal decision making on whether or not they should work outside the home, a large number of them experience conflict with their spouses regarding the wives' ability to balance work and home obligations. Several of the women complained that while husbands "let them work," they would become upset if dinner was late or their clothing not ironed. Sofia describes such conflicts:

Manuel me dice que está bien que yo trabaje. Pero a veces salgo muy cansada y compro comida ya preparada para la cena, él no me dice nada pero luego anda con cara larga y se pone a hablar de lo bien que cocinaba su madre.

[Manuel says that it's all right for me to work. But sometimes when I'm very tired after work, I buy fast food for dinner. He doesn't say anything, but then he walks around with a long face and talks about what a good cook his mother was.]

Table 3

Issues Over Which Marital Difficulties Arose

Problem	Number (percent) women reporting			
	Has Had Problem		*Never Had Problem*	
Work	18	(64.3)	10	(35.7)
Money	20	(74.1)	7	(25.9)
Children	16	(61.5)	10	(38.5)
Responsibility over child rearing	14	(51.9)	13	(48.1)
In-Laws	11	(39.3)	17	(60.7)
Religion	8	(44.4)	10	(55.6)
Alcohol	8	(28.6)	20	(71.4)
Drugs	4	(15.4)	22	(84.6)
Friends	11	(37.9)	18	(62.1)
Infidelity	5	(17.2)	24	(82.8)
Coming home late	6	(20.7)	23	(79.3)
Housekeeping	11	(40.7)	16	(59.3)

Despite the difficulties, however, 83.9 percent of the women described their marriages as happy. For those respondents not in a relationship, 54.5 percent reported dating frequently, but few (9.1 percent) indicated they wanted to remarry.

Symptomotology. By and large this sample appeared emotionally healthy, as compared to the general population. However, there was some indication of anxiety, somatization, and depression among the women (see Table 5). Specifically, most of the women scored in the significant range for feelings of depression, anxiety, and physical manifestation of stress.

Relationship among Variables. A Pearson Correlational Analysis was conducted to assess the relationship of the various outcome variables (see Table 4). Most notably, sex-role positively correlated with decision-making patterns and couple problems and negatively correlated with couple activities, so that women in *traditional sex-role arrangements* tended to have less egalitarian decision-making patterns and fewer couple problems and engaged more in couple activities. In sum, women who described traditional marriages experienced greater marital harmony and cohesion than women in transition towards greater equality in sex roles. Women experiencing *marital difficulties* tended to have more egalitarian sex roles as well as decision-making patterns and fewer couple activities than women low in marital difficulties. Thus for women, the major difficulties were in the marital arena.

Table 4

Intercorrelation Outcome Variables

Scale	Who Does	Who Decides	Marital Problems	Couple Activities
Who Does	1.00	0.62***	0.61	-.35*
Who Decides		1.00	0.36	-.75***
Marital Problems			1.00	-.57***
Couple Activities				1.00***

*p<.05
***p<.001

An analysis of the relationship of marital satisfaction, marital conflict, and symptomatology found that female symptomatology had a negative correlation with couple problems. Thus women experiencing psychiatric symptoms did not express having marital difficulties. It seems that women did not make a connection between their depression and perceived marital conflict. The findings do indicate that women in traditional marriages experienced greater symptomatology than women with greater egalitarian relationships. Women who indicated having fewer couple problems had more symptoms than women who reported greater marital difficulties. Perhaps when the women did not confront the marital problems directly, the conflict was expressed through somatic concerns, anxiety, or depression. Several of the women indicated that they suffered from migraines, backaches, and gastrointestinal distress, which they associated with job stress. In the course of the interview they related conflicts with their husbands as affecting job stress but did not make a connection between their physical symptoms and the marital conflict, much of which appeared related to the women's involvement in wage labor. Dolores expressed it this way:

> I work in order to give the family a better life. My work is hard [cannery work] and has no security. Eso me preocupa, I think por eso tengo tantas migraines. Y luego Carlos me hace pleito porque la casa anda descuidada y que los niños no lucen limpios. Pos qué se va a hacer, así es la vida de mujer casada [laughter].

> [That worries me, I think that's why I have so many migraines. And then Carlos fights with me because the house is not clean and the kids are not well kempt. Well, what can one do, such is the life of a married woman.]

An assessment of the interrelationship of female symptomatology (see Table 5) indicated all three scales as highly interrelated so that women experiencing psychological distress did so through psychosomatic concerns, anxiety, and depression.

Table 5

Intercorrelation Symptomatology

Scale	Somatization	Anxiety	Depression
Somatization*	1.000	0.524	0.644
		(36)	(36)
		$p=.001$	$p=.001$
Anxiety		1.000	0.826
			(36)
Depression			1.000

*Physical manifestation of stress or psychological and relational difficulties.

Generational Differences. A comparison of first- and second-generation women in terms of outcome variables found that first-generation women evidenced a higher degree of somatization than second-generation women. No differences were evident between first- and second-generation women in terms of marital satisfaction. It must be noted that the restricted range of acculturation in the sample, as measured by generation and other indices, may have attenuated potential differences between variables and among the women.

Hypotheses

This study proposed that acculturation and changes in family characteristics would have an impact on sex roles, marital satisfaction, and symptomatology among the women. The findings suggest that level of acculturation was primarily reflected in changes in familism and ethnic identification. Furthermore, the study indicates that acculturation may bring about changes in the meaning of the family, although not necessarily in the structure of the family itself. In particular, women with greater academic attainment continue to value a strong, interdependent family but voiced a strong preference for egalitarian marital partnership, rather than the traditional marriages they observed in their families of origin. Thus, while the informants appeared low in socioeconomic indicators of acculturation and highly familistic, a move toward preference for egalitarian marital arrangements and greater political consciousness was evident.

An analysis of variance of outcome variables by acculturation found that differences in ethnic loyalty (as measured by the value dimension) most affected communication problems with spouses so that a move away from traditional gender role values was related to marital conflict. An examination of the relationship of the value dimension of acculturation with outcome variables found a negative correlation with intergenerational conflicts, so that for women changes in value orientation resulted in greater consonance with their children's level of acculturation and thus fewer problems. Increased acculturation per se, however, did not result in increased marital problems, but a preference for more egalitarian marital arrangements did correlate with marital distress. Furthermore, increased value changes away from a traditional sex-role orientation were associated with increased somatization and anxiety, particularly for women who worked outside the home.

The study partially supported the hypotheses that increased acculturation would be reflected in a preference for more egalitarian family and marital arrangements. Furthermore, the findings suggest that, for this sample at least, moves away from traditional sex roles resulted in marital difficulty and increased psychological distress, often expressed through somatization, anxiety, and depression. Of note is the fact that the focus of marital discord was the husband's dissatisfaction with the wife's work involvement.

These findings suggest that Chicanas continue to face the triple bind of economic inequality, racism, and sexism. The women in the sample who preferred or wished for more egalitarian sex roles in their marital relationships also experienced conflicts with their spouses. The conflict often centered on the wife's involvement with wage labor and the extent to which her work outside the home detracted from her role as a housekeeper. While the husbands seemed not to complain about this directly, the women "sensed" or "read" their displeasure, as evident is Dolores's comments.

On the other hand, women who described their marital arrangements as traditional and claimed to prefer these were more symptomatic, perhaps because gender conflicts were not overtly expressed. Many traditionally raised women do not feel entitled to complain about their lot in life and appear only to have physical symptoms as an outlet for their distress. Petra offers an example:

> Yo soy muy feliz en mi matrimonio. Mi esposo es bueno. El no toma ni bota el dinero. No me ayuda con el quehacer, él dice que el oficio es cosa de las viejas. Sólo cuando yo ando mala de la espalda, o cuando se me afectan los nervios se pone él un poco cariñoso y hasta a veces me ayuda.

> [I am very happy in my marriage. My husband is a good man. He doesn't drink or waste money. He doesn't help me with housework, he says that's woman's work. Only when I have problems with my back or my nerves, he becomes affectionate, sometimes he even helps me.]

Discussion

This study elucidates the complex interrelationship of acculturation, family structure, marital satisfaction, and psychiatric symptomatology in a sample of Mexican and Chicana women. The degree to which the work role had an impact on the marital relationship emerged as a central focus of the investigation. The study found support for the relationship of acculturation to marital satisfaction, work satisfaction, and gender roles. Specifically, while the sample was not highly acculturated in terms of sociological indicators (economic status, employment, income), some cultural values appeared in flux. The informants endorsed highly familistic values but preferred egalitarianism in their marriages. In addition, the informants appeared knowledgeable and supportive of Chicano political issues and educational struggles.

The participants in the study are blue-collar workers, low in acculturation, who describe their marriages as happy and traditional. The findings indicate, however, that a shift away from a traditional value orientation with regard to gender roles is associated with marital distress. In particular, the husband's perception that his wife's work demands made her unavailable emerged as a central theme of marital discord. Furthermore, the relationship of symptomatology (anxiety, somatization, and depression) to marital satisfaction is intriguing. Women who described themselves as egalitarian in terms of gender values faced more marital problems but evidenced few symptoms of psychological distress. In contrast, women in traditional marital arrangements, and who claimed to favor these, experienced fewer marital difficulties but demonstrated greater psychological distress. While this study cannot unequivocally propose a causal relationship between traditional gender values and psychiatric distress for women who work, the data support the importance of assessing the psychological realm of Chicana workers. The extent to which role fragmentation, as reported in the literature, is related more to domestic conflicts than to job difficulties per se needs further investigation. Furthermore, it is important to elucidate whether cultural loyalty may make it difficult for women to complain about their husband's attitudes toward their work, particularly if "he is a good man." Several women stated that they were chastised by female relatives for working outside the home *and* enjoying it. Many of the relatives feared that the man might be alienated if he found out that the wife enjoyed her work. (The message seemed clear: If the work is for the benefit of the family, great; if it also brought pleasure to the women, that was problematic.) To what extent the perceived lack of support the women experienced from other women affects their mental health needs further study.

The small sample size and homogeneity of the sample precludes vast generalizations. Moreover, this study points out the importance of assessing the value dimension of acculturation, and the possible relationship of value change, work status, marital conflict, and psychological distress for female workers. The most significant finding, perhaps, is the fact that even women who described egalitarian relationships in their marriages did not perceive themselves to have equal influence. Furthermore, the majority of the married women described a subjective experience of *disrespect* in their family relationships. While job status historically accords respect to men, the experience of wage labor, including professional employment, did not earn the women respect from their partners. The message from extended family was more complex. Often, white-collar workers and professional women privately received support from other women, but publicly they were chastised if they did not conform to the cultural ideal of the good wife and mother. One graduate student in psychology reported that her father told her, "tal vez después del doctorado puedas aprender algo útil, como coser" [maybe after your doctorate you can learn something useful, like sewing], even though at family gatherings he often expressed great pride in her accomplishments.

Clearly we have a long way to go before we can truly understand the psychological context of Mexicanas/Chicanas and the influence of their roles as workers in their overall well being. It appears, however, that before Mexicanas/Chicanas can attain economic parity and satisfaction in the world of work, their fundamental integrity as individuals must be respected within the institution that they continue to value and in the roles that they continue to fulfill.

Works Cited

Broverman, I. K., S. R. Vogel, D. M. Broverman, F. E. Clarkson, and P. S. Rosenkrantz. 1972. "Sex Role Stereotypes: A Current Appraisal." *Journal of Social Issues* 28, no. 2: 59–78.

Cartwright, C. 1978. "Occupational Stress in Women Physicians." In *Stress in Health Professionals*, ed. R. Payne and J. Firth Cozens. New York: Wiley.

Castro, F. G. 1977. "Level of Acculturation and Related Considerations in Psychotherapy with the Spanish-Surnamed, Spanish-Speaking Client." *Occasional Paper No. 3*. Los Angeles: Spanish-Speaking Mental Health Research Center, UCLA.

Cohen, J. B., and R. Lazarus. 1977. "Social Environment Questionnaire." University of California, Berkeley. Photocopy.

———. 1977. "Social Support Questionnaire." University of California, Berkeley. Photocopy.

Cowan, C. P., P. A. Cowan, L. Coie, and J. Coie. 1978. "Becoming a Family: The Impact of First Child's Birth on the Couple's Relationship." In *The First Child and Family Formation*, ed. W. B. Miller and L. F. Newman. Chapel Hill, NC: Carolina Population Center.

De La Torre, A., and B. Pesquera. 1993. *Building with Our Hands: Directions in Chicana Scholarship.* Berkeley: University of California Press.

Derogatis, L. R., R. S. Lipman, K. Rickels, E. H. Uhlenhuth, and L. Covi. 1974. "The Hopkins Symptom Checklist (HSCL)." *Behavioral Science* 19: 7–15.

Ducker, D. 1983. "The Career Patterns of Mid-life Women and Men Physicians." Paper presented at the meeting of the American Psychological Association, Montreal, Canada.

———. 1987. "Role Conflict for Women Physicians." In *Heal Thyself: The Health of the Health Professional*, ed. D. D. Scott and J. E. Hawks. New York: Brunner Mazel.

Flores-Ortiz, Y. 1982. "The Impact of Acculturation on the Chicano Family." Ph.D. dissertation, University of California, Berkeley.

Flores-Ortiz, Y., J. C. Coyne, and A. V. Mesa. 1978. *A Measure of Acculturation for Raza.* University of California, Berkeley. Photocopy.

Gibson, G. 1983. "Hispanic Women: Stress and Mental Health Issues." In *Women Changing Therapy*, ed. J. H. Robbins and R. J. Siegel. New York: Haworth Press.

Griffith, J. 1983. "Relationship Between Acculturation and Psychological Impairment in Adult Mexican Americans." *Hispanic Journal of Behavioral Sciences* 4: 431–59.

Keefe, S. E., and A. Padilla. 1987. *Chicano Ethnicity.* Albuquerque: University of New Mexico Press.

Nieva, F. V., and B. A. Gutek. 1982. *Women and Work: A Psychological Perspective.* New York: Praeger.

Pesquera, B. M. 1984. " 'Having a Job Gives you Some Sort of Power:' Reflections of a Chicana Working Woman." *Feminist Issues* (fall).

Roberts, R., and C. R. Roberts. 1982. "Marriage, Work and Depressive Symptoms Among Mexican Americans." *Hispanic Journal of Behavioral Sciences* 2:199–222.

Szapocznik, J., M. A. Scopetta, M. A. Aranalde, and W. Kurtines. 1980. "Cuban Value Structure: Treatment Implications." *Journal of Consulting and Clinical Psychology* 46: 961–70.

Valtierra, M. 1989. "Acculturation, Social Support and Reported Stress of Latina Physicians." Ph.D. dissertation, California School of Professional Psychology, Berkeley/Alameda.

Ybarra, L. 1977. "Conjugal Role Relationships in the Chicano Family."
Ph.D. dissertation, University of California, Berkeley.
Zavella, P. 1984. "Work Related Networks and Household Organization
among Chicana Cannery Workers." *Working Paper Series*, No. 2.
Palo Alto, Calif.: Stanford Center for Chicano Research, Stanford
University.

Part Three:
Situating Stories

Engendering a "Dialectics of Our America": Jovita González's Pluralist Dialogue as Feminist Testimonio

María Eugenia Cotera

In the spring of 1935, a few months before her marriage to educational activist Edmundo Mireles (July 31, 1935), folklorist Jovita González stole a few moments for herself and penned a short story. Jovita had been awarded a Rockefeller grant to study ranching communities on the Texas–Mexican border the year before and was putting together a manuscript compiled from her fieldwork notes as the guest of a prominent Rio Grande City family. In spite of the "family's efforts to have [her] work in the house," Jovita opted to stay by herself in a "garage room," which she decorated with "relics" gathered from her "quest for stories of the ranch folk."[1] The short story, titled "Shades of the Tenth Muse," is set in this "room of her own," and narrated in the form of a dialogue between the spirits of Sor Juana Inés de la Cruz and Anne Bradstreet, two preeminent poets of colonial America. "Shades of the Tenth Muse" bears analysis as both an example of an entirely unique narrative departure in Jovita's oeuvre and as a remarkable document that testifies to the complex positionality of early Chicana feminists. Contemporary Chicana writers can well imagine the pressures that Jovita must have felt on that spring afternoon of 1935 when she took a break from her university work and her wedding plans to write what could only have been a farewell letter to a "room of one's own" and the comforts it represented.

The notes on folklore, family structure, and history that Jovita gathered on this, her last independent "quest," resulted in two manuscripts that were not to be published until after her death: *Dew on the Thorn* (1997), a collection of folklore loosely connected through a continuous narrative; and *Caballero: An Historical Novel* (1996), a historical romance set at the eve of the Mexican American War and written in collaboration with an Anglo woman, Margaret Eimer. These texts, discovered over sixty years later as part of a recovery project,[2] have reinvigorated academic interest in this important Mexican American intellectual and recuperated her work for feminist studies, especially in relation to the groundbreaking theoretical work of a new generation of Chicana feminists.[3] Before these remarkable manuscripts were brought to light, Jovita's work had been commonly understood as the product of a painfully acculturated intellectual, deeply influenced by the style of folklore practiced by dominant Anglo academics at the University of Texas in the 1920s and 1930s.[4] And even though the discovery of *Caballero* (in particular) has lead scholars to challenge this impression, most critical analyses of her writing still situate Jovita's work within the context of mainstream Texas folklore studies, creating the impression that this was the only intellectual community in which she operated.[5]

I propose a different reading of Jovita's work, one that does not center on her position as a colonized intellectual trapped in the "prison house" of colonial discourse. My extensive research into the fragments of essays, speeches, and personal letters that comprise her archive[6] reveals a much more complex picture of an organic intellectual, who in her writing (both fiction and nonfiction) spoke to many audiences at once. In the sort of reading I am proposing, Jovita's work must be understood as operating at a number of discursive junctures. Read within their "primary institutional context," her folklore studies may be understood as the work of a repressed and "disorganicized intellectual" whose "political unconscious" is revealed in the subtle attempts to assert a distinctly Mexicano or Tejano voice against a primarily Anglo vision of Texas culture (Limón 1944, 60–75 *passim*). However, when read against the backdrop of Mexican American political ideology and rhetoric of the 1930s, her work emerges as a pluralist intervention elaborated by a self-conscious "Mexican American intellectual" against monocultural notions of American history.[7] Finally, when read within the context of a tradition of Chicana feminism that traces it roots to the writing of colonial poet Sor Juana Inés de la Cruz, Jovita's fiction stands as a critique of the limitations on female creativity in both Mexican American and Anglo culture. These three interconnected but often competing discursive domains—Texas folklore studies, Mexican American politics, and an incipient Chicana feminist theory—form the terrain of influence within which a properly contextual reading of Jovita's work may take place.

"Shades of the Tenth Muse" proves a particularly productive text for the mode of reading I am suggesting above. Created, as it was, on the eve of Jovita's transformation from independent female and institutional intellectual to wife and political helpmeet of Edmundo Mireles, the story offers an almost autobiographical picture of the multivalent contexts that shaped Jovita's life and work. A review of her correspondence with Edmundo Mireles and J. Frank Dobie between 1934 and 1935 poignantly reveals the overlapping obligations to family, politics, and intellectual activity that increasingly placed demands on Jovita's time. Both Jovita and her husband-to-be were in their thirties and feeling the pressure to settle down and start a family. More important to both of them (and especially to Edmundo Mireles) was the work they were about to begin, and to which they would dedicate their entire lives: the fight for educational equity for Mexican Americans in south Texas. Edmundo's letters to Jovita bristle with impatience at the delays in their union caused by both of their demanding careers. In a letter dated April 15, 1935, Edmundo describes his long hours as the principal of an adult education night school in Del Rio, Texas, but laments:

> All these things are naught compared to what I could develop and at the same time enjoy fully, if you were with me and helped me in my work. I need you so much; I feel that we are the first to be considered and as long as we are not together I am always of the opinion that whatever I do has no positive value, that it has no foundation. That it is worthless and meaningless, whereas it would be quite the opposite if you were with me, for then we could talk about it so much and you could do so many things that would make us both much happier. (Mireles 1935)

Added to the pressure to materially and ideologically *reproduce* Edmundo Mireles' labor was the pressure Jovita felt from

Rockefeller Foundation to *produce* a text that could be submitted for publication. In a letter to the Foundation dated May 29, 1935, Jovita requests a six-month extension of her grant, stating that while she has "completed almost three hundred pages" of notes for her manuscript, she needs more time to "see beyond the facts" and create an "artistic whole" that offers a "comprehensive presentation of the customs and beliefs of the Texas-Mexicans, with the spirit of the people themselves" (González 1935b). Last but not least, Jovita was anxious not to disappoint J. Frank Dobie and Paul Taylor, the distinguished scholars who had written letters of recommendation to the Rockefeller Foundation. Her letters to Dobie regarding the first drafts of the manuscript demonstrate this desire for approval.

> I know the thing is poorly done, in fact I am a little ashamed of it, but I have this advantage, I know it is poor and I know what I want to do, and when it is properly done, it will be something that will make you proud you were my *padrino*. I can visualize what is to be done, I know the type of thing I want and I am going to do it. Like the oak I may get bent but not broken. This is no boasting Don Pancho, I mean it, and even though the first reading might have been discouraging and disappointing, please have confidence in me and in *Dew on the Thorn, the poor thing is having such a difficult time being born.* Your good opinion has always meant much to me and I want that above everything, and *when Dew on the Thorn comes out you will be proud of it* (emphasis mine). (González 1935a)

The criss-cross of tensions invading her life are manifested in Jovita's metaphorical conflation of *creative* and *procreative* activity and in her desire to make the intellectual "father" of her manuscript proud. The multiple pressures to complete her work—to be done with it so that she could join Mireles in his battle for educational equity, to produce a publishable manuscript for the Rockefeller Foundation, to fulfill the expectations of her mentor and friend J. Frank Dobie—might well have given Jovita reason to muse upon the multitude of restrictions limiting the intellectual horizons of women.

When Jovita took those few moments for herself in that "close and smoky" room, she wrote an imaginary dialogue that narrativized the contradictions brought on by her complex social location at this particular moment in her career. Though not purely autobiographical, "Shades of the Tenth Muse" functions as a *testimonio* in that it illustrates the multiple demands determining the life choices of intellectual women like Jovita. At a basic contextual level, the story may be read as a literary homage to Jovita's Anglo colleagues and to her own intellectual engagement with Texas folklore studies itself, a farewell letter of sorts. At a formal level, the narrative style of the story, especially its dialogic form and its rhetoric of plurality, mimics the ideological stance and political goals of Mexican American intellectuals at the time. Finally, Jovita's use of the female voice, whether articulated through Sor Juana Inés de la Cruz, Anne Bradstreet, or the narrator herself, points to a deeper analysis of the limitations placed on female creativity by patriarchal norms and thus frames the ideology of pluralism within a problematizing feminist discourse.

The dialogue form offers the perfect narrative device for Jovita to elaborate her gendered vision of the "dialectics of our America" (Saldívar 1991). In the classic literary tradition, the dialogue, one of the oldest rhetorical genres, generally takes the form of a philosophical debate in which two or more notable figures engage in an extended dialectical examination of a subject. In the classical mode, the dialogue form is most often adopted for didactic purposes, but in later usages, it is often employed to comic or satirical ends (Cuddon 1979). The dialogue that takes place between Sor Juana Inés de la Cruz and Anne Bradstreet in "Shades of the Tenth Muse" serves both these purposes. As a model for a properly dialectical vision of American culture, it insists that this vision be understood as a conversation between women based on reciprocity, plurality, and, perhaps most importantly, on the recognition of a shared oppression. As a comedy that engages in a discussion of social norms from both a gendered and a racialized perspective, the dialogue slyly critiques not only the ethnocentric biases of American culture but also a patriarchal system that limits the creative possibilities of women throughout the Americas. What emerges is a somewhat didactic but engaging text that not only offers a uniquely feminist interpretation of the political strategies of Mexican American intellectuals in the 1930s but also attempts to dialectically resolve the seemingly contradictory life choices pulling at Jovita's consciousness.

"Shades of the Tenth Muse" is related in the first person and begins on a curiously autobiographical note. Narrating in the present tense (which gives immediacy to the tone), Jovita describes the room where her writing takes place. In this "room of her own," a "faded Saint Teresa" and "a Virgin of Guadalupe" serve as symbols to "remind" Jovita "daily" that she is "the descendant of a proud and stoic race." "An old crude treasure chest" holds her "only possession, a manuscript," and in the place of honor above her desk, sits a framed "prayer," written by a colleague and friend, Frost Woodhull. Two dreamlike figures enter the room and commence a dialogue about aesthetics and spirituality initiated by Woodhull's prayer. This initiatory dialogue defines the characters of Sor Juana Inés de la Cruz and Anne Bradstreet by introducing the reader to their dissimilar cultural contexts and by highlighting their historical significance as creative females within these contexts. After a short debate on the merits of wit and humor in religious faith, Sor Juana and Anne discover that they have something in common: They both bear the descriptive title of colonial "Tenth Muse." And although they emerge from different social contexts (Sor Juana from colonial New Spain, and Anne from colonial New England), they share a love of knowledge, a trait generally discouraged in women of both colonial cultures.

That Jovita selected these two singular women to voice this internal dialogue is significant. Each is a foundational figure in the two distinct feminist traditions. Sor Juana Inés de la Cruz (1651–1695) is a familiar cultural archetype in Chicana feminist writing. Her life, characterized by a singular passion for knowledge and a rebellious stance against patriarchal norms, has provided many contemporary Chicana feminists with both a model and a metaphor for engaged intellectual creativity.[8] Sor Juana, whom Jovita calls the "spirit of her epoch and race," is not only regarded as one of the greatest poets and playwrights of her time but was also one of the first writers on the American continent to argue for the intellectual abilities and social rights of women. Sor Juana opted out of marriage and chose instead to pursue a life of learning within the cloistered walls of the San Jerónimo convent, an order known for its leniency. At San Jerónimo, Sor Juana assembled a library of over 4,000 volumes, conducted scientific experiments, and wrote poems, songs, and religious and secular dramas. Eventually, her outspoken nature and open criticism of patriarchal norms earned her the reprobation of high officials within the church. In the end, faced with impending charges of heresy, Sor Juana was forced to give up her library, sign a confession in her own blood, and cease writing for public performances. She was only 44 when she succumbed to an epidemic while nursing her sister nuns (Cotera 1976).[9]

Anne Bradstreet (*c.* 1612–1672) is also a foundational figure in the literary genealogy of Anglo feminism. Recognized by many Anglo feminists as the first American poet, Anne Bradstreet also suffered from the limits placed on female creativity by patriarchal norms. Anne married Simon Bradstreet at the tender age of 16, and two years later she and her husband accompanied a group of Puritans to America, settling on Massachusetts Bay. Anne was one of the few published females at the time and was prolific considering the fact that she raised eight children in the rugged and somewhat stultifying environment of seventeenth-century New England. Anne's first volume of poetry (published by her brother-in-law without her consent) was written during the first few years of her marriage and focused on intellectual subjects and philosophical abstractions. Her second volume of poetry was published after several years in the New World. The subjects in this volume include her family, their home, and their faith. Like the other members of the Puritan faith, Anne Bradstreet believed she should lead a life guided by the principles of Grace, Plainness, and Divine Mission. She is known primarily for writing poems that deal with domestic life and religious life (Mainieo 1979–1994).

These two very different women engage in a dialogue that highlights their distinct approaches to life, religion, and social relations. They share ideas on a variety of subjects, all of which serve to illustrate the epistemological differences between Anglo and Mexican culture. While Sor Juana feels at home in this New World, singing the praises of the cultured metropolis of Mexico City with its "palaces" and "distant volcanoes," Anne is "repulsed" by this "new country" with its "savages" and "discomforts." Sor Juana speaks of English "pirates" sacking Spanish galleons loaded with gold, and Anne implies that these men are patriots for the cause of England. "I do not like to contradict," Sor Juana responds, "Pirate or patriot, it is the same. It merely is a matter of point of view." Here the narrative's appeal to pluralism is most evident: Sor Juana's freewheeling and liberal approach to spirituality and life presents the perfect foil for Anne's xenophobic Puritan ethos. Sor Juana and Anne's dialogue thus creates a vision of "American" culture that does not begin with "Plymouth Rock" and the "Pilgrims," and that recognizes that culture and commerce existed for generations before the English arrived. In fact, Sor Juana's shade seems more like an older sister to Anne than an equal, symbolically manifesting what Jovita and other Mexican American intellectuals argued was the true role of Spanish America with regard to North American history and culture (Garcia 1989, 231–290 *passim*). By contrasting Sor Juana's more modern liberal ideas against Anne's old-fashioned Puritan beliefs, Jovita registers a subtle pluralist argument against the ascendancy of Anglophile culture in the Americas.

Interestingly, Sor Juana and Anne are able to bridge the epistemological gap that divides them by sharing their poetry. The conflict created by their opposing world views is thus temporarily resolved in their common love of art and culture and through their mutual recognition as women who "like knowing." But even in these tentative steps toward sisterhood, Sor Juana and Anne represent oppositional approaches to female creativity. While one has entered the convent to escape the burdens of conjugal duties and motherhood, the other has written odes to domesticity and wifely duty. When Anne shares her poetry extolling the superior virtues of men, Sor Juana asserts that she considers herself "superior to any man," and offers in exchange her famous verse diatribe against the patriarchal double standard, "*Hombres necios.*" This poetic sparring not only reveals their philosophical differences regarding issues of gender and sexuality but also illuminates their differing strategies for contending with the limitations placed on women's creativity by patriarchal culture. The choices are made clear: Either pursue a "life of the mind," as an independent intellectual exiled from the domestic sphere or combine the *creative* and the *procreative* in odes to domestic motherhood.

Sor Juana, broadminded, sensual, and impeccably modern in her sensibilities (she quotes from Mae West at the close of the story) is clearly Jovita's ideal model for female creativity. She enters first, is the last to leave, and generally dominates the dialogue. Sor Juana's physical features, her "patrician" face which resembles an "ivory cameo" and her contrasting eyes like "black diamonds shining in the dark," are reminiscent of Jovita's description of the matriarch of her own family, her beloved great-grandmother "Mamá Ramoncita," whose "clear-cut ivory features contrasting with her dark, sharp eyes," serve as Jovita's reminder of the Mexican legacy in Texas.[10] Moreover, the picture Sor Juana draws of convent life is a romantic idealization of an aristocratic and imminently sociable "room of one's own," and seems more wish-fulfillment on the author's part than accurate description of convent life in colonial Mexico. Sor Juana's dominant role in the narrative, her linkage with Jovita's matriarchal legacy in Texas, and her idyllic description of the "life of the mind," all seem to indicate Jovita's preference for her as a model of female creativity. However, we cannot forget (as Jovita surely must not have) the tragic outcome of Sor Juana's independence: She died alone, ministering to her "sisters" after being stripped of her intellectual tools, her books. Given this unspoken tragic ending to Sor Juana's story, Anne's return to her husband to "tuck him in" for the night seems less of a naive revocation of female intellectual independence and more of a realistic though somewhat depressing compromise.

In the end, the dialogue expands our vision of American history and culture from both a racialized and gendered perspective, offers an idealized vision of female creativity in the image of Sor Juana, and critiques the limitations placed on women's creative lives by patriarchal culture. In her dialogic illustration of the different material conditions under which Sor Juana and Anne forged their individual creative worlds, Jovita seems to outline the conditions of possibility limiting her own creative world. "Shades of the Tenth Muse" thus offers the student of Jovita González' work a unique metaphor for the multivalent discursive contexts that shaped her world. Created at the juncture between these contexts, at the moment of separation from her life as an institutional intellectual (with all of its contradictions), and on the eve of her final political commitment to the work of her husband in the arena of Mexican American politics, the dialogue serves as a fictional testament to Jovita's difficult passage from the world of Sor Juana, to that of Anne Bradstreet.

Notes

1. Jovita González, "Shades of the Tenth Muse," AM. E. E. Mireles & Jovita González de Mireles Papers, Special Collections & Archives, Texas A&M University–Corpus Christi Bell Library.

2. The discovery of *Caballero* and *Dew on the Thorn* was part of a recovery project undertaken by Jose Limón and myself after a review of Jovita's correspondence with J. Frank Dobie revealed that she had sent him several chapters of an unpublished manuscript. After consulting a bibliography of her published work, I discovered that the manuscript she described in her correspondence with Dobie had never been published. A recovery project was initiated by José Limón through Art Público Press (Recovering the U.S. Hispanic Literary Heritage Project) that resulted in the publication of not one, but two, manuscripts written by Jovita between 1935 and 1940. For more information on the project, see Limón 1996, xii–xxvi.

3. For an analysis of González' gendered critique of nationalist ideology see Cotera 1995, 151–70.

4. This style of folklore is perhaps best expressed in the romantic regionalist folklore of J. Frank Dobie. For more information on Texas Folklore Studies during the early twentieth century, including a detailed examination of J. Frank Dobie and romantic regionalism, see McNutt 1982.

5. For both a thorough account of Jovita's life and work and an example of a critical reading that contextualizes her writing within the discourse of Texas folklore studies, see Limón 1944, 60–75.

6. Archival resources on Jovita González are divided among three major collections: The J. Frank Dobie Collection, housed in the Harry Ransom Humanities Research Center at the University of Texas, Austin; the Carlos E. Castañeda, E. E. Mireles, and Jovita González de Mireles Papers at The Mexican American Library Project of the Benson Latin American Collection, University of Texas, Austin; and the E. E. Mireles & Jovita González de Mireles Papers, Special Collections & Archives, Texas A&M University–Corpus Christi Bell Library.

7. While space limitations do not permit a thorough discussion of the rhetorical strategies and political imperatives of Mexican American intellectuals of the 1930s and 1940s, it is important to note that I draw my conclusions from the historical review of this era offered by Mario T. García 1989. His analysis of the work of Carlos E. Castañeda, George I. Sanchez, and Arthur L. Campa provides the groundwork for my placement of Jovita González within this intellectual milieu. According to García, Mexican American intellectuals of the 1930s, most notably Carlos E. Castañeda, whom Jovita regarded as both a family friend and a mentor, believed that the "plight" of Mexican-Americans could be alleviated by transforming dominant conceptions of history, culture, and language. By articulating a pluralist vision of American culture that recognized the important historical, cultural, and linguistic contributions of "Spanish America" in the development of "American" society, Castañeda hoped to combat the racist stereotyping that he identified as a primary factor in

the uneven social, educational, and economic development of Mexican Americans. For a more thorough account of the work of Mexican American women during this era, see Ruiz 1998.

8. Critic Tey Diana Rebolledo (1995, 58–62) charts the appearance of Sor Juana Inés de la Cruz in Chicana writing from Estela Portillo Trambley's theatrical representation of her life in "Sor Juana" to the poetry of Lydia Camarillo and Pat Mora. Rebolledo notes that for many Chicana writers, "Sor Juana remains an important image of female intellect and striving for knowledge."

9. For a detailed critical analysis of the writings of Sor Juana Ines de la Cruz and her ideological engagement with colonial discourse in seventeenth century Mexico, see Franco (1989).

10. In her autobiographical statement, Jovita recalls the last visit she paid to Mamá Ramoncita, her great-grandmother. During this visit, the matriarch urged Jovita and her siblings never to forget that Texas once belonged to Mexicans: "'Your mother tells me you are moving to live in San Antonio. Did you know that land at one time belonged to us? But now the people living there don't like us. They say we don't belong there and must move away. Perhaps they will tell you to go to Mexico where you belong. Don't listen to them. Texas is ours. Texas is our home. Always remember these words: Texas is ours, Texas is our home.' I have always remembered the words and I have always felt at home in Texas" (Limón 1997, xi).

Works Cited

Cotera, María. 1995. "Deconstructing the Corrido Hero: *Caballero* and Its Gendered Critique of Nationalist Discourse." *Perspectives in Mexican American Studies, Mexican American Women: Changing Images* 5: 151–70.

Cotera, Martha P. 1976. *Diosa y Hembra: The History and Heritage of Chicanas in the U.S.* Austin, TX: Information Systems Development.

Cuddon, J. A. 1979. "Dialogue." In *A Dictionary of Literary Terms*, rev. ed. London: A. Deutsch.

Drinnon, Richard. 1997. *Facing West: The Metaphysics of Indian-Hating & Empire-Building.* Norman, Okla.: University of Oklahoma Press.

Franco, Jean. 1989. *Plotting Women, Gender and Representation in Mexico.* New York: Columbia University Press.

García, Mario T. 1989. *Mexican Americans: Leadership, Ideology, & Identity 1930–1960.* New Haven, Conn.: Yale University Press.

González, Jovita. 1935a. San Antonio, Texas; letter to J. Frank Dobie. ALS, 8 April. J. Frank Dobie Collection, Harry Ransom Humanities Research Center, University of Texas, Austin.

———. 1935b. San Antonio, Texas; letter to Dr. David H. Stevens, Director for the Humanities, The Rockefeller Foundation. TLS, 29 May. Jovita González File, Rockefeller Archive Center, New York.

———. 1997. *Dew on the Thorn*, ed. José Limón. Houston, TX: Arte Público Press.

———. n.d. "Shades of the Tenth Muse," AM. E. E. Mireles & Jovita González de Mireles Papers, Special Collections & Archives, Texas A&M University–Corpus Christi Bell Library.

González, Jovita, and Eve Raleigh. *Caballero: An Historical Novel*, ed. José Limón and María Cotera. College Station: Texas A&M University Press.

Limón, José. 1944. *Dancing with the Devil: Society and Cultural Poetics in Mexican-American South Texas*. Madison: University of Wisconsin Press.

———. 1996. "Introduction" to *Caballero: An Historical Novel*. College Station: Texas A&M University Press.

Mainiero, Lina, ed. 1979–1994. *American Women Writers: A Critical Reference Guide From Colonial Times to the Present*, 5 vols. New York: Ungar.

McNutt, James Charles. 1982. "Beyond Regionalism: Texas Folklorists and the Emergence of Post-Regional Consciousness." Ph.D. dissertation, University of Texas at Austin.

Mireles, Edmundo E. 1935. Del Rio, Texas; letter to Jovita González. TLS, 15 March. E. E. Mireles & Jovita González de Mireles Papers, Special Collections & Archives, Texas A&M University–Corpus Christi Bell Library.

Rebolledo, Tey Diana. 1995. *Women Singing in the Snow: A Cultural Analysis of Chicana Literature*. Tucson: University of Arizona Press.

Ruiz, Vicki L. 1998. *From Out of the Shadows: Mexican Women in Twentieth-Century America*. New York: Oxford University Press.

Saldívar, Jose David. 1991. *The Dialectics of Our America: Genealogy, Cultural Critique, and Literary History*. Durham, N.C.: Duke University Press.

Shades of the Tenth Muse

Jovita González de Mireles

The air in the room is close and smoky. I can still smell the rosemary and lavender leaves I have just burnt in an incense burner to drive out the mosquitoes that have driven me insane with their monotonous droning music. For, in spite of the family's efforts to have me work in the house, I prefer my garage room with its screenless windows and door, its dizzy floor, the planks of which act like the keys of an old piano, and walls, hung with relics which I like to gather as I go from ranch to ranch in my quest for stories of the ranch folk. A faded Saint Teresa, in a more faded niche smiles her welcome every morning and a Virgin of Guadalupe remind me daily that I am a descendant of a proud stoic race. Back of the desk, a collection of ranch spits is witness of my ranching heritage, an old, crude treasure chest holds my only possession, a manuscript which will sometime be sold, if I am among the fortunate. Hanging from a nail above is a home-spun hand-woven coin bag, the very same which my grandfather was given by his mother on his wedding day with the admonition, "my son, may you and all who ever own it keep it filled with gold coins." It hangs there empty, for the descendant of that Don has never seen a gold coin, much less owned one.

In the place of honor, above my desk in a gold and black frame is a prayer, a letter written to the Almighty by my good friend Frost Woodhull, in which he asks for rain, not for himself, but for his friends in the ranches of Northern Mexico — "Dear God in Heaven," it begins "Give us rain" —and ending "Yours Truly . . ."[1]

It is late, too dark to write, the smell of Rosemary and Lavender is soothing and I fall, can I say asleep; or am I transported three centuries back?

A figure glides in. It is a woman. She does not see me, or if she does she does not acknowledge my presence. She sits in the vacant chair by my desk. A radiance surrounds her, and I can see her face. She is beautiful her features patrician and classical in their perfection resemble an ivory cameo, and her eyes are like black diamonds shining in the dark. I am not a bit surprised at the unexpected entrance of my uninvited guest, I seem to know who she is. She takes paper and pen and begins to write. I don't have to read over her shoulder, I know. She is Sor Juana Inez de la Cruz the spirit of her epoch and her race. I don't know how it happened, I don't even remember having left my place at the desk, yet I find myself resting on the couch. I cannot be dreaming; the song of the mocking bird on the telephone post by my window tells me I am awake. And yet another figure equally strange has entered my room. She is a stately matron, her somber dress and serious expression mark her out as one who is always mournful and sad. She sits in the empty chair with a sigh and looks around the room. Her eyes become fixed on the prayer. I can see terror and consternation on her face as she reads—"Oh God, our cows are dying; we are not crying. Our tears are dry much like our land. Its rained on every other land." She clutches at her heart. She gasps at the sacrilegious words. She cannot even utter a word.

A clear, silvery laugh bursts from the lips of the nun. "The prayer has shocked you has it not?" she asks.

"You call that prayer? It's blasphemy! Who dares to address God in such familiar terms?"

"I wouldn't say that," answered the nun in a careless drawling tone, "the man no doubt asks for what he wants in his own way. Let me see, who is the author? Frost Woodhull, Judge of Bexar County,"—not one of us; but I would like to know him. He's witty, I can see and wit my dear, is a gift from the Angels."

"How can you!" gasps the somber figure. "What did you say his name was?"

"Woodhull, English perhaps, one of your colonials. Do you know him?"

"The Lord deliver me from that! He must be one of the pagan dwellers of Merrit Mount, one of Morton's infidels."[2]

"Its a clever piece, nonsense though," the nun continued, but seeing the look of anguish on her companion's face she said laughing, "Perhaps he was merely joking."

"Joking about God? That's a sin that would bring fire and brimstone from heaven. Don't you have any religion?"

"Do I have any religion?" laughed the nun, "don't you see these garbs of a servant of the Lord?"

"A nun! And you'd like to meet that awful man?"

"My dear, religion and virtue should wear a happy face."

"I don't understand at all. You say you serve the Lord, don't you fear his wrath?"

"I have confidence in His love."

"Who are you? Your words and attitude dismay and yet surprise me."

"Who am I? I am Sister Joan of the Cross. I serve the Lord, and I also write when my duties permit me. People call me the Tenth Muse of New Spain."

"They call you that? What a coincidence! I am also called the Tenth Muse, but of New England."

"Then we should be friends, and know more of each other. Where are you from? Where do you live?"

"I live in Massachusetts, the governor of the colony is my husband, but I was born in England, dear England," Anne Bradstreet, for she is no other, replied sighing again, a tear rolling down her cheek.

"Why do you weep?"

"For England, for my lovely home, for the friends I left there."

"Don't you like this new place where you live?"

"How can I like it? How can I like the savages, the discomforts of a new country? The ways are so strange! But I am convinced now that it is the way of God and to it I must submit. Do you like your country?

"Do I like it?" answered the nun with the shining eyes. "You've never seen anything like the greenness of its valleys, and the blueness of the sky. The air is warm and soft, and the first thing my eyes see at dawn are two volcanoes in the distance covered with perpetual snow! I was born there just twelve leagues from the city of palaces, that's what we call Mexico, and there I would be now had it not been that my thirst for knowledge brought me to the city."

"Oh you like knowing too?"

"Yes, I was but three when I learned to read and write, and when I was thirteen my parents presented me to the viceroy who had heard of my learning."

"And when I was seven," answered Anne, "I had as many as eight tutors in languages, dancing, and music."

"Strange isn't it that we should like the same things! I love music too; often have I composed selections for the viceroy and his wife and the Mother Superior."

"Somehow I cannot see you as a nun. You are so gay, so happy, so carefree. Why did you enter the convent?"

"In the first place to serve God, and then too, I needed a retreat, a quiet place to study, where I might work without interruption, and in the convent I found the things I longed for."

"Aren't you ever lonesome? Don't you crave for the companionship of others?

"My dear Anne, you don't know much about us do you?"

"No, I must admit I don't. I have always looked upon nuns and Popish things with distrust, even with fear. Won't you tell me about your life?"

"Delighted. We live in a big beautiful convent surrounded by luxurious gardens. We never leave it, but we have a life of contentment and leisure. You see all of us there belong to the nobility. We have over two hundred servants who do the work and we lead a life of proper and innocent pleasures. We are quite expert at making pastry, cakes and sweets which we send to our friends in particular to my friend the Viceroy. During our leisure hours we embroider altar clothes, converse or play the harp. In the afternoon after vespers we hold open house. The viceroy, the notables, and their ladies come. We discuss the events of the day, the gossip of the town, comment on the sermons preached, the last religious festival. There are times though when the conversation is not so pleasant, and that is when we hear that an English pirate ship has captured a Spanish galleon loaded with gold and silver bars."

"English pirates! We never have been that. Our seamen might capture a Spanish treasure ship but always in a good fight!"

"I do not like to contradict. Pirate or patriot, it is the same. It merely is a matter of point of view. What was I saying, I've lost the trend."

"You discussed the events of the day."

"Oh yes, our guests sing to us the latest songs, ballads, romances, provincial tunes, and they also delight us with the latest dances."

"Dances? Dances? Dear me; dear me, and you a nun! Dancing is an instrument of Satan himself. And I always though living in the convent was dull."

"Not when you realize your Spanish convents have not been invaded yet by northern prudery and Puritanism. But tell me, how do you employ your time?"

"I am the mother of eight children.

'I had eight birds hatch in one nest,
Four cocks there were and hens the rest,
I nurst them up with pain and care,
nor cost, nor labour did I spare,
Till at the last they all had wing.'
And then I have my husband,
'If ever two were one, then surely we,
If ever man were loved by wife than he;
If ever wife was happy in a man,
compare with me you women if you can,'
Did you ever want to get married ?"

"No, I cannot say I ever did. Many suitors wooed and made love to me, but no one would I have. I always thought myself superior to any man."

"You astound me, Juana."

"Why should they be our superiors? Have we not a mind like they? Do we not have a soul? Can we not think? Can we not love the same as they? Are they made of finer clay?

"Let Greeks be Greeks, and women what they are,
Men have precedency and still excell,
It is but vain unjustly to wage warre;
Man can do best, and women know it well."

"I don't know such things! They are weak, silly creatures who can not take the blame for the sins they commit. 'Foolish, foolish men who blame women for the evil things they do, when they themselves are to blame for the sin women commit! Tell me who is more to blame, although both I think, are sinners, the one who hungry, sins for pay, or the one who pays to sin?'"

"Stop, stop!" Anne called out covering her ears with both hands. "Your evil words pollute me, contaminate me! Have you no decency, no shame?"

"My dear Anne, there is nothing more decent than truth, and there is nothing shameful in seeing life as it is! However, if such things hurt your tender, sensible heart, we shall no more discuss them. When you came in you told me you were the Tenth Muse; I am curious to know what you've done to merit such title. Have you published any of your poems?"

"I don't like to talk about it. It's too much like vanity, and vanity as you no doubt know, is a thing of Satan. But if you'll tell me what you've written, perhaps I shall consider—

"I don't mind telling you. I have written three plays and my poems have been published under the title of, 'Works of the only poetess, Tenth Muse, Sister Juana Inés de la Cruz, professed religious in the monastery of San Geronimo of the Imperial city of Mexico, which in various metres, languages and styles, discusses many matters with elegant, subtle, clear, ingenious and useful verses; for teaching, recreation, and admiration.' It was published in 1689."

"Your title is as verbose as mine, ' The Tenth Muse lately sprung in America. Several poems compiled with great variety of wit and Learning full of delight. Wherein specially is contained a complete discourse and description of the Four elements, Constitutions, Ages of man, Lessons of the Year. Together with an exact epitome of the Four Monarches, viz, the Assyrian, Persian, Grecian, Roman, Also a dialogue between old England and New, concerning the late troubles, With diverse other pleasant and serious poems."

"As high-sounding as mine. What style did you follow?"

"At first I imitated the 'fantastic school' of England, but in spite of that, I am told that I made use of ingenious arguments. I would have liked to express my poetic nature, to set forth all that my heart felt, to express my loneliness for England, but I dared not."

"But why, why? Don't you know poets should express their feelings?"

"I dared not, I was touched with maladies of conscience. My Puritan instinct repressed me."

"Pooh, pooh! My dear Anne, you talk like an old woman! I've never been ashamed or afraid to express anything I wish. I discuss earthly love with the same freedom as I do love divine. Love is the spark that keeps us happy."

"Please, Juana, if you talk that way, I shall be forced to leave you. What time is it now?"

The nun looked out the window and without hesitation answered,

"Its eight o'clock by the evening star."

"Dear me, dear me, Simon must wondering what has become of me. He loves his pipe early, and I must tuck him in bed by nine!"

"Simon must be tucked in," giggled the nun to herself, and aloud to Anne she said, "It has been a great honor and a pleasure to know another Tenth Muse. I though I had the monopoly to the title. Come up and see me again."

"Come up and see me! Where have I heard that before?"

"Never mind, you wouldn't even recognize her name if I told it to you; but do come again."[3]

"That I will my dear Juana," answered the New England Tenth Muse, kissing the nun on the forehead, "but please put that sinful prayer away, I shudder at the levity of it!"

"The one written by your countryman? I really must meet that man; he may not be a poet, but I bet he has a sense of humor and is clever."

Anne faded away. Sor Juana stood up, yawned, looked at me with what I thought was a wink, and following her companion, disappeared in the dimness of space.

—Apt and Just

Notes

The original manuscript of this story is in the E. E. Mireles and Jovita González de Mireles Papers, Special Collections & Archives, Texas A&M University–Corpus Christi Bell Library. Copyright Texas A&M University–Corpus Christi. All rights reserved.

1. An original copy of this prayer, dated April 9, 1935, was located in a box along with other personal correspondence dating from the same period (1934–1935). It appears to have been sent in a letter from Woodhull to Jovita while she was residing in Rio Grande City and finishing up her Rockefeller research, and he himself was visiting friends in Coahuila, Mexico. The typewritten prayer reads:

> Dear God in Heaven: Give us rain./ Oh, please, Sir, give us rain. God, must we ask in vain?/God, do what you think you must, but give us rain, and no more dust./ Oh, God. Our cows are dying; we're not crying; Our tears are dry much like our land. Its rained on every other hand./ God, what shall we do? Pray more to you? We're praying: 'God, fix up these things which ail us'./ Yours Truly, Helen and Max Michaelis/ P.S. Our two year olds have never drank from well or stream or muddy tank. Oh, please, Sir, give us rain.

At the bottom of the letter/prayer are two handwritten notes, one from Frost Woodhull which reads: "To Jovita González, Is this heresie [sic]?" and a second note apparently inscribed by Jovita herself upon receipt of the prayer. Jovita's inscription reads: "Composed by His Honor, Judge of Bexar County by the Grace of the Middle Class Americans and God. Pending Approval of His Holiness."

E. E. Mireles & Jovita González de Mireles Papers, Special Collections & Archives, Texas A&M University–Corpus Christi Bell Library.

2. A historical reference to Thomas Morton (c. 1590–c. 1647), an early Anglican settler in colonial America who ridiculed the strict religious tenets of the Pilgrims and the Puritans. Morton arrived in Massachusetts in 1624 and established the settlement of Merrit Mount in which he erected a maypole, encouraged conviviality and merrymaking, wrote baudy verse, and engaged in free trade with the local Indians. This historical figure has survived as the epitome of the anti-Puritan in literature and in the popular imagination. In *Facing West: The Metaphysics of Indian-Hating, & Empire-Building* , historian Richard Drinnon (1997) describes Morton as a rebellious colonial subject whose early espousal of pluralist notions concerning the humanity of New World "savages" flew in the face of Puritan ideology. "Morton asserted the superior humanity of the Indians and then went dangerously far toward establishing that claim by living among them in amity. As a living example he undermined, just as they were establishing it, the colonizer's notion of the treacherous savage and their need to see themselves as a tightly knit armed band of Christians perched on the edge of hostile territory."

3. An obvious reference to the infamous Mae West (c. 1892–1980), American stage and film actress who wrote, produced, and starred in her own theatrical and film productions. West was both reviled and adored for her "frank sensuality, regal postures, and blasé wisecracking." The sexually charged line "come up and see me sometime," uttered in "She Done Him Wrong" (1933), a film adaptation of her play *Diamond Lil* (1928), became her trademark. For more information see "West, Mae" *Britannica Online*.

Three Stories

Mary Helen Ponce

Campesinas

The walnut season has ended; the dusty tents struck down. Wagons teeming with tired children, soiled bedding; the workers take their leave. Footprints dot the hard packed dirt where early this morning our canvas tent stood. In the silent camp the trees stripped of fruit stand tall.

Two women hover next to our loaded wagon, their walnut-stained hands clasped to dry breasts. Behind frayed bonnets of mismatched calico, their tired eyes slide past me to the pale November sky. As father straps a worn suitcase atop the wagon, I watch them from afar. "Old maids," someone whispers. "Hermanas," says another.

Campesinas, they call themselves. Pickers of nuez, chabacán, uva. Over-ripe fruit. A family of two, they yearly follow the crops to Reedley, Parlier, Cucamonga. The hot summer sun, el sol caliente, has sucked dry their youth, muted girlish laughter. Their bonnets open to reveal reddened cheeks, parched lips, listless hair. Old-fashioned dresses with high collars and muddied hems brush against boots tightly laced against the elements.

The women whisper to each other. Soft Spanish words drift past my head. They wait as father, strong hands gripping at a twisted rope, pulls tight the worn canvas that shields their worldly goods. The brass-studded trunk that followed them from Mexico groans against a sack of walnuts. Homemade quilts of unmatched cotton snuggle next to scorched frying pans. Cardboard boxes crammed tight with *tiliches* lie on the wagon floor.

The women clamber atop the open wagon, hug tight bal-
looning skirts, fluff dark shawls devoid of fringe, give a pull to
bonnet strings. Father whistles to the horses, reins in the
leather straps. High atop the buckboard, I jam my boy's hat
tight against a sudden wind. A white cloud drifts across the
California sky. The horses strain against the heavy load, then
settle down to a familiar trot. The camp behind us, we disap-
pear behind the walnut trees.

Onions

"There was nothing to eat," she tells me, a frown on her round
face. "The Carrancistas set fire to the wheat, the corn. They
left only the onions, las cebollas. We ate roasted onions, fried
onions, onion stew, onion tacos, onion gruel. Onions, onions,
day and night, I ate onions."

"I was pregnant again—and afraid. My babies all had died
as infants, the last one was only two. No sé por qué se me
morían," she sighs, then covers her wrinkled arms with a dark
shawl. "I feared not so much for myself, but for my unborn
child, but onions is all we had. I made atole from onions
ground on a molcajete. Each day I drank atole, never hating
the taste. It was for my child that I ate."

"When my time came I knelt on the floor, gnashed my
teeth, stifled my cries with rags. I birthed her myself; her father was in the fields digging for onions. I cut the cord,
swaddled my child, then gave her my breast."

"Nunca se me enfermó," she smiles, "but lived past two,
and when twelve, stood taller than her father." She sighs,
smooths a wrinkle in her cotton apron, and squints into the
sun that cuts through the kitchen window. "I think it was the
onions."

Granma's Apron*

The funeral is over; the guests fed on pan dulce and choco-
late say goodbye. Tired of sitting still, the children run freely

in the noonday sun. Inside granma's old house mother rinses the cups and dishes given free with Rinso soap. They were granma's pride and joy. She straightens the velvet cushions sent from Korea with love. Anxious to leave, I pace the worn linoleum, peek out the window, surprised to see robins nesting in granma's trees.

Long before granma began to die, her garden started to wither. One cold winter, the apple tree, planted when I was a boy, shivered, then split in two. In a sudden windstorm, the walnut tree nurtured by granma, held up by boards that from afar resemble crutches, groaned, then stooped over, never to rise again. Yet steadfast geraniums, cuttings from neighbors and friends, blistering red with glossy green leaves creep along the old picket fence.

Mother calls me indoors to sift through dusty boxes. High school yearbooks in tissue paper secured with twine brought home from the work fields, football programs yellowed with time, postcards from Korea. My fingers brush a crocheted doily, manteles of bleached flour sacks, a baby blanket smelling of mothballs, and come to rest on thick dark canvas.

"This was your granma's," mother tells me, as she rubs her tear-stained cheek against a faded apron. "She wore it when she picked cotton. ¿Te acuerdas?"

Memory floods my tired mind: Granma in the cotton fields of Shafter, McFarland, Delano. Granma straining beneath the cotton sack to which, between dusty rows, I hung on for dear life. Granma sharing tacos of fried potatoes, weenies, carne asada, rolled at five in the morning while I still slept, food washed down with coffee kept in an empty jam jar. Granma sitting upright in her rocking chair, worn Bible in hand, thanking her God for a job well done.

"She was over fifty," mother reminds me, "pero se fue al fil. I was en el Keene with TB; the social worker tried to take you from her. We were poor, míhijo, so alone." From far off mother's voice drifts past me like dust swirls along a country road.

"Yo puedo trabajar," she told the craggy foreman who looked her up and down, then snickered loudly. "She strapped the cotton sack around her shoulders, plunked you at the very edge, staked a row for herself. All summer long she worked with you at her side."

The apron feels heavy in my hands, its sulphur smell clogs my every pore. Granma, of peasant stock, short and wide, her strong arms covered with dust. Granma in the sweltering July heat sipping water from a dented canteen. Granma in a faded dress, thick frame hoisting high the sack that slithered up and down the dusty field. Granma's calloused hands that reeked of mentholatum, wrapped each night with clean white rags. Blistered hands that held me tight.

I cradle the apron in my smooth hands, empty the side pocket of lint, looking for pieces of granma. I see granma at the kitchen table, her wide feet resting on the worn linoleum. The tin sewing basket stands next to the kerosene lamp that sheds its steady light. Spools of colored thread, assorted pins and needles, the round pincushion stitched from scraps. The apron, sewn late at night, was cut from old work pants, stitched after she first mended shirts, torn jeans and worn socks. As she sewed, granma hummed church hymns sung at the Apostolic church. Spanish words of faith, compliance, perseverance. In the dim sunlight I touch the sturdy material, poke with my finger the wide buttonholes, feel the double-stitched seams that held our home together.

I say goodbye, hold tight mother's thin frame, make vague promises of visits to come. I hold the faded apron, smooth down the creases made by time, roll it tight in Sunday's news, then slowly drive past cotton fields of childhood, granma's apron by my side.

*In memory of Granma Pepita (Josefina Altamirano), who in the 1930s picked cotton in the San Joaquin Valley.

Mexican Migrants in North Carolina: María Salas Shares Her Story

Margarita Decierdo

As part of the Smithsonian Institution's oral history project, "An Oral History of Southern Agriculture," I conducted a number of interviews with Mexican migrant workers in North and South Carolina. The Mexican migrants' reception in the South as well as their motivation in choosing to migrate to this area were explored during these interviews. Interviews with African American sharecroppers conducted by another researcher made it clear that there were ambivalent feelings toward these Mexican workers, ranging from welcome acceptance to a belief that their presence threatened the sharecroppers' livelihood ("Oral History" 1989).

Mexican workers have come to North and South Carolina from as far away as Michoacán, Guerrero, and Zacatecas to work and eventually settle. Some came to find a better life, while others wanted to reunite their families. In telling their stories, the farm workers seemed a little shy, as if surprised that anyone would be interested in learning about them. Through these interviews they offer us a glimpse of their perspective on this new environment.

One woman spoke of her husband's three-year absence from Mexico while at work in North Carolina. She had remained at home with five of their six children. During this period, he had sent money and written letters, but by the end of the third year, he wrote to say that he was tired of being alone and tired of worrying about his family. He asked if she would brave the journey to "el otro lado." Married at nineteen and a homemaker in Mexico, this woman traveled from Nayarit, where she was born, to the United States with her children. Her experience illustrates the situation facing many Mexican migrants as they start a new life in the South.

How did you get here [North Carolina]?
We came here like all the families that come who don't have their papers. He [her husband] contracted someone to bring us. We crossed the river, and this person brought us here to the house where he was working with another boss. My husband has always worked on a dairy farm.

Can you please tell me how your crossed into the United States?
Well, we came with other families, and we went to the border where he was waiting. And because he was familiar with the area, he brought across the river in a canoe. When we got to the other side of the river, the *migra* (Immigration and Naturalization Service) caught us.

And did you return? Did you cross again?
Through Piedras Negras. But it wasn't the same like those that they take to jail. They caught us and brought us back to the border. We went back to the hotel where we waited until we could cross the river again. We crossed, and the person who brought us across told us where to go, and we spent several days walking, we endured the heat and hunger, we did not have any water.

So you walked?
Yes, once we crossed the river, we had to walk to where he was waiting for us in a car. We walked more because we had to take another route because the immigration had caught us before. The youngest boy, who was six then, cried and cried because he wanted water and was very hungry. Until we finally reached where he was waiting with the car.

And how many days did you walk?
We walked about six days. We suffered a lot. And there were so many snakes. At night while we walked we could hear the snakes hissing, the noise was awful. During the day while the sun was very hot, we would seek refuge under the small bushes, and just when we were about to sit down there in front of us were two or three snakes coiled, and I would

scream, "Let's go, there are snakes here." And now that we are here, I ask the girls if they want to go back to Mexico. They say they wish to return but not if they have to walk back. But now we can go back, because we got permission to return for six months.

Is this the amnesty program?
Yes, and we are about to apply for permanent residency. And because of this we can return to Mexico and cross the border.

The youngest, how old was he when you crossed?
He was six, and now he is fourteen.

Do the children remember much about the crossing?
Yes. My daughter, the one you saw with the black skirt, she is the oldest. We talk about the time we spent walking in the desert, and when they ask Norma, that's her name, if she remembers, she says she will never forget that.

And when you reached the man waiting with the car, where did you go?
He brought us here to North Carolina.

Do you remember where you crossed to get to North Carolina?
We crossed through Texas, through San Antonio.

And then you came to North Carolina?
Yes. And we have not moved from here because he (her husband) has always worked here. And ever since he brought us here we have been here.

And what kind of work does your husband do?
I don't know what you call it in English, but he works in a dairy, milking cows.

Has he always worked on a dairy farm?
Yes, always.

With the same man?
No, he had been working with a dairy farmer for five years. He worked those years with him. But he sold his farm, and my husband had to find another job, and so he has been here with this farmer three years going on four.

Have you always lived here, close to Chapel Hill?
Yes, we used to live about fifteen to twenty minutes away from here [in a trailer park].

Did your husband ever work in the tobacco fields or pick cucumbers?
Yes. Before he got this job, milking cows, he tells me he worked in tobacco, cucumber, and tomato fields.

You take care of your children and now your grandchildren. Have you ever worked in the fields?
No, I have not worked. I have always depended on him. He has always been responsible for me and my family. The others help him, they work too. Right now we have only two left that can't work. When we first arrived, it was only my husband and my oldest son, they were the only two working. It was very hard because of the expenses, but we survived. Many people have had the help of the government; they receive food stamps, but not us. When we arrived the youngest was six, and we had no right to ask for help.

And when you came here from Mexico, how was life here in North Carolina?
Well, the one that just left, she was aready fifteen years old when we got here, and my other daughter was thirteen years old. They had a hard time because they went to school and could not understand English, it was very hard. But then they learned to speak and understand English, and it was much easier, they got used to life here.

How about the Mexican customs? Did you have a hard time finding Mexican products?
No, it wasn't difficult. But for those families where the husband and wife work—they cook their food in a hurry. But I have always been home so I have time to cook a good meal, the way we like it. When we first got here there were no stores that sold products from Mexico. Well, it was like that for two or three years, we could not find anything. Now we can find everything. In many places there are stores that sell Mexican products, and one doesn't have to hassle. I went three years without making tamales and other things that we liked because we could not find the necessary ingredients. Now you can find everything you need, like the corn husks, the

264

flour, and all the other things you need to make tamales, now I make them. It has been okay. My oldest son was the only one with a license to drive. It was difficult because he would work very late and would come home very tired and didn't have the energy to take us shopping. Afterwards, when the oldest daughter was in her second year of school, she got her license too. There are three now that have their license to drive. My other son comes home from work, he stays about four hours, eats, and then it is time for him to go to work again; he works in a dairy too.

And your daughters?
The girl that just left, she works in a restaurant and the other two girls started working in a factory while they are not in school. And when they get out of school they go to a restaurant part-time. When they get out of school, they go to work and get out of work about nine at night.They do their homework, but it's very hard because they are still in school. But they have to work and earn some money; that's how it is. It is still better here, because in Mexico there is no work.

So you just got back from Mexico?
Yes. We left here on the tenth of June and came back the ninth of July. Yes, over there everything is so expensive. Many people come, people that are from the same place. We get together, pass the time with family and friends—happy moments.

Is there a Catholic church that conducts mass in Spanish?
Yes. We have always attended mass. Here in Burlington there is a Catholic church, but they conduct mass in English. Sometimes they conduct mass in Spanish. Before they used to conduct mass in Spanish every first Sunday of the month. But we have gone to Greensville, there, every week they conduct mass in Spanish, but only during the summer. But when it is very cold and the weather is bad we don't go. We are also going to another church in Kernersville; there they conduct mass in Spanish every week. We continue to practice the Catholic religion.

Well, what do you think of life here in North Carolina? Is it very different from life in Mexico?
Yes, but I like it here.

And the Americans, how have they treated you?
Well, you see, wherever you go, you will find all types of people, and if you like the people, fine, but not everybody gets along. And you will find people you like wherever you are, here or in your own country. We have been comfortable here.

Can you please describe a typical day?
I get up at 6:30 or 7:00 in the morning, because at that hour they bring me my grandchildren, so I get up to care for them. I make breakfast for those who are going to work. Then I clean the house and cook for those who work. When they get here around noon or one o'clock, they eat, then go back to work. My husband goes back to work around twelve-thirty, and the other son leaves for work around one-thirty. When they leave I stay around the house, cleaning and cooking. When the kids come back from school around three or four, they eat because at school they eat around eleven-thirty and are very hungry when they get here. So the whole day I am very busy with the house chores, washing the clothes. If I have a little time I crochet.

And you take care of your grandchildren?
Yes, their mother comes by around three-thirty or four to pick them up.

And what time does your husband come home?
Late afternoon, he comes home around six-thirty, he works hard.

And where do you do your laundry? Here?
Yes, here. I have a washing machine. When I was in Mexico this last time, I washed by hand. My mother-in-law has a washer, but you wash the clothes twice and the water stays. So I told her that it was better for me to wash them by hand. Here, you put them in the washer, and it does all those things, it rinses, but not over there. You have to wash the clothes on a washboard and wring the clothes yourself.

Does you husband work on Sundays?
Well, on Sundays we go to mass, and then he goes out to watch baseball games, he likes to play too.

How old is your husband?
He is forty-eight years old and will soon be forty-nine.

And how old are you?
I just turned forty-six. When I was in Mexico to see my relatives, everyone was telling me that I had not aged, that I was still young. And that they wanted to come to the United States just to become young [laughter]. But the years pass and you do notice your age—but one ages differently in Mexico, who knows. We watch TV and we pay attention to the news from around the world.

Is there a TV channel that presents the news in Spanish?
Yes, it comes from California, I think.

And do all your children speak English?
Yes, all of them. The son that got married, he went to school only up until the tenth grade. He had to work. He was responsible for the work and could not continue going to school, but he knows how to speak English. The oldest son, he didn't attend school here because when he came here he was already sixteen years old, and it was work, work, work after that. He didn't go to college, but he understands and reads English. It hasn't discouraged him from going back to school. He'll go back for a short period of time, but then he has to start work again, he has to quit. He works very hard in the dairy, but he also works out in the field, preparing the land for planting. He has a lot of work. And when he doesn't have work, he'll go back one or two months. He's young, so all of that will come in handy some day. We are going to school too, but it is not the same as when you are young. But we learn a few words.

Are you going to school to learn English?
Yes.

You and your husband? Where do you go?
Yes. Very close to here, past the Dixie factory. It looks like a church, they give classes there. We go on Tuesdays and Thursdays at six-thirty in the evening until nine. When I get books I can read a few words. When one is younger, however, one can learn [laughter]. But whatever word you pick up, it's important. My daughters say, "We can't speak in English anymore because mother understands everything we are saying" [laughter]. Before, they would not speak in Spanish, instead they would speak to each other in English so that I couldn't understand, but now there are a few things I understand and

sometimes when they are talking I tell them, "Hey, you'd better stop talking because I can understand everything you are saying." And then the oldest one says, "Now we can't even speak in English because Mother understands everything we are saying" (laughter). One understands, but to speak it, it's difficult. Sometimes my husband comes home tired from work and does not have any energy to go to the classes, but I encourage him, and then we go. He says that whatever word that one learns is an advantage. They give you a book to read, and they ask you questions, or you present them on the blackboard. They write words, and one makes note of them. I think it's fine even if it's just a little.

Who is in charge of the English classes? Is it part of an organization?
Yes. The woman who gives us classes is from Argentina. She knows how to speak Spanish and English, and whenever we can't understand something in English, she will explain it to us in Spanish. I like that.

How do you see the future? Do you think that you will stay here? And your daughters, do you think they will get married here?
Yes. I am happy because before we came here, all of their friends and family that were the same age as my daughters have gotten married and have four children. None of my daughters have gotten married. As I told my husband, the work begins when they get married. But right now the sons are the ones getting marrired.

Does it matter to you if your daughters marry Mexicans?
Like we have told them, they will be the ones to decide whom they marry, but they will have to give it much thought, because marriage is not just for a little while but a lifetime. Mexicans are Catholic and are not of those who only get married and then they are divorcing for whatever reason and then they leave each other. That's why we tell them to look carefully and be very cautious, because marriage is not for a little while. And they reflect and say, " I'm not going to get married right now." And we tell them no one is forcing them to get married. I believe that their time has not come, but it may just happen soon enough, no one knows. One can't say, "I'm going to get married," and then get married. Like father used to say—it just happens. And I believe that's true, because as they get

older, they no longer listen to the advice one gives them. If one has made up her mind to get married, she'll get married. That's why I am pleased with my daughters. They may not be living an exciting lifestyle, but at least they are not married so that they may be prevented from getting somewhere. We don't give them that much freedom, but at least we give them more consideration.

Do you continue with the customs of Mexico? Is your husband very strict with your daughters?
Yes, yes.

Do they have to ask permission for everything?
Yes, that is what he tells them. They don't give me trouble, but he tells them if they want to stay here with us they will have to do as he says. It's okay with me that they go out. Sometimes we go with them or I go with them. But alone, we don't give them that much liberty.

Has it been difficult to continue with Mexican customs?
They were taught the Mexican way since they were small and began to comprehend.

When your son got married, did you have a big celebration?
Yes, we celebrated in Mexico. He got married in Mexico, but his wife stayed over there. He has to arrange the proper documentation to bring her over here. He wants to have the immigration papers so that she can cross the border through immigration rather than crossing like we crossed. That's why he left her over there, for, perhaps, two months.

What does the future look like for you? Will you be staying?
Well, I think we might at least stay a little while longer. Like my husband says, maybe after he can't work anymore, maybe we'll go back.

Do you want to go back?
Well, like I told him, wherever you go, I'll go. He is very tired of working, but there is no other way but to keep on working, especially if one is poor. How will one live? But it's not going to be soon. We would like the youngest to be out of school and then, maybe.

And your visions for the future?

Well, according to what the children want to do also. But he tells them that one day we may return to Mexico, and those that want to come back with us are welcome. Those that want to stay and make a life and career here, that will up to them, it will depend on their wisdom. If it's a job or study, something that will allow them to work. Not this difficult work, because my husband and I have worked very hard because we had no education.

Work Cited

"An Oral History of Southern Agriculture." 1989. Washington, D.C.: Natural Museum of American History, Smithsonian Institution. Project Coordinator, Dr. Pete Daniels. Principal Investigator, LuAnn Jones.

Part Four:
Taking Charge

The Synapses of Struggle: Martha Cotera and Tejana Activism

Mary Ann Villarreal

I began my research about the women of the Texas Raza Unida Party in the archives of the Benson Latin American Collection at UT Austin. There Margo Gutierrez, head librarian of the Mexican American Library Project, introduced me to the papers of Martha Cotera. I had the opportunity to interview Cotera, a wife, mother, writer, librarian, political activist, and most important to my work, an active member of Texas's first Chicano third political party, La Raza Unida Party. LRUP emerged as a third political party seventeen days after the end of the Crystal City school boycott in January 1970. One of the original members wrote that LRUP "sought to implement social change in the barrios and to improve social conditions for La Raza by mobilizing its massive political potential and making its influence felt at the ballot box."[1] For eight years, the Texas Raza Unida Party had a profound affect on Texas politics.

Through my research and interview with Martha, I discovered the ways in which Tejana feminists transcended gendered, racial, and political boundaries, fusing together their own feminist strategies by hosting their own conferences and organizing Chicana caucuses in both settings and on their own terms. They ultimately carved out their own public space to address issues previously ignored by Chicanos and Euro-American feminists. Periodicals and other primary sources illustrate how Texas Chicanas utilized public space. Their names appear handwritten on anything from torn

273

pieces of paper to conference literature. Other Chicana activists who gave them recognition for their work list a majority of them in speeches or articles. Newspaper articles highlight the themes of conference workshops and panels, ranging from women's legal rights to their responsibility for cultural identity. Many of the Chicanas who joined the Texas LRUP brought to the table a wide spectrum of interests and concerns. They represented occupations from educators to artists and from the beginning Chicanas occupied leadership positions within the party.

On February 25, 1996, I arrived at Martha Cotera's home for our 11 A.M. interview. The informal part of our interview began with a trip to the home of Magarita Muñoz Simon. On the way, Martha explained to me that she and a group of people had worked to have Mrs. Simon's house fixed after they had discovered that her home was in need of repair. In the meantime they had moved her into an apartment, and Martha was in the process of having Mrs. Simon's belongings moved back into her home. Mrs. Simon was well known throughout the community, especially for her work as a radio commentator, editor, and publisher of *El Democrata*, and as a founding member of the Austin chapter of LULAC. Mrs. Simon was 90 years old when she died of heart failure on September 8, 1998. In her obituary, Martha Cotera described her as "a giant, especially among women."[2]

After gathering a few items, putting them in the car, and taking them to Mrs. Simon's, we headed back to Martha's home for our interview. I learned that she had been interviewed countless times without any concrete results. Indeed, I had found little written about her. I made a mental note that I would see this interview through to the end. Two years later, during which time she experienced the loss of a child and I of a parent, I turned my attention back to the significance of writing about her life. This is only the beginning of her stories, her life.

TESTIMONY FROM A TEJANA FEMINIST

I was born January 7, 1938, in Nuevos Casa Grandes, Chihuahua, Mexico. Don Miguel Valdez Martinez, that's my grandparents, and Doña Romanita Martinez de Valdez Martinez. My mother is Santagracia, now her name is Catano, but she was Santagracia Valdez Martinez. She was married to [my father] who was an out-of-towner, unknown. It was a very unhappy event, a very unhappy occurrence. He cut out of our lives when I was two and a half years old, and he went to California. We migrated to the United States when I was nine years old, and I was very unhappy about migrating. My mother had remarried, and we were coming to live with her new husband. I was very unhappy about moving. I talked to my grandfather about it. And my grandfather said, "Well, just remember, as long as you're in the southwest, you're in our extension area. This is our growth area. They can never stop us. This is ours. You're just going to their territory. As long as you're in the southwest, you're in your land. Don't let that worry you." And that has always stayed with me. As long as I'm in the southwest, I'm OK.

My grandparents were very revolutionized. My grandparents were my second parents! First of all, we spent a lot of time with them when I was little. My grandfather taught me to read when I was four. Being a revolutionary and a progressive, he became a preacher. He was a very religious person, so he converted to Protestantism. That was the progressive thing to do in the thirties. I grew up with my grandparents. Of course, he came up to see us at least once or twice a month to El Paso, and we spent all our summers with them. At first [there were] four of us, two brothers and two sisters, then my two brothers died. One was six, and one was just eight months, a year old perhaps. My sister is about four years younger than I am. She and I grew up together with a single mom, because my mom became a widow within a year of remarrying. So we grew up with a single mom. She was only twenty-six when she was widowed. She was single from then on. We were living in El Paso. She was middle class by upbringing, because my grandparents were very well-to-do in Mexico. But she was working class by necessity, having to work in El Paso in the garment industry. She worked in the garment industry for about forty years before she retired when she was sixty. So I have a very unusual upbringing.

My mother always went to great pains to make sure we were starched, and ironed, and curled. We went to school like little princesses all the time. I don't know how she did it; she worked sixteen hours a day. My mother was working class in position, but middle class in upbringing. So it was kind of hard. We went to live in a middle-class neighborhood, in the worst housing in a middle-class neighborhood, the worst housing, but in a middle-class neighborhood because my mother was very concerned about safety. So all the romanticism about living in the barrio, I'm sorry. Sometimes it can be a very unsafe place for single mothers and small children. You know you can have a mixture of classes and you're very safe. In this city [Austin] you have to be very careful before you take your children and try to raise them in the barrios.

I did everything with my mother! I admire single mothers a lot because, as a married woman all my life now, since I was twenty-five, I've had a companion. I don't think we did half the things with our children, except bring them to movement activities, as my mother did with us. My mother worked two jobs, and I don't know how, most of the time when we were little, I don't know how she had time to take us to church, to carnivals, on trips. But we always had our trips. I had a really nice childhood. She still lives in El Paso. My husband's very supportive. His parents are deceased, so he doesn't have any obligations, and he puts in a lot of care and attention and love towards my mother. She's our only surviving parent. She's on the go. She's seventy-five years old. I don't think of her as seventy-five years old. She's always on the go. She's a very active person, really funny.

I went to school in Mexico, and then when we came here I went to school here. You're not going to believe this, but all of my elementary school, when I graduated seventh grade, I had perfect attendance. I got a certificate for reading worth $166. When I came from Mexico, they skipped me up to two grades. I started first grade, then they skipped me up to third grade right away. I loved school. We grew up with Anglos and U.S.–Mexican children. The U.S.–Mexican children were very cruel, just like they are to immigrant children today. They would call me "basement roach," because we lived like in a house basement. They called me all kinds of ugly names. They were very ugly to us, to the children that were Spanish-speaking, and to the children that were bilingual. And we were totally bilingual. I was the interpreter for the other kids that came new to the school. And, yes, they put us down a lot. We were really discriminated against. The teachers in my elementary school were very good. It wasn't until junior high that I got my first dose of racism. The teachers in elementary school were very good. But I just thought schools here were so beautiful. That's why I believe in beautiful buildings for children, beautiful buildings that are well kept, because sometimes children live in less than ideal situations from their school. But if their schools are beautiful, they have that as a thing to look forward to. I really thank the fact that the schools were really beautiful, and they were a beautiful part of my life.

I wanted to be a journalist when I was younger. I wanted to be a writer, but journalism's what I wanted. We had a lousy School of Journalism at University of Texas at El Paso. So, instead of doing that, I went into English. But I daydreamed about becoming a writer. My Mexicana role models, I have two, three: Doña Josefa de Ortiz Dominguez, because my grandparents spoke about her; Elena Vicarro, that I write about in my book, *Diosa y Hembra*. Those three were my role models. And my grandmother, from the Mexican side, she [grandmother] was so hard working, and so brave, and so together. And of course, my mother, because she was so brave, and so hard working.

I had a best friend in junior high. In junior high it was the pits. There was a girl from a Catholic school that spoke up for me. And my mother couldn't speak for me. My mother wouldn't understand. My mother felt, like, well, maybe there's something wrong. Maybe this person's right. This person is your teacher, after all. You know how it is. We run this authority thing. And this girl was able to help me, and I'm very grateful to her. She remained my friend throughout high school, and I learned from her how to be very assertive and how to depart from listening to my Mom. I had to take a different step. I learned from her how to get around; how to use the PTA [Parent Teachers Association]; how to have a good relation with the principal; how to speak up; how to defend myself; how to defend others; and if everything else failed, how to be downright nasty. And this girl came from a Catholic school. She was Irish Catholic, and she was totally nuts. But I learned from her in junior high. I remember I was very frustrated. I guess I was in a front desk at school, and crying. And she just came up and she said, "What is the problem, and why is this woman treating you this way? Why is the teacher treating you like that?" I told her, "I don't know." Anyway, this girl said, "I'll go to my mom. And we'll take care of it. And you'll get this straightened out." And they did. They took me out and put me in another class. That was also very important. That taught me that peers can be rather important resources. And that taught me that there were things that we could do as

Mexicanos, there were ways of getting around it, and it was my turn, many, many times after that, to help others. I just watched her. I watched what she did. I watched how she did it. I went with her. We talked to PTA. We talked to influential people in the community. We talked to the principal. I just picked up and said, "Well, bullshit! I'm not gonna let this happen anymore." Junior high, I mean, in elementary, it never happened. Never happened. So I didn't know what it was. So that was real important. I guess you learn along the way that there are times when people come and help you; and there are times when you can help others. That was very important to me, a very important experience. And as anti-Anglo as I am, that there have been good people in my life. That is so important. That's something that nobody considers in leadership or, at least, in activist. I like to use activist instead of leadership because you're not a leader all the time. If you're lucky, you're a leader when people say you are. I became an interpreter; in fact, I'm still an interpreter. That's one of my, it's been one of the most productive things in my life, money-wise. This is a role that you never abandon. I'm not saying everybody does it; but I'm saying that with certain personalities, I've got that personality, this is something that you carry through all your life. *Las formas*, I can look at them, I can do them. I can get a whole application package for this guy that's suffering a lot, and I don't know anything about his situation.

I have very successful high school records. I did a lot of stuff in high school. I was school editor with my friend. We were editors and then I went on to UTEP. I graduated from there in 1962, and I got married in 1963. I knew my husband's family before, from work in the community, especially in the cultural arts area. His family's from Juarez. I met him [again] when he came back from the Air Force. I met him from those activities and in college. We met in 1959 and got married in 1963. We had our first child in 1964. We had a very good financial situation because my husband and I are college graduates. We were college graduates in the sixties. We were probably one of the first totally modern marriages. It didn't start out that way, but it became that way very early, because I was just like a total bitch. He tried to put on some real reactionary stuff on me, and I just always responded in a joke. I always made him see how silly it was. He became very supportive. He's a very smart guy, so he knows crap when he sees it, when I point it out to him. So, there was never any question about which way we should go in our relationship. If we're gonna have any kind of a relationship, it was gonna have to be on a real equal relationship.

We got our education on our own. Besides scholarships and all that, I've paid for my own education in El Paso by working full-time. He wanted to study architecture here. So he paid for his own education. We worked really, really hard. We were two people with college degrees. That should give you a head start, that you've got the raw material there. So I made sure that I married the first guy that really argued with me. That was my standard. I said, "If I could ever find a man that argues with me, that discusses things with me, that's the guy I'm gonna marry. If I can't find somebody like that, I'm not gonna bother." I couldn't stand these guys, "yes, yes." Just give you your way so they could have their way with you. I said, "Shit, no." And so I never really had any serious boyfriends. Then this guy, he really argued with me, whether he knew what he was talking about our not! Most of the time, he didn't know what he was talking about. So he'd argue with me, and I said, "Oh, this is something very interesting; imagine arguing back! Oh good, OK. I think we have something here." We went together for about four years, and we finally got married in 1963. He wanted somebody that was really mental. And I don't know whether he meant, mental, mental crazy; or mental, mental intelligent.

We got along fine. And after he got over a lot of the early macho stuff, I just didn't let him get away with it. He'd say, "You know, my socks; they never matched." And I'd say, "Who cares? There's a war going on; there's people getting killed; there's things to be done. There's a lot going on here in this city, between Anglos and blacks and Chicanos! And you want me to sit there and worry about whether your socks match? Get real! Get real! What's the deal? Do I ever complain that my socks don't match?" That was a real turning point in our lives. I said, "Get pantyhose. Your socks don't match, get pantyhose." So that's how our relationship evolved from there. He was very supportive because he was smart. And he was supportive because he could make it too. He's a very ethical and very moral person. So all of the decisions that we made about everything, we made together, and we would think about them and then just say, "You know what? I wonder should we do this?" And we were, like, at the same time, say, "Well, should we do this?"

1964 was our first getting involved with PASSO [Political Association of Spanish Speaking Organizations]; 1966 getting involved with farm worker movement and march; 1967 with police brutality issues. We started working with the upholsters' union. So we had been recruiting for the Crystal City walkout. I had been very active in recruiting tutors and walkouts. Nevertheless, he was used to, "OK, we'll do it as long as it's convenient. We'll be activists as long as I don't have to move from our little home." When it came time to go, because all the schools blew out, and there were a series of walkouts in Crystal City, we planned the walkouts. And when it was time for the tutors to go to Crystal City and do a teach-in with the students, we had a two-week vacation period that I could take from my job. He didn't wanna go. Well, it was gonna be uncomfortable. It was gonna be cold and wet and uncomfortable. I think he wanted to do something else with his time off. That was a real serious discussion that we had. I said, "Of course, I'll go." And that was, of course, unthinkable because everything we did we did together. We had a baby. Well, she was about three years old or two [Maria]. So we had her, and there was a problem as to what we were gonna do with her. I told him, "I'm going." I felt that it was tutti-frutti to be recruiting people and then not to show up. You'd be recruiting people that were gonna go over there, God knows where they were gonna sleep, what were they were gonna eat, what were they gonna do, how to drive around.

We were in the network. We had formed in 1964 or 1965 a Texans for Educational Advancement for Mexican Americans (TEAMS). We had formed chapters to look at the situation of education in our own particular community. From TEAMS we had a network of educators throughout the state, and when these walkouts started at the community level, at the grassroots level, it was naturally up to TEAMS that was composed of primarily teachers, elementary, secondary parents, and college students to respond. Who else was gonna respond? We were the ones that were up on education on a day-to-day basis. I was working as Information Director for the Southwest Educational Systems. Before that, I had been for four years Head of Documents at the State Library. I told Juan, "I can't have been recruiting and sending people here there and all, and now I have a chance to go to Crystal City [Texas] and help." And I wasn't gonna be one to stay home and be warm and have a wonderful trip. And so I said, "I'm sorry. I'm going, and I'll hitch a ride." And I didn't even drive! "I'll hitch a ride with somebody." And so he decided, "Well, now, if that's what you wanna do, we'll go." We'd already met Angel [Gutierrez] that summer. And we thought Angel was totally nuts. I remember Juan came home one day and said, "I met this guy from the university who's nuts, and his name is Jose Angel Gutierrez. And he's talking revolution; I mean, real revolution." And I said, "Oh, bring him to the house." And he brought him to the house, and I thought, "Yeah, this guy is nuts." We just agreed that we'd stay in communication, and if anything happened in Crystal City he'd let us know. When the walkout happened, it happened in the fall, in the winter that year he called us and said, "We want you to help get us volunteers to come and teach-in."

We went to tutor while the walkout was going on, and then we came back. Everybody went to tutor at different times. And we went to tutor so the kids could complete the semester. TEA (Texas Educators Association) told us, "If you get enough tutors so classes can be meeting, then, we'll give them credit for the semester." That was a big concern, especially for the high school students. So then we went to do that. And then Angel wanted us to go, Angel said, "We're gonna take over, really take over, the school district. Would you consider coming?" We said, "No, not now." Because we were considering going with some of the court tutoring groups, considering setting up a Mexican American teacher's training college in the valley. So, we couldn't go, that's when we were writing position papers for Colegio Jacinto Treviño. So that's when we went to the college for six months. After Crystal City, believe it or not, that spring, we went to the valley to set up; he left the university, and we went to the valley. I left my job, and we went for the valley to set up a college through Antioch University. So we were involved in Colegio Jacinto Treviño. Well, we went to the college, and we had a commitment to stay for a year or two, but through Antioch. In fact, Juan was hired through Antioch. I was doing my master's through Antioch. Part of my master's project was to be at the college and to render information, do the library, and do stuff like that and then get my master's and teach. But what happened at Colegio Jacinto Treviño is the knowledge; por eso te digo que los de California estan bien tontos [and that's why I tell you that those from California are real dumb]. I mean, they came from California, and they screwed everything up. Then we had a . . .

because some guy from Colorado, from Corky's, Crusade for Justice, his son-in law, was one of the directors of the Colegio. And another director was this crazy guy, also from Colorado. And they're both totally nuts. And added to that pair came the knowledge from California. And it was, like, total chaos. Juan was so fed up. He can take everything except bullshit. He couldn't deal with that bullshit, so the Colegio split after six months. Some people stayed in the valley, and some people went to north Texas. We went to Crystal City. This was 1971. Angel offered Juan the urban renewal director's job, and they offered me the city's public library job. When I first went, I volunteered in the high school library, got it organized, and then I went to the city public library job.

I was involved before I became an U.S. citizen in politics. I was involved in El Paso in the Viva Kennedy campaign. So when we came here [Austin], the first thing we did was check in with the [Raza Unida] Party and start getting involved here. I hated the Anglos here in Austin. I hated the way they worked because of the racism that we found here. But we started working on black campaigns here in Austin. We did fund raisers for black candidates. The blacks were the larger community, about 15 percent of the population, and we [Mexicans] were 10 percent. So we supported black candidates, hoping that we could make it 25 percent. And they never won. We worked with mainly local candidates here in the 1960s. So we left in 1969 and came back in the winter; we came back in 1973. See the time was going by so fast.

We did not go to the Denver 1969 conference, but we were pissed when Enriqueta Vasquez called us after the conference and she said, "Well, they voted not to be liberated" (laughter). I said, "I'm not surprised." It didn't surprise me one bit that they would do that, not one bit. There's a lack of collective consciousness, and we cannot have a collective consciousness, and that's what I kind of in a small way, along with Enriqueta Vasquez, Betita Martinez, Bernice Zamora . . . Francisca Flores, definitely the leader of the pack did; went to try to establish a connection. After that conference, it was shocking. They were the Crusade women. A lot of them were very young women and very much under the thumb of Corky [Gonzalez]. The prevailing winds were that, to be a cultural nationalist, you had to live up to the stereotype that the Anglos had shown these kids, because this was not something that was developed in our community. This stereotype of the culturalist nationalist passed to the Mexicano was acquired knowledge at U.S. universities. It was believing and listening to Anglo media about us. It was listening to sociologists in Anglo society, that's what it was. These were young people, a lot of them were groupies. Now we did have in the movement the problem of young groupies. I'm sorry to say, but we had the groupies that dropped in and dropped out. We had the opportunists that dropped in and dropped out for whatever reason, because they had a political agenda.

The 1969 [Denver] conference I missed just by a few days because I was in and out of the Crusade a few days before that, but I didn't go to that conference. And the main reason I didn't go, I mean, I just felt like it was gonna be a lost cause. I didn't realize, I should have known that there would be a woman's caucus because we were beginning to caucus; we were beginning to have conferences, and out of the conferences, we would caucus. I just didn't realize the issue of what was gonna come up. We used to go to conferences, big conferences, civil rights conferences, and I would just publicly say, "You guys are really dumb. If you would bring your wives and your girlfriends, we would have three times the number of people here!" They were *bien viejajeros*! [womanizers]. And I said, "Ok, bring us your wives and girlfriends, and we'd have three times the people here." "Ha, ha, ha!" They thought it was really funny, but it was true. The fact is that it's that acquired stereotype and the lack of a collective consciousness about what a reality is. But that was very important to get us on the road. That attitude, that pervasive attitude was very important to get us on the road to document some history. And also about pushing us out of stages in civil rights conferences. Where, literally, they attempted not to let us speak. Like in Houston. The Chicano conference in Houston. I think that was 1970. Just like a statewide conference. Where they tried to boo Hernandez, and that really pissed me off. That was in Austin in 1970, because she's a woman. We almost to have fistfights with the guys on the floor. So that's when I decided that I was the one person in the Texas movement that was the most, the best trained in research. So I would go ahead and start with my positive role models and expand on that.

When La Raza Unida was formally organized, I guess the first meeting was 1971, or 1970. The first meeting San Antonio, we went. We were already in Crystal City. From Crystal City, we were calling everybody, everybody was to call their friends that they had in various cities. And we had a lot of friends in many cities because we had been involved in the boycott movement. And we had been involved in all the civil rights conferences. Everybody went to civil rights conferences. It was like, not an organization. But if you had a civil rights conference in Houston, everybody went. It would be the local Houston committee. We had one in Austin, in El Paso; that was one government function, in 1969, we didn't go to that. But we went to a Houston conference. There was one in San Antonio and one in El Paso, and always there was talk about a party. Mario [Compean] was the one in charge of that. They were the ones to bring the party idea to the forefront, and Crystal City as a community was the forefront for the party. Because Crystal City had a background in political activism and they had had people working that had run for office in the 1950s. So Crystal City was the focal point.

See, there were lots of movements going on. And keeping in mind too that there were different people involved for different reasons. Maria Elena Martinez; Virginia Muzquiz; Carmen Lomas Garza, the artist; Nick Tovar, the writer; Betita Martinez, the writer-journalist . . . Enriqueta Vasquez; and others—Alma Canales, who's running for Lieutenant Governor. Maria Hernandez was in her seventies when she joined the Raza Unida movement. I need to add to this Rosie Castro, of San Antonio; Anita Compean; Raquel Orendain, farmworker [activist] with Raza Unida from the valley. I'm talking about Texas women primarily with few exceptions. But that's the perspective, and then you will have other people with other agendas. The same people that were doing el Colegio were also working along with others to lay the groundwork for the party.

MAYO [Mexican American Youth Organization] was concentrating on the college on the party. We were concentrating on the college, but networking with the party. And the artists were with the college and with the party and with the writers and the university people like Americo Paredes. Some people from all these networks joined the [Raza Unida] Party or started laying the groundwork for the party. If you look at the party platform they include a lot of issues. There were housing specialists who were Raza Unida people. There were educators that were Raza Unida people. There were poets, there were writers, and there were farmworker organizers. There were anti–law-enforcement agency people, Raza Unida people working to clean up the [Texas] Rangers. It was a lot of people. We were at the college, and we were working with the Raza Unida organizers. By this I mean, we were in touch. And always, like, "How far are you along? How ready are we to have our first convention?" And, of course when the first convention came about, there was no doubt that everybody was going to participate. It was expected that everybody that was in the movement would be Raza Unida. That was just a given. That was like the next progression. And, of course, some people did not. Some people, like Gonzalo Barrientos here, and some of his friends, waited it out with the Democrats. Raza Unida was a reaction against the Democratic Party not opening up, not allowing people to have meaningful positions.

The way it spread was through the network. MAYO is ready. We were getting it together, and here is where the first conference is coming. The first conference was in San Antonio in 1970. It was a very busy year because we had had a conference here in Austin. And we had had smaller meetings of people like [Jose] Angel; we had people at the college that were part of MAYO. We were not part of MAYO. We were always five years older or more. We were only in our thirties when all of this happened. So we were kind of like in an awkward age. And MAYO was more, was very youth oriented. People were mobilized through a network. The movement had many networks. The movement had the writers and artists, the academicians, the grassroots people. But the grassroots people were the oldest. They're the ones that gave us a lot of credibility, as well as the academicians. And then we had the political arm; the Raza Unida Party was seen as the political arm of the movement. Oh, then we had the farmworker movement [Texas Farm Workers]. The farmworker movement was extremely important, and along with the farmworker movement we had the labor. We had communication workers and so forth. So we had all together about ten networks. The state conventions were real hands-on, and out of Raza Unida came excellent political leadership. People that are still in state legislature, people that were coming up. Raza Unida provided more leadership for the longest period of time in this state than anybody else has done.

Our objectives were to help the grassroots communities in south Texas. The prime objective was to break the stronghold of the Democratic party in communities where it was 90 to 95 percent of the Mexican Americans had no representation. The Democrats will give you leaflets and let you leaflet, but that's all; they're not gonna teach you the ins and outs of politics. They're not gonna teach you how to run a campaign, how to organize a campaign, and how to preen candidates; they weren't teaching us that. We really needed a party of our own where we would learn everything from the ground up, and we could really learn political structure. La Raza Unida was an excellent way to learn the political structure in addition to preparing politicians to take over in the twenty-first century.

The purpose was to help South Texas, and to develop a catered politician in south Texas and that definitely happened. The objectives were to empower the people and to win elections. That happened in towns like Carrizo Springs, Pleasanton, Crystal City, Floresville, all of these towns where we organized the community, we instituted the party, we trained people how to get elections, all of those towns are now run by Mexicanos. That was our first objective. We felt that if we could gain that objective and empower people at the grassroots in those southern Texas communities and others, then we would have representation at the state eventually. Eventually, if the party survived, there would be representation at the local level and the state level so that Mexicanos would start getting some representation, because they seemed, like, hopeless. It seemed like, even if you had like, 95 percent of the community, you were not getting political representation. If you couldn't get it at 95 percent, what could we in Austin do at 10 percent, or 15 percent? We had no hope.

Now for anybody who wants to do any analysis, all they have to do is look at the representation before Raza Unida, look at the representation after Raza Unida, and not focus on whether the people today feel Raza Unida was effective or not. That's immaterial! The fact is that you're in control, buddy! And you weren't in control before Raza Unida. Without Raza Unida, those doors, those barriers, would never have cracked. Or if they had, we would have awful crutches there, because the only people that were being allowed in were people that would play the Anglo game. And we, Raza Unida, liberated the Mexicano community because when they came into this community, they came in on their own terms. They did not, they don't owe shit to the Anglo structure! And I think it would have been very different if the Democrats had let them in. When you open your own doors, you don't owe them anything! And that's what Raza Unida did. And that's one thing that people still don't understand.

I ran for State Board of Education, a very reluctant candidate. I ran because they didn't have a candidate. My son was eight months old. I had to train him to hand out literature. It was very traumatic. I ran in a very rural district out of Crystal City for State Board of Education. I think I got like 28 percent of the vote. It was very hard to beat established Democratic candidates. We had organizations in all of the counties. It was not my intention not to run for office. It was never my intention to be a leader. I would much rather be known as a thinker. But all my life I've been drawn to activism. I'd much rather sit and think, and figure things out, and write things out. I really enjoy that. I can't imagine why people don't see the connections. I didn't want to be a candidate. When you're a candidate, and when you're in politics and in electoral office, it takes a very special kind of person. It takes a person that is not an absolutist, the way I like to be. It takes a person that is able to compromise and able to negotiate, and that's a very special skill. And also a person that is able to take a look at the big picture and love everybody. I always feel like, I only have one lifetime and I want to concentrate my love in one direction, and I would not be a very generic politician. I have had to learn because of Juan, because my husband is so good at looking at the whole picture, that he tells me, "Look, if the politician does 10 percent of what you want him to do, thank your lucky stars." If you can accomplish something, one or two little things, that's enough. So you have to be real special to think that way, and I've learned to accept that.

The happiest that I've ever been is with Mujeres de la Raza Unida [Women of the Raza Unida]. That was the happiest that I've ever been, because I was doing what I really wanted and that was consciousness raising. That's what I groove on. I really love that. We always had support for Mujeres por Raza Unida. Always. I have to say one thing about Raza Unida, we always had a lot of support from the guys. Now, one-on-one, we had to work things out with Angel in Crystal City. We came across attitude. We came across bad attitudes on giving women credit and sharing the glory and all of that stuff. But these are things that for either, right or wrong, they didn't matter to us. Maybe they should have mattered to us, but what mattered to us was the position of the movement in relation to accepting women, women's input or not. That's what really

mattered and our ability to work within the movement unfet-
tered. That's what mattered to us. The recognition or lack of
recognition and all of that, we weren't looking far enough into
the future, and we were not looking into our place in history.
We were looking into what was happening there, today, and
eventually what would happen in politics in the future.

Our political projections into the future are fabulously
accurate in that in our elected officials we have just about as
many women as we have men right now in Texas in electoral
politics. That was really good. Where we got cut out were in
things that didn't matter us as much. Like I said, looking at
it from your perspective maybe they should have mattered,
but they didn't matter . . . that was, who got the credit. It just
didn't matter. What mattered to us were other things: coop-
erativeness, bringing the women in, making sure that the community was aware, incorporating the eradication of sexism as
part of the movement. He [Ignacio Garcia] has a paragraph
on women. Of course it's all missing. He's missing on the
people that made the party possible. That's OK. He's got a
superficial piece [United We Win] that is going to take a lot of
revisionist history. Which is good, it gives you a job. It gives
you something meaningful to do. But it goes to show you how,
despite a lot of our work . . . maybe the women were aware of
what we were really doing. Enlarge the ranks, and sensitize
at least that generation of men to women making history.
Maybe there's a way without destroying the souls of activist
women to put ourselves in that history without destroying the
real issue, which is to act.

It [Mujeres por Raza Unida] started kind of for the same
reasons that we better start doing some consciousness raising today. It did have its roots in things like the Denver Youth
Conference, and it did have its roots in other civil rights conferences we had in the seventies; where in the 1970, that's
the precise year, where we would let the guys be the ones to
plan the conferences. Then our agenda never got on. Our
agenda was real simple, our agenda was child care, health,
you know the usual female-oriented issues. Opening up political opportunities to men and women, so that issues would
get there. Our agenda a lot of times had to do with writers
and poets, never really given their own time, like we had a
knock-out drag-out, because we wanted Carmen to do a presentation on Latina artists in Houston. That is one of the
things that made us so angry, that they would not include [us].

We were beginning to notice that, because we were not demanding, it would never occur to these guys to include the female agenda. Not only that, that it wasn't just important to include the female agenda, but it was important to include female bodies presenting that agenda, so that others in the community would see that activism and leadership could come from both genders, that was the main thing. We felt that if women in the community didn't see women on the agenda or presenting issues, then women would think that there wasn't room for them to become activists. So that was the main reason why we started pushing for the specific inclusion of women in the conferences. It was because we were not included, like in Houston we presented a list of demands. I don't know if we ever wrote them up or if I have them, but a list of demands. We had not decided who was going to do it, and they wanted me to do it and I said, "No." I mean I didn't really didn't want to be the one to do it, but no one else wanted to do so I was the one that got up there and gave the demands. Then in Houston that's another . . . where one of the young kids screamed, "Why don't you go home and do the dishes where you belong." It was one of those "why don't you go back to Mexico" kind of things. So then I just decided that these people are acting out of ignorance, they just do not know. They are cultural nationalists, but these people don't know that part of our culture is the participation of women. This is not something that is not part of our culture. And that's when I started putting that first book together.

The very first thing I wrote is, on an emergency basis, is that thing in *Event* magazine on women and activism. That was the first thing before the book [*Diosa y Hembra*] and then I started working on *Diosa y Hembra*. We realized that it wasn't just failure, *como te dijere* [how should I say it], it wasn't just oversight. These guys honestly believed that women did not belong in the movement other than to do as they were told. There was a certain attitude, a lack knowledge, of the men *and the women* about our history. I felt that we were on the right track on a lot of issues, except for the inclusion of women. Too it was the fact that we really very strongly believed that the home was a very good basis for educating the children, and if women didn't have a self-concept about themselves and the meaning of being Mexican, then what it meant to be a Mexican American woman. They were not going to be able to impart the kind of strength that had been imparted to us in our homes and our situations.

The other thing was that if we didn't carve out a significant growth for women to where there would be visible models and movement activity, that it would be very difficult for us to recruit women to come into the movement, to come into the party and run for office. Guys wanted us to run for office not necessarily because they felt that we had any good issues to carry forth or a different perspective, but because they were running out of guys. Like in Crystal City, a lot of the times men couldn't run because of their jobs, they were vulnerable to being dismissed. So we needed wives to run, we needed women to run that weren't as vulnerable or maybe even didn't have jobs. So it was also a logistical, a matter of numbers. For me, it was a matter of numbers, bringing more numbers into the movement. The more people we brought, the more successful we would be in carrying our agenda and in electing people to office at the local level and having a better chance of electing even Anglos that were more in tune to the movement. But we needed the numbers. Also, I felt that we needed the consciousness. I wanted that revolutionary consciousness that women are so good at imparting, especially when women can reinforce that consciousness, as my grandmother had done with me.

Being a good researcher, one of the first things I did was lock myself away for a long time, for a while at least with my little children, and really study, research, get my facts. I knew my facts, because my grandmother was a very strong imparter of that information about women's roles. I had grown up with some very strong role models, but I didn't have a lot of details. So the thing that I did was do that research. I have been analyzed and I have been criticized for writing contributory history, which was *Diosa y Hembra*. *Diosa y Hembra* was never meant to be any kind of academic history, *Diosa y Hembra* was a propaganda piece, it was just a background for a book. I was supposed to provide this story, and somebody was supposed to write it. I wrote it so somebody else would find it, but we never had the money. We never got an editor, so they published it the way I'd given it to them. And then they put in a lot of misspellings in the text, and I didn't realize that. *Diosa y Hembra* was to provide the facts, with the sources; irrefutable sources to give us a way in to cultural nationalism, to give us a position in cultural nationalism as women, and to strengthen our position within the movement that so that these men would not destroy the movement by running the women away.

What these [women] didn't know is that they could destroy the movement. They could've brought it to a screeching halt if the women, like myself and others, had just gone home. If the women went home, the men would never go to the meetings. Who controls the meetings? We figured out that if the woman said, "¿Para que vas viejito? Mira, quedate. Quedate en la casa y te hago una cenita. Y luego despues de la cenita . . ." I need you to be home. They would not have come. If the woman . . . we understood the power of women within the family and in the community. We understood that the movement would survive as long as the women were there. I understood that I was biggest promoter of our family being in the movement. Our family could basically take or leave the movement. I was living spirit, the soul behind it. That if I didn't want to go to a conference, we'd never go. If I didn't want to go to a meeting, I'd make sure Juan never went. We controlled the social environment. We could make or break the social environment. We decide what's gonna happen socially. We felt that if we empowered the women, if women felt really good about participating, especially if . . . to expand the movement we needed to expand the participation of women. We needed to make the participation of women totally tied to cultural nationalism, I mean totally tied. That the people who said that women should not be involved were the people who were *agringados*, not us. If they wanted to make those accusations, they were the ones that had learned stupid things from American sociologists, not us. We were not going to allow anybody to drive us away from what was our culture, so we made feminism part of cultural nationalism. We made it OK to be Chicano and OK to be a feminist.

I know there were guys in Crystal City who would tell Juan, "Hey, why don't you do something about Martha? Look at that which she's doing. She's out there working on this training and bringing women in. Look at what she's saying and reading." Juan would just say, "Hey, if you feel that you can do something, fine! I don't pretend to be able to rule Martha's life. But if you feel up to that, be my guest. I don't have any problems; you talk to her. I think Martha's going to do whatever she feels she has to do, just like I do too." He was talked to a lot, "Pull her, bring her, rein her in." He would say, "What's there to rein in? You do it. You feel that she's doing something out of line, you talk to her."

We went to all the conventions. Well, the El Paso convention was later, in 1972. And it was very hard when we came together as a national movement to get a national agenda going. The national convention; it was so stupid! Such a waste of time! Well, we couldn't get anything done! All the guys were playing politics, walking around, strutting. The most productive convention, would you say, was the state convention. They were real. There were real issues. And we didn't let the guys bullshit. "OK, you can bullshit, but let's get real here. Let's do some work." And that's what we did, the real political organizing. We talked to communities. And we helped them strategize their campaigns. I think for the most part, most of us could see the national impact further down the line. We were looking down the line at developing this leadership so that Texas, today, and we do have an excellent group of legislators, so that we could have legislators that we could count on. I don't think we were looking at the national picture, if we didn't fix the local and statewide picture. I think when we got together as a national movement it was a little premature at that time, so a lot of the people that controlled the situation were the people that wanted to become the national leaders. Then it became a circus. To me, the national meetings were always a circus opportunity.

The union people were very supportive. In fact, sometimes we even convinced them to come along and promote issues within the women's movement as a whole, that were minority issues. Sometimes we would talk them into the gay and lesbian coalitions. Sometimes I regretted that we talked them into it, because these things weren't worth going to, but sometimes we felt that maybe we could promote the ERA agenda or the pro-choice agenda. I'm thinking of specific people involved in the union movement, particularly locally and statewide, and then people involved in the gay and lesbian movement that sometimes wanted to protest. The other thing is that the more radical movements were the ones that generally supported La Raza Unida and would vote Raza Unida, like the Young Socialists. We had to depend on those camps to help us, we had to depend on the working-class movement. The union movement, we had to depend on some people from there, some people from the Socialist movement to come and help us. They [Freedom Socialist Party] were very, very supportive of Raza Unida and they did work and vote for Raza Unida. This is what I meant, that for the radical feminist, usually, we were a much more mainstream group than they were used to dealing with so they were very supportive of Raza Unida.

Now the mainstream feminists, we were eons away from them. These people were not interested in radical change. These people were a careerist, that's what it is. They were not there because they were committed to change. They were careerists, anything that would benefit their careers. Anything that would give them more money and better jobs and access to credit. Look at the issues. The only real issue that the feminist's movement has is the pro-choice issue. That's the only real noncareerists, nonopportunists, clean-cut issue, is the pro-choice issue. Everything else is careerist, even the military crap. Think about it. So what happened? I just told our women, "Don't worry about the feminist movement. Whatever they get, we're gonna get. If we need to support them whenever we can, live with it. We can support them." We tried, we really felt like, oh these women, the NOW women, we should really work with these women. I tried and I thought to myself, "If they're putting out all this propaganda, maybe they have some real issues in mind. Like eradicating sexism and racism in the schools, that was one big issue." Economic opportunities, especially contracting opportunities where we were getting totally ripped off, because we were paying taxes and never getting anything back into the community capsule. We couldn't get them involved—No! No way! They were not interested. The only thing they were interested in, things that would advance their political careers or things that would line their pocketbook. Period. So I told our women, "Let's just work with them cuando lo convenga, because they're going to that and we can get it. That's easy." Things like that they're easy to get. Credit, stuff like that, they're easy to get. Real power and substantial change—that's hard work.

That's why I'm saying that the radical group we found to be more consistent in ideology with what we wanted to do, like working on the right for working class women. For example, NOW, they were not interested in firefighters, getting into the fire department. Not unless they could be chiefs, you know? They were not interested in poor women being discriminated, poor women being discriminated against in the police academy or women being discriminated in the labor union. That's

why we turned and worked with radical women and continued to work with gay and lesbian women a lot. I think if gay
women, lesbian women have a problem with the community
. . . I've told my daughter this, we're all going to have one-on-
one problems in whatever stands we take for the people we
love, there are people we cannot lobby. There are people we
have to accept the way they come, their little attitudes. We
accept them because we love them, we go about our business.
I think a lot of lesbian women suffer those one-on-one experiences with their family. Then they take these experiences and
put them on the whole community. I've never known of an
antilesbian movement in our community or in our group
[women's] or any kind of discrimination in our group against
lesbian women, not even jokes. I mean, not in MABPWA (Mexican American Business and Professional Women's Association), not in HWT (Hispanic Women's Texas Network), not in
Raza Unida, in anything. Never a protest, never a hate crime
that has come to my attention. So I don't know where these
feelings are coming from that the community does not love
lesbian women or gay men.

I wrote that [a letter to Chicano studies] as president of
MABPWA. We were just furious that the women who had
worked so hard to set up the Chicano studies movement,
worked so hard to set up everything. The people that didn't
get it the worst were academicians, they were the most insu-
lated class when it came to eradicating the sexism. She [Anna
Nieto-Gomez] suffered a lot, because California had a hard-
core group of antifeminists that are a hard-core group of
"groupies." It's what we called them, movement groupies, and
it's kind of mean. The women that were there to please the
men, at the pleasure of the men. The women that were there
to find guys. Women that were there for whatever, that's a legitimate role, it's just that the guys used them to interfere with
the women who were involved for a reason, for a real reason.
I'm talking about a group of women that were very committed
to the development of the community and then there were the
groupies, then there were the opportunists.

The opportunists, the academicians that joined the movement to get something else from it. They didn't stay very long,
or they came in and out from the movement. And I think that
reading Anna Nieto-Gomez, however maligned she has been
outside of the state of Texas, specifically in her own state, in
our state, how she opened our eyes, in terms of the readings

and struggles that she had, out of that, she becomes one of our heroes. The other is Francisca Flores from Los Angeles and then Bernice Zamora. Some of the movement writers, they made a contribution to our consciousness, to our collective consciousness. I guess I'm talking about a collective consciousness of a certain category that has held together. And sometimes it does slip away. And that's why you saw me today doing something very concrete that we do with our women, together with our women. For example, it's very important to us, because if you're not involved in concrete day-to-day activism or activity, even if it's just for each other at times, even if it's just something as simple as going to the city council and talking against [Proposition] 187, or English Only. If you don't do one-on-one, day-to-day concrete things, it slips away. You start losing your sharp focus on group consciousness, and that's what we need to do some work on right now, is in listening to this group consciousness persistent in the movement. It seems that these women are the ones that supplied our nerve endings, you know, the last of the nerve endings, but that are constantly reconnecting with our bodies. I think that's what the 90s did, we lost that involuntary movement; there's very little connection. And it's not so much our brain and our body, it's more our brain and our soul. A lot of these women are the nerve endings still alive in the movement. And these are the nerve endings we need to reconnect to the community as a whole.

Works Cited

Compean, Mario. 1989. "Foreword: A Legacy Untold." In *United We Win,* ed. Ignacio García. Tucson: University of Arizona.

"I Want to Be Treated as an Equal": Testimony from a Latina Union Activist

Guadalupe M. Friaz

Latinas have been active participants in the struggle for a better life wherever they might be: in the fields, factories, service establishments, or in their own homes. Historically Latinas have looked to trade unions to provide an important avenue for the creation of social change, as well as for individual career advancement.

As the proportion of Latinas in paid employment grows, we are beginning to see a greater percentage of Latinas represented by unions. For example, in 1991, 16 percent of employed Hispanic women were represented by unions. Still, Latinas' proportionate representation in union is below that of black, white, and Hispanic men and below that of black women. The rates of union representation for these groups in 1991 are 28 percent, 21 percent, 19 percent, and 21 percent, respectively. Not surprisingly, Latinas as presidents, vice-presidents, or secretary-treasurers of their local, national, or international unions are few and far between.[1] This author's 1991 preliminary survey of union leaders in northern and southern California verifies this statement.

The voice of one Latina union activist richly illuminates the barriers that keep Latinas out of leadership positions within their unions as well as those factors that can facilitate their advancement into these positions. In the following pages, a forty-one-year-old Chicana, mother of two, relates how she became politicized as a result of her participation in the Great Society Programs of the 1960s and how she came to join a union. She details the difficulties she encountered at home when her husband wanted her to "be normal." She describes racism and sexism within her union and tells how being Chicana gave her added insight into male interracial relations; this insight allowed her to mediate a potentially explosive issue within her union. Finally, she tells of Chicanas' internal struggle to put themselves first.[2]

TESTIMONY FROM A LATINA UNION ACTIVIST

I went to a high school in the San Francisco area that was full of Latinos and blacks and Asians, and I had no idea there were that many white people in the world, until I got to UC Santa Cruz. Where did these people come from? Culture shock! . . . They didn't dress, no makeup, you know we were Chicanas looking great and dressing up in high heels. And they were like with holes in jeans, it was the height of the hippie era, and they were like flower children. I really went through a lot. . . .

Actually when I was looking for a job it was for my husband who was going to school and we needed some extra money. I was on a mission to get out of poverty. When I talked to the guy [at METRO] he says, "you know this is like a contest, you would have a better chance at winning this than him, because we need Spanish-speaking women." I got caught up in working for METRO, I mean, like my salary doubled when I went to work there.

It was the first time I ever joined the union. The first time I joined the union was when I came to work for METRO because it was a closed shop . . . so I paid my dues. I was a station agent, I still am. So when I first joined the union, I wasn't really thinking about becoming involved. I just wanted a good job.

By that time my daughter was about two-and-a-half, because I had her in '73 and I started working for METRO in 1975. You have to understand that at that time I was married to a guy who was very much like my father [laughter]. You always have to marry guys who are like your dad. Yes, he was dark, he was a Filipino Latino—no Spanish—and he was a musician. And he didn't like me doing community work! He wanted me to be normal, to have a regular job, and be a wife, take care of the family, and not go to meetings at night, and not to do a lot of stuff that didn't have to do with anything, he said.

I was going to go to work and not do anything else. Be a family person, take care of him, and all that kind of stuff. Because he had been bugging me and complaining since we got married that the community work that I did was not important or relevant. Basically I was never home. Well, I was home, but not what he considered home, because even at home I worked. I was on the phone, or writing, or reading and preparing.

I would take her [the baby] with me [laughter]. [Four months after] I had her I went back to work [for the community agency] so she came with me. She was in her little baby stroller, and that was the only way I would come back to work. She always hung out with me. It wasn't as though I was a negligent mother. The decision to go work somewhere else didn't come from him [her husband], it really came from me because I started looking at her and wondering what I was going to do about her medical care and all that.

So when I went to work for METRO I realized it was a really good job. And it came with benefits, I was really excited about that. You know at the time I got paid I cashed the check and I wanted it all in cash. And I went home and I just laid it all over the carpet. It was really exciting for me to have that much money.

Because being a station agent, especially when you come in as a new person, you are working very different shifts all the time, and because I had such junior seniority I had to work nights. Still I took care of my daughter and took her to preschool about three o'clock, and my husband would pick her up at five-thirty; that's when my shift started. So I thought OK, this will work for a little while. Then I started going to school again, but I started taking things like music. You know, trying to find things in common with my husband, things like art. . . . I was kind of bored, seeing that I wasn't doing very much, and I kind of let go of the community work. After about two years of that, I was really out of my tree.

I was always an opinionated person, so this guy, his name was Tim, he was a shop steward, and he said, "You know, Sandra, I think you would be a good shop steward, because you sure know how to talk a lot, and you know how to argue." He was black, and he recruited me. "I want you to be my shop steward." He was a chief steward. I said, "Well, what do I have to do?" He says, "What you do naturally, you argue for people when they have been wronged." I said, "That's all?" He says, "Yeah." I said, "OK, that's no big deal."

Before that time I went to union meetings, and I remember not knowing parliamentary procedures too well. And not knowing when to speak up or how to speak. And just kind of standing up and raising my hand, and then I realized there was a way in which you did it. And I learned that kind of process early on, but I started comparing it to organizing, that it wasn't really very much different than the community organizing that I had done before.

There's a lot to compare, you still got people together, you still ask for people's opinions, and you facilitated discussion, and that I was used to because of the community organizing that I had done with the young people, only this was between more diverse groups.

I guess the first thing that I realized was that the power, the leadership of the union, was male, and at the time that I was a union member in my early years, the union itself was young. I came to METRO in 1975, and it had only been there since 1973, so it was a relatively young union, and the leadership was just beginning to emerge. And so there was a power struggle going on between the white males and the black males, as to who was going to control the union.

I only know that now. Back then I was oblivious to it. I would go to meetings to see what was going on, but I didn't go that often. It wasn't until I was asked to be a shop steward in 1977 that I started going regularly, because that's what you have to do as part of being a shop steward, you go to the union meetings and find out what is going on. That's when I realized that the union was pretty much run by a black guy, John, who now is really like a mentor to me . . . .

In 1977, I started becoming a pretty active shop steward, going to meetings, and then in 1979 we had our first lockout, and I was actually a strike committee chairperson. I organized the strike committee of people, and I made the assignments and the picket assignments. I mean, I was really involved.

My organizing skills became relevant then because I knew how to do that based on organizing other things. My writing skills were kind of important. I did utilize my writing skills to help the president who took over John's job after he resigned; I helped him out with strategies quite a bit because of my background in community organizing. I enjoyed the role.

I guess part of it is cultural too, because Latinas, we like helping, we like thinking that [it] is really where it is at. At the time I didn't strive for leadership in the union, I never even thought about being in a leadership position, but because of my background, my educational background, and my organizing skills, I was plucked naturally. The president was more than happy to have me work, unions always need people to volunteer to do stuff, and since I volunteered to do this and did it so well, they said, "Oh great, what else can you do!"

After the 1979 lockout . . . the president was not reelected, and a white regime was elected. I remained a shop steward, and I probably did my best work, because this white guy was such an asshole I refused to be kicked out of the union. Because that's what happens, when a new regime comes in all the shop stewards resign, because the new president gets to appoint their own shop steward. Well, I didn't know that, and I didn't resign!

A lot of people choose to go to the affirmative action department instead of going through the union process [when dealing with racial discrimination on the job]. And they can choose to do either/or. As a matter of fact I was pretty instrumental in mediating a crisis during 1981, when Latinos at METRO began to get pretty ticked off about the lack of promotional opportunities for Latinos in METRO management, and it was true, there were fewer Latinos in management— and there still aren't [opportunities for Latinos].

They [Latinos] were very vocal—a community forum was organized to support them. There were Latinos in the union who actually started pointing the finger at the union, saying that the union was also being really racist, that they encouraged the promotion of blacks and not Latinos. I never believed pointing at another race for promotional opportunities and saying "look what they are getting and we are not getting" was a good idea.

I spoke up and said we were all in this together. I remember meeting the members, Latinos, in the union. The union needed to change but attacking another minority was not good. We should be applauding the fact that there are blacks in management, and we should strive for the same. But not point to them as the enemy, because that was not the enemy. It was difficult, and kind of a touchy situation, and I give a lot of credit to the community-based organizing experience in mediation that I got.

I remember going to the Board of Directors and talking about the recent Martin Luther King program that we had implemented and how we had all been really in harmony, and now we are coming before you and obviously there are some problems. But this has to do with fairness, and where Latinos are, that we were proud that blacks had that, and that we wanted to have the same opportunities. This kind of helped the tension in the room between the blacks and the Latinos; otherwise we were going to have a big problem. It could have easily gone that way. It could have been explosive, but it didn't [happen that way], and I always feel good about that. Ultimately, a program to recruit Latinos was implemented, including hiring a Latina outreach coordinator.

But it is not enough that you are skilled. When you get to the level of leadership that I attained, you are still a woman, and the racism and sexism is very subtle. . . . Latinas need to be given credibility. They need to be told that what they do is important, to be confident. A lot of the work requires going out to places where Latinas are not welcome. So you are going to be isolated, and you are going to be by yourself, and you don't find a lot of people to talk to or work with that are going to be like you. You are probably going to be the only one. So you have to kind of know what you are doing is good and you are OK at it. So from your family and from your Latino brothers and sisters, you need that encouragement. You need that support, that what you're doing is important.

It is not difficult, it is just that you feel insecure about it. But if you have done other things in the world, you can do that too. A lot of what motivated me was anger. Like, "I'll be damned if they are going to get me out of here!" [laughter] I mean the best work that I have done is because people didn't want me there. Some white guy didn't want me there, and I was going to be there anyway. And so, I insisted, and to me anger is what motivated me. And funny, I say you need support, you need love, you need attention, you need encouragement. But, I guess because I didn't have that, it was my own anger that motivated me. . . .

[Union] leadership cannot be afraid of bringing in new blood—bringing in the future. A true leader cannot be afraid to let go of power. You say you're too busy running the organization. Men particularly, if you don't agree with them, they blackball you. . . .

When women run for office, you must sell yourself, women are good at selling others, but feel too shy to sell themselves. I ran for secretary-treasurer, my president was supporting me. He told me, "You have to go out to the yards and talk to the men." I didn't do that, I felt too intimidated. I sent out flyers instead. I lost by six votes. At that time I was working on Jorge's campaign, he was running for supervisor, I made his campaign a higher priority over my own.

The white women's leadership has come from a different ground that has allowed them to gain skills and status in society, that we have not just naturally been given. You know we have had to fight our way to that kind of level and so, that's the one thing that I don't appreciate from white women—I can't stand the patronizing. I want to be treated as an equal, I don't want to be treated like somebody's little sister.

Notes

1. I was unable to locate any statistics on Latinas in union offices. The literature on women and unions largely ignores Latinas and occasionally considers black women. See, for example, Melcher et. al. 1992 or Chaisen and Andiappan 1989. Certainly women such as María Elena Durazo, president of the Hotel Employees and Restaurant Employees Union, Local 11; Alicia Sánchez, Founder of the Sonoma County Industrial Union, which later became affiliated with the Service Employees International Union; Felisa Castillo, secretary-treasurer of the Bakers Union, Local 24 in San Jose; and of course, Dolores Huerta, who served for years as vice-president of the United Farm Workers Union are notable examples.

Unions have made great strides in recognizing that it is essential to institute programs to hire a diverse staff and to reach out to Latina/o workers in order to make unions more closely reflect the composition of the labor force in terms of gender and race/ethnicity. Unions such as the International Union of Electrical Workers (IUE); the United Automobile Workers (UAW); Communication Workers of America (CWA); the American Federation of State, County, and Municipal Employees (AFSCME); the Service Employees Industrial Union (SEIU); and other unions have been at the forefront of organizing and advocating on behalf of women within their respective organizations and in society at large. Nevertheless, we have a long way to go before the composition of these unions and their leadership reflects the composition of the force.

2. Some of the particulars have been changed to protect the identity of the speaker.

Works Cited

Chaisen, Gary N., and P. Andiappan. 1989. "Analysis of the Barriers to Women Becoming Union Officers." *Journal of Labor Research* 10, no. 2 (spring).

Melcher, Dale, et al. 1992. "Women's Participation in Local Union Leadership: The Massachusetts Experiment." *Industrial and Labor Relations Review* 45, no. 2.

"No se raje, chicanita": Some Thoughts on Race, Class, and Gender in the Classroom

Gloria J. Romero

Let me begin by explaining the title of my essay: "No se raje, chicanita" is the title of the final poem in *Borderlands/La Frontera: The New Mestiza* by Gloria Anzaldúa, a compañera in the struggle to make known the voices of women of color. The poem details the strength of la mujer despite the attempted destruction of mestizo lands, history, culture, and spirit. Gloria reassures Missy Anzaldúa, her niece, to whom the poem is dedicated, that the pride of being Mexicana-Chicana will never be broken. Our voices will be preserved.

I chose this title for a number of reasons: to acknowledge the struggle to revolt in order to survive; to acknowledge the impact of the voice of a working-class woman, a Chicana, on our disciplines of study; to assert that in the destruction of an old way a new way will emerge; and to persevere with the belief that we shall endure. It is a message that I sometimes myself do not believe when I feel the weight of the ivory tower upon me.

I want to share with you my thoughts on race, class, and gender in the classroom and their impact on the transformation of social knowledge and scholarship. Although I now hold a tenure-track position, most of my years of teaching were spent in the margins of academia—as an "intellectual migrant worker" traveling from campus to campus in search of work. Typically, wherever I have taught I have been "the first," and I usually count twice: as a woman, and as a Chicana.

This essay is based on my combined experiences teaching in departments of psychology, sociology, Chicano studies, and women's studies. Please accept them as thoughts, just thoughts. Perhaps at times my passages will have a stream-of-consciousness quality, like journal entries of experiences that have shaped me and the work I do. My thoughts reflect my life experiences, which, I am sure, would not be the same were I not a Chicana, a woman, the working-class daughter of a railroad laborer and a domestic who once cleaned the houses of rich New Mexican "Spanish" women; who came of age during the Vietnam War and who felt anguish the day I learned that Clarence Griego—a twenty-year-old Chicano from my hometown—was killed by a grenade in an unjust war. We were from a town where Chicanos, blacks, and poor white working-class men dutifully marched off to war as cannon fodder, not one burning a draft card. Clarence's twenty-year-old pregnant widow survived him. She eventually gave birth to a daughter, Clarissa, who will probably never read in history textbooks why her father's name is really inscribed on "the wall" in Washington, D.C. They are thoughts shaped by participation in the Chicano movement, the civil rights movement, and the death of Dr. Martin Luther King, Jr. (the name of the hall where I teach most of my classes today). I remember the lectures my father gave me from the very beginning: that there are only two kinds of people in the world, the rich and the poor, subsuming both race and gender to class. He assured me that the poor would rise up one day and enjoy the fruits of our labor in a society that I could somewhat imagine while I was still a young girl accompanying my father to a picket line or meeting. My mother occasionally reminded him that there were women in the world as he organized for this new society, not always in the most egalitarian way. They are thoughts shaped by deep hopes and pains reflective of women's lives, and through it all a passionate commitment to the belief that "soy del pueblo, del pueblo soy."

In the beginning race, class, and gender sometimes seemed like separate, even contradictory worlds I knew I inhabited. Over time, I grasped their intersections in the production, dissemination, and enactment of social knowledge for social change.

Race, Class, and Gender in the Classroom

The last course I taught before leaving UCLA as a Rockefeller Foundation Fellow was titled, "Culture and Personality."

From the catalog description it may have appeared to the student that, upon enrolling, he or she would study the "natives in the jungle." After all, when one thinks about culture and personality, especially in the ivory tower, one often envisions the study of "primitive" peoples in their native habitats and the existence of matriarchal societies that existed prior to "civilization."

The first day of class I warned the students that we would not study the natives in the jungle. In fact, I explained, we would turn the magnifying glass on ourselves: in a sense, to study the natives of Los Angeles in the urban jungle of a twentieth-century advanced monopoly capitalist society. Chicana sociologist and dear friend, Mary Pardo (1987), has observed that in this modern day and age, universities, when they address the topic of culture, do so with an anesthetically benign view: University administrators prefer to project culture as quaint. As demographics in the country change rapidly, particularly in California, universities have jumped onto the multicultural bandwagon. They celebrate culture and offer workshops on "managing" diversity. In these workshops, conflict rarely arises. Culture is projected with a positive affect. Culture does not offend (Romero and Arguelles, 1991).

Our classroom discussions typically mirror such benign approaches to the study of culture, with cross-cultural studies having become sufficiently sanitized for classroom discourse. Yet, as Caulfield (1969) reminds us, the most important force for culture change, for the development of race, class, and gender relations in the history of the world today has been Western expansion, or simply put, "imperialism." In reality, the anthropologists, sociologists, psychologists concerned with culture and personality have largely studied men and women, entire societies that exist under some form of colonial or neocolonial domination.

Yet, what appears remarkably absent from their works is overt acknowledgement of colonialism. The central role of exploitation when looking at culture and personality, when attempting to understand psychological growth and development, for example, is rarely addressed in the classroom. My experience has been that readings on culture, imperialism, and personality development wind up on the syllabi of the Marxists and the leftists at the university—if any will survive the purge of "political correctness." The typical course on culture and personality in a psychology department (which even my

own department has failed to develop) presents harmonious
views of culture as though east and west, north and south
had met . . . and all had gone well. Likewise, we can extrapo-
late when we consider race relations in U.S. society. In sur-
veying texts used in the course "Race and Ethnic Status
Groups," which I also taught while at UCLA, not one of the
texts built a theory of race relations on U.S. political economy.
One could read about individual prejudice and race discrimination, certainly, but no text argued that the fundamental
contradiction upon which race is socially constructed is the
economic and social fabric of U.S. capitalist society. Hence,
we could, had I chosen any of those popular texts, have had
a very polite, sanitized, "nonpolitical" discussion about race
and race relations without ever challenging the social order
of which we all partake on a daily basis.

Women's studies, likewise, has contributed to such a fal-
lacy with respect to race and class. Bell hooks, in *Feminist
Theory: From Margin to Center* (1984) critically points out that
the feminist "classics" have seldom been based upon race and
class exploitation. Betty Friedan's *The Feminine Mystique*
(1963) is often credited as a major feminist work—must reading for every women's studies major. Yet, as hooks points out,
Friedan ignores class and race, as they are ignored in many,
if not most, of the feminist "classics." I most likely will never
use *The Feminine Mystique* in any women's studies class I ever
teach. My reality, like the reality of hooks, has been that every woman I have known in my family lineage has worked,
painfully hard, both inside and outside the home. And the
history of middle-class white women has (but should not have)
a monopoly on how feminist theory has developed. Indeed,
most histories of white women have even left out the reality
of most white, working-class women. Hooks laments how feminist theory has been retarded in its development by the mar-
ginality of women of color and the exclusion of class.

So, I chose to teach the UCLA course. After all, the Sociology Department, through which the course was offered, expressed interest in "integrating" more ethnic minority faculty and
certainly more women of color into their curriculum, and to have
me, a Chicana, teaching a course on culture appeared perfect.
They wanted to "integrate" issues of race into the curriculum.

I intended my course to be a third-world perspective on
culture and personality. By virtue of the historical processes
that have shaped who I am, and how I have come to understand

the world, even had I not consciously recognized it as an attempt to present a third-world perspective, it still would have been. When I study personality, unequal social relations becomes the key to understanding, so I subtitled the course "a study in alienation, domination, and the psychology of oppression." As in any movement, there arose resistance. A number of the white students, both male and female, quickly dubbed the course "Oppression 151." It was my impression that they subtitled it in reference to themselves—their own oppression at being forced to turn the magnifying glass on themselves, and I—a Chicana (rarely seen teaching at UCLA)—became their "oppressor." For I am firmly convinced that the U.S. educational system functions in a way that systematically reinforces and reproduces the existing social and class inequities. It reinforces and seeks to reproduce that which has already been declared as "knowledge" (Aptheker 1972). Students are encouraged, taught, and rewarded to expect the expected. It was Upton Sinclair who noted that the system of public education in the United States is not intended as a public service to advance humanity but rather to keep America capitalist.

Aptheker's (1972) classic work on rebellion in the academic factories provides a succinct historical overview of these processes. Historically, intellectuals and the intellectual factories have provided the philosophical and theoretical foundations for the existing social relations needed to control not only domestic social processes but international ones as well. Analyses of most university governing boards lend support for these "subversive" observations. For more than a century universities have been governed by corporate representatives (Aptheker 1972), with many institutions owing their very survival to the "philanthropy" of the ruling class. They enable us to contemplate democracy in the academy due to apartheid and neocolonialism in the world.

However, educational propaganda has been premised on concepts of equality and objectivity. As Aptheker (1972) makes clear, information and the corpus of knowledge exchanged on a daily basis in the college classroom has been obfuscated— painted as the presentation, discussion, and free exchange of ideas (the philosophical foundations of the free market itself). If an idea is not sound or does not approach truth, then it will not be purchased and subsequently abandoned. Hence, the law of supply and demand operates in the marketplace of the classroom. After all, education does attempt to reach the "truth." Psychologists, in particular, pride themselves on the basis of their scientific method, on objectivity, and value neutrality. Yet, a fine line can be drawn between education and propaganda (Aronson 1988). For what remains unsaid, unacknowledged, is whose truth? Whose paradigm, through whose tint of glasses do we view the world and come to understand its contradictions? And with whom do we go in search of truth? As W. E. B. DuBois said so long ago, "The problem of the twentieth century is the problem of the color line," and the color line parallels very closely the class line in the United States. And the color line, particularly for me, becomes painfully clear in the college classroom, regardless of the department in which I have taught. For example, when I first arrived at Women's Studies at San Diego State University, I developed a course on race, class, and gender, the first time the course had ever been offered. Yet, ironically, the Women's Studies Department was preparing to celebrate its twentieth-year anniversary—twenty years.

Adrienne Rich wrote, "All silence has meaning." Still in the process of birth, the color line has left an unsightly stretch mark on women's studies. Just look at the curriculum—in the topics discussed and the textbooks chosen, in who teaches, and who enrolls in courses! For if scholarship and social knowledge can ever be transformed with a liberatory effect, it must interlock all aspects of ourselves—primarily race, class, and gender. Let me explain.

Not too long ago I reviewed a 400-plus-page book recounting the history of the U.S. women's movement written by a white feminist—someone I respect. A mere three paragraphs were devoted to Chicanas. Native American women were acknowledged in no more than three sentences. African American women fared better: They received a whole three pages. I do not recall any discussion of Asian American women.

I teach psychology of women and I have yet to find a textbook that does not insult me as a woman of color. An almost universal presumption of these texts is that there exists a female experience that composes half the human experience. That female experience is white, middle-class, and lives in the United States. One can find no presumptions of structural barriers based on race or class in these textbooks, as if the psychology of the black woman in South Africa might be any different than the psychology of the white woman in the United States.

In these texts, which thousands of introductory psychology students read each quarter, women do not live under conditions of apartheid. In these texts, women do not live under conditions of neocolonial domination. In these texts, women do not live under conditions of civil war and occupied territories. In fact, just months have passed since my retention committee—comprised of three white men (a jury of my peers?)—reprimanded me for acknowledging on my syllabus the existence of a march against apartheid on the Martin Luther King, Jr. holiday. I was politicizing, not educating, I was told.

I recall a textbook on child development written by a feminist in the psychology department where I received my degree—someone I respect. She wrote about the need to "humanize" the childbirth experience. Her well-received book surveyed the research literature on the mother–infant bonding practices following birth. The bulk of the studies reviewed had employed a methodology in which an infant was removed from its mother immediately following delivery and placed in a nursery as opposed to allowing the infant to remain with its mother.

Who were the "subjects" of the research (please note the archaic yet standard aristocratic language of psychological research)? Women from Guatemala. In scientifically controlled studies, researchers deprived half of the Guatemalan mothers of contact with their infants immediately following birth, while the other half were allowed to remain with their infants. Researchers examined the bonding processes and, not surprisingly, they concluded bonding is facilitated when infants remain with their mothers. The author graciously went on to draw public policy implications for the design of hospitals to guard against dehumanization in childbirth. Hooray! Guatemalan women were used as guinea pigs so that, in the application of the work, North American women can enjoy more humane conditions of childbirth. Not one word was even written about the use of third-world women to advance the standard of living for North American women. Not one word questioned the ethics of such research. But our understanding of childbirth has advanced, and the white feminist professor eventually received tenure. As Chicanas in the department we celebrated her tenure, but we questioned the parameters of our sisterhood.

I remember when I gave birth to my daughter, Soledad, now nine years old, at Los Angeles County General Hospital— a depository for poor women, for immigrant women, for women without health insurance. The Mexican American Legal Defense and Education Fund unsuccessfully sued the hospital in the late 1970s for the forcible sterilization of poor Mexican women. Many of my courses include readings on such topics, and I always refer to these very real conditions of womanhood for poor, working-class and immigrant women, primarily women of color. The nurses were amazed when they learned I had a Ph.D., one of them asked incredulously (remembering the lawsuit, I'm sure), "Are you conducting a study?" "No," I reassured her after having sat alongside mostly Mexican and Korean immigrant women almost four hours to see a doctor for ten minutes, "despite my degree I live in the margins."

The contents of textbooks on the psychology of women continue to reflect their class bias: Entire chapters are devoted to "gender differences," comparing and contrasting empirical results of contrived laboratory studies on how men and women behave, for example, on competitive games tasks. Some of my colleagues may criticize me, but I skip these sections entirely when I teach "Psychology of Women" or "Gender Differences." I refuse to spend my time essentially teaching crap. Sure, I am "denying" the students some "classic" works, but then I view social knowledge through a different shade of the lens.

In teaching psychology, I find it imperative to understand the impact of racism on the development of one's psychological growth and development. I have never read a chapter on this in the so-called psychology of women "classics." Students usually consider these "biased" readings, and my "bias" in teaching usually manifests itself at this point in the quarter. As I continue to teach "Psychology of Women"—indeed, all psychology—increasingly I have internationalized the curriculum. Sisterhood is global, and women live under varying moral and political conditions of life. My psychology courses emphasize the role of, and the effects of, multinational corporations, political torture, military occupation, and impoverishment on human behavior and consciousness. My interpretation of the psychology of women will soon look very different from what is currently published. Publish my own? I certainly hope so, but how will I be evaluated by my "colleagues" in psychology? I once had an article rejected, an essay on how Chicanas and white women view the role of affirmative action policies in our employment and retention. One reviewer's written explanation for the rejection centered on his/her observation that Chicanas "are an abnormal population."

Upon arrival at my present university, my assigned faculty member advised me to forsake my research on women and minorities. After all, she cautioned me, university committees are still controlled by white men who do not value such. I told her I refused to sell my soul in order to make it in the ivory tower. We argued. One week later she called me to say she had been moved, declaring, "Hold on to your principles!"

Yes, the color line is painfully clear, and once one recognizes it, one confronts it on a daily basis. The color line becomes excruciatingly obvious when I walk into a classroom and face a sea of white faces and one or two Chicana, Asian, or black students. When I first arrived at women's studies, I asked some Chicanas why they hadn't taken women's studies courses. I knew the answer even before I had asked it. Sure enough, they responded, "because it's a white woman's thing," which at the moment is both painfully true, but painfully inaccurate.

The Transformation of Social Knowledge

Historically, if we examine the academic rebellion that paved the way for the "integration" of Chicano studies, Afro-American studies, American Indian studies, Asian studies, labor studies, and women's studies, we know that the academic rebellion that created space in the university has been intricately intertwined with the liberation movements of these same communities. In examining the rise of Chicano studies in the late 1960s, it was, at times, led by Chicano students—in the high schools and colleges that in the process of the Chicano movement significantly altered the fabric of both U.S. politics and education (Muñoz 1989). Any review of the history of civil rights, women's rights, and the free speech movements acknowledges that colleges have generally been an arena of intense and sustained political activity (Aptheker 1972). The classroom should be no different. In particular, the initial creation of black, brown, and womens' student organizations marked a period of attack upon the racist and sexist foundations of the university and its attendant curriculum. Mounting pressure was exerted to force university administrators to respond to demands for knowledge arising from the marginalized, the excluded men and women of color.

313

These demands represented more than the traditional curriculum. We wanted access in the dissemination of information, but more significantly, they were demands for knowledge that would assist in the development of our movements. We insisted on participating in the production of new paradigms and their dissemination, which would seek more than "integration" into the curriculum but liberation from the curriculum. The radical, indeed revolutionary potential of Chicano studies, African-American studies, and women's studies, would entail a new history, a new psychology, a new social science—a new paradigm by which to view the quest for truth (Aptheker 1972).

Confrontation with the world invites dissent, and the dissenting individual is then forced to move from mere protest to resistance (Aptheker 1972). For only by breaking out of the operational model altogether can education be more liberatory. Thus, one moves into an intense political struggle—one that unfolds not only in life, but in the classroom, on a daily basis. It becomes both a theoretical and a practical struggle— between those who service the ideological and practical needs of race, class, and gender subservience and those who resist. As a leader of the free speech movement declared:

> There is a time when the operation of the machine becomes so odious, makes you so sick at heart that you cannot take part, you can't even tacitly take part. And you've got to put your body upon the gears, and upon the wheels and upon the levers and upon all the apparatus and you've got to make it stop. And you've got to indicate to the people who own it, and the people who run it that unless you are free, their machine will be prevented from running at all. (Cited in Aptheker 1972)

Full Circle Return

So, in preparing to teach "Culture and Personality" at UCLA, I recruited third-world students, men and women, with whom I wanted to enter into a dialogue. One can "integrate" rather easily, but once the decision moves beyond "integration" from protest to resistance and the creation of alternatives, then the material is deemed "political," and one meets the full-scale resistance launched by those who maintain a personal stake, a social entitlement, in the status quo. And just as in any liberation movement, one does not embark on a solo venture but amasses and aligns the forces with those one feels one can enter into alliance.

This should not surprise anyone. Discourse in the classroom is as much conditioned by the content of the curriculum as the student composition of the class, and the significance of those numbers. The classroom represents a microcosm of national and international struggles and issues. As social beings, we personify the social relations of production in all of its grand contradictions. Thus, education can be painful. Education can be offensive, especially in a system that leads students to expect the expected.

So, on opening day of "Oppression 151" (as I fondly learned to refer to it), 220 students entered the classroom, a significant number of whom were third-world students from working-class backgrounds. By the second week of class, the number had pared down to a manageable 180. Interesting to note, the Sociology Department, so interested in integrating culture into the curriculum, canceled all discussion sections for the course.

Over the ten weeks we talked, we discussed, we listened, we refused to listen. Over the ten weeks temperatures rose. Oppression 151 exploded the session immediately prior to the midterm, as we began to summarize the meaning, the significance of all that had taken place. Like a woman giving birth, sensing the next contraction, our dialogues, our sessions, I felt, propelled forward a breathing, living vision of our historical selves. And like birth, it gave both pleasure and pain.

Students argued. Some cried, some threatened. One white female student warned, "We've given you your civil rights, but now you're pushing us, you're pushing us too hard." Some students were asked to step out into the hallway.

Race, class, and gender—when intertwined—do not necessarily make for pleasant polite discourse, and we need to allow for that. I do not advocate for a policy of containment. Anger, I have always felt, is part of education and has its proper expression in the classroom. For how does a student of color separate her/himself from the color line? When one seizes the meaning of Frantz Fanon's colonial dependency complex, how can one merely view it as a potential multiple choice item on a midterm: "Excuse me, Dr. Romero, but do we need to know Fanon's theory of violence for the exam? Do you think you could format it as a true/false item?"

Oppression 151 advanced, with anger, reform, resistance, and eager anticipation—just as it does everywhere around the world. From my unique position behind the podium, I could see the sea of faces enrolled in Oppression 151, just as we who stand there see students on a daily basis. We see their faces, just as we should see the social histories behind those faces, often hidden behind elaborate masks. In their faces, I saw the continents and social histories of Latin America, Africa, Asia, the Middle East, North America, and Europe.

By the final day of class, I could recognize the students who represented national liberation forces, and those who represented the solidarity internationalists. Even in seating arrangements, I could see Soweto and Pretoria. The ten weeks had been intense, for all of us.

Regardless of which side of the podium one has ever been on in a classroom, one walks into the class and personifies or expresses the historical and political contradictions of the collective existence. After the experience of Oppression 151, I am convinced that it is not just the content, but the recognition of class, of race, of gender—and their numbers in the classroom—which exert a profound difference on how scholarship becomes transformed. "Culture and Personality 151" became "Oppression 151" in direct correlation with the increased numbers of men and women of color in the classroom and an accompanying consciousness of race, class, and gender structures. This has important implications for women's studies, indeed for all of education, for as long as only one or two faces of color are present in the sea of students, transformation of our scholarship will be delayed, if not denied.

I recall that as a college student I often sat in the back of the classroom and never said a word. However, as more students of color entered college we began to speak up, to assert, and to challenge. Collectively, we knew our numbers counted. We resisted and, with numbers, could validate our resistance. As long as women's studies remains "a white woman's thing," there remains little hope.

And so we "integrated" into the classroom. The beginning of each class session, I often imagined, was probably much like the opening of a session at the United Nations. With the world present, we were embroiled in the problem of the twentieth century—in all of its race, class, and gender contradictions. Does it surprise me that anger erupted? Students walked out, and students struggled it out. Like some people in the world, some students chose to remain oblivious to it all and slept it out.

At times I sincerely worried about a first strike weapon. Just as globally we, too, drop bombs in order to forcibly "integrate" our ideas on the world. In the end, we survived the ten weeks without overt physical violence, though I will admit that there were times when I felt like throwing a molotov cocktail in the form of white chalk. For even though I was the professor, I, too, cannot be expected to divorce myself from my own concept of humanity and morality. I am a part of the political struggle in both the world and classroom in which I live.

Some of you may wonder how Oppression 151 ended. On the final day of Oppression 151, as we summarized the ten weeks, one student, who happened to be a Chicano male, stood up and spoke. In effect, it was a soliloquy about his identity: a product of neocolonialism. But he said, "Today, I am not speaking to you out of an inferiority complex of a colonized person. . . ." Tension greeted him, yet he continued to speak, asking the world around him to work with him in the destruction and reconstruction of a new humanity. He spoke so eloquently, and when he finished the hall was filled with such silence that you could have heard a pin drop. As a citizen of the world first, I was moved. I felt tears well up in my eyes. No further words were needed. I began to clap, and before long, the room was loud with applause. I knew that I and the others who clapped that day were applauding for more than his words and his summation of who he told us he was, who we all were even when we might not want to see how the unfolding of history had crippled all of us and what it promised us if we dared to hold that magnifying glass to the shaping of our beings. That day we knew we clapped for a vision of a new world he so eloquently represented. And we left the room that had, for a moment in time, captured the essence of our interrelated oppression.

I do not quite know how to conclude. As I indicated to you from the beginning, these are thoughts, just thoughts: like journal entries of experiences that have shaped me and the work I do, and which I am sure, would not be the same were I not a Chicana; a woman; the working-class daughter of a railroad laborer and a domestic who once cleaned the houses of rich "Spanish" women of northern New Mexico; who came of age during the Viet Nam War and who felt anguish the day I learned that Clarence Griego—a twenty-year-old Chicano from my hometown—was killed by a grenade in an unjust war. We were from a town where Chicanos, blacks, and poor white working-class men dutifully marched off to war as cannon fodder, not one ever burning a draft card. . . . I also dedicate Anzaldúa's poem to his daughter, Clarissa. I dedicate it to mine, Soledad: ¡No se rajen, chicanitas!

Note

Portions of this paper were originally presented as a part of the New Views Lecture Series at San Diego State University, and as part of the Distinguished Lecturer of Color Lecture Series, University of California, Berkeley.

Works Cited

Anzaldúa, G. 1987. *Borderlands/La Frontera: The New Mestiza*. San Francisco: Spinsters/Aunt Lute Press.

Aptheker, B. 1972. *The Academic Rebellion in the United States: A Marxist Appraisal*. Seacaucus, N.J.: Citadel Press.

Aronson, E. 1988. *The Social Animal*, 5th ed. New York: W. H. Freeman and Company.

Caulfield, M. D. 1969. "Culture and Imperialism: Proposing a New Dialectic." In *Reinventing Anthropology*, ed. D. Hymes. New York: Pantheon Books.

Friedan, B. 1963. *The Feminine Mystique*. New York: W. W. Norton Co.

hooks, b. 1984. *Feminist Theory: From Margin to Center*. Boston: South End Press.

Munoz, C. 1989. *Youth, Identity, Power: The Chicano Movement*. New York: Verso Press.

Pardo, Mary. 1987. Personal Communication.

Romero, G. J., & L. Arguelles. 1991. "Culture and Conflict in the Academy." *The California Sociologist* 14.